111901/tom

LIBR

D0494301

GROWING YOUR OWN HEROES

The commonsense way to improve business performance

JOHN J OLIVER OBE
&
CLIVE MEMMOTT

LIBRARY
EDUCATION & RESEARCH
WYTHENSHAWE HOSP

Acc. No.	Class. No.
19528 ✓	HD 61.1 OLI ✓

UHSM Academy Library

R00278F4989

Published by
OAK TREE PRESS
19 Rutland Street, Cork, Ireland
www.oaktreepress.com

© 2006 John J Oliver & Clive Memmott

A catalogue record of this book is
available from the British Library.

ISBN 1 904887 06 6

All rights reserved.
No part of this publication may be reproduced or transmitted
in any form or by any means, including photocopying and
recording, without written permission of the publisher. Such
written permission must also be obtained before any part of
this publication is stored in a retrieval system of any nature.
Requests for permission should be directed to
Oak Tree Press, 19 Rutland Street, Cork, Ireland.

Printed in Ireland by ColourBooks.

CONTENTS

FIGURES

DEDICATION

This book is dedicated to the millions who find the daily grind a drudge – there is hope!

AUTHORS

John J Oliver OBE is a 'used to be'. He used to be the Chief Executive of Leyland Trucks, as well as Chair of Runshaw College for 10 years and Chair of Business Link North & West Lancashire for four years. All three organisations were transformed using the principles described here. His first book *The Team Enterprise Solution* has been used extensively in organisations seeking to replicate the experience.

Clive Memmott is Chief Executive of Business Link Lancashire. He has spent most of his career in international manufacturing companies and first became interested in enterprise and providing business and skills support for smaller companies during a stint as Chairman for a Business Link. Clive is a director of a number of organisations/agencies, a College Governor, an Honorary Research Fellow in the Lancaster University Management School and Chairman of Progress Recruitment Limited, a charity that provides supported employment opportunities to people with disabilities.

FOREWORD

Business life has always been subject to change, but today's businesses are experiencing unprecedented change. Not only do they face rapid technological development and increased competition, they are also managing in a volatile economic environment. For many businesses, 'survival' is a major pre-occupation and they are actively seeking help with this challenge.

Clive Memmott recently introduced a stake-holder meeting on the future of business support with a succinct statement of fact:

> In a rapidly changing economy, businesses must adapt
> and innovate to gain competitive advantage and grow.
> (Leyland, October 2005).

Such adaptations and innovation are driven by people at all levels of the firm, not just leaders and owner-managers but the whole work-force, irrespective of their role. As a manager who started her career in R&D, and more recently as a Business School Dean, I am passionate about the role of people within the innovation and growth process. Unless business leaders understand (and are managerially competent) to release this potential, their businesses will not thrive. Management and leadership capability is thus a key factor in both survival and growth.

However, much of the leadership development activity to date has focussed upon larger organisations, despite the fact that a large proportion of managers operate within small and medium-sized enterprises (SMEs). The key differences between large corporate and SME leadership development, not surprisingly, are context dependent. The context of the large organisation is one where a relatively large number of managers (a community of practice) share a career path in which their desired and acceptable goals are to lead. Structures are in place both to enable and to support career progression, and all the appropriate facilitative activities are made available to ensure that they have the necessary skills. These activities may occur naturally through peer-to-peer learning or they may be formally structured through development programmes, counselling or shadowing and secondments. The SME context is very different: the owner-manager and the business are almost two sides of the same coin. As a consequence, the structures reflect the owner-manager's perspective. Their development is limited through isolation, and the naturalistic learning that is available to their large firm counterparts is very restricted. Furthermore, the quest for self-development (and, particularly, leadership development) is often subjugated to survival needs. So what is needed by way of support for SME managers?

The LEAD programme developed in my Business School, with the support of Business Link, has addressed the isolation issue and has provided a natural SME network and bespoke leadership development programme. However, only 74 owner-managers have participated to date and they are hungry for even more knowledge.

Growing Your Own Heroes is a book developed by two people who are well-placed to provide such knowledge. Clive Memmott and John Oliver have collaborated to address a key leadership issue: employee engagement (see earlier). They have agreed on three guiding principles:

♦ First, that there is a need for all business managers to understand the practicalities of people management skills to ensure that employee engagement is optimised.

♦ Second, technical competence may be suitable but is not, in itself, sufficient for business survival. SMEs need to achieve both people and process excellence to be effective.

♦ Finally, the book will be directed at all sectors and presented in a style that is straightforward with concepts that are readily implemented.

I am pleased to say that they have more than met these goals. I strongly recommend you read the book, quickly at first, so as to get a general understanding of employee engagement. Then reflect upon your own situation, phone a friend if you can or try and engage with a SME network. Then use the book, step by step, to inform you and your team on the journey of self-improvement. John's first book, *The Team Enterprise Solution*, was used in this fashion and was a great success.

To return to the survival challenge, the best adaptation and innovation comes from people at all levels in the firm. You cannot afford for their talents to remain hidden. Your competitors may already be addressing their employee engagement issues. It will cost you relatively little, and could reward you greatly.

Professor Sue Cox
Dean
Lancaster University Management School

1
INTRODUCTION

A famous travel writer once remarked that living in Britain was like squatting inside an 'inverted Tupperware box'. Presumably, he was referring to our rather damp climate. Sadly, there is nothing we can do about it, apart from moving to Spain to join the sangria and bingo set.

The same metaphor could be applied, much more appropriately, to the world of work for most employees in this country. It doesn't seem to matter whether you are public or private sector, big or small, daily life for so many people is total greyness. Surrounded often by what they see to be stultifying bureaucracy, employees across the nation find the daily grind dull, uninspiring, stressful and unfulfilling. They feel no affinity to their companies and dutifully limit themselves to their job description, no more – and no less, unless they can get away with it!

Each year, the authors visit scores of companies and find that this pessimistic picture is far more commonplace than we, or they, would like to admit. Most organisations seem to suffer from this general malaise and yet few, very few, do anything about it.

Over the past four decades, life in business has become appreciably harder. In the private sector, global competition has increased to a level where scarcely any organisation has avoided its icy blast. Add to that pressures emerging from macro-economic changes, technological advances by the day, not to mention an increasing tendency by governments to micro-manage, and it is little wonder that alternative lifestyles have become so popular in recent years! The practice of private sector management has never been more difficult.

There is little respite in switching to the public sector. Whilst once this may have been seen by some as a comfortable retreat, the steady march towards best value has introduced these organisations to the same stresses and strains as their private sector equivalents. The worlds of regional / local government, education and business support seem to be characterised by incessant, and often unnecessary, restructurings, reorganisations and redirections.

Change is not just constant nowadays, but seems to be increasing exponentially. We are exhorted daily, not just to accept the inevitability of change but to go out actively and to seek more of it – and, whilst we're at it, to learn to love it. Add to that the spectre of increased pensionable ages in the not too distant future and it is little wonder that the sparkle in the eye of our average manager no longer represents a glint but is more likely to be abject fear!

It should not surprise us then that most managers constantly seek an easy way out. We are all searching for that elusive Holy Grail, that miraculous snake-oil, which liberally sprinkled across our organisation, will make it at once strong, robust and impervious to competitive pressure. Profitability, productivity and quality then will flow in easy profusion.

You may have noticed that there are plenty of candidates for this utopian application. The bookshops are full of alternatives. Your mail is crammed each day with invitations to courses, seminars and books that entice you to the promised land of certainty, predictability and control. At a recent CIPD conference, one speaker confided that he had gone to the trouble of counting all the alternative initiatives and methodologies currently available to management and was already at 17,642! Most of them were described by the usual ubiquitous three letter acronym: for example, TQM – Total Quality Management; BPR – Business Process Re-Engineering; SPC – Statistical Process Control; MRP – Management Resource Planning; ABC – Activity Based Costing; and on and on and on.

If you are a reader of any maturity, you are likely to have encountered several of these big ideas in the recent past. There is a fair chance that you may be a fan of, or even be an expert in, one or more of the more popular methodologies. Sadly, however, in our limited but painful experience, you are likely to have concluded that the majority of these approaches tend to have three things in common:

- ♦ First, they all WORK as one would expect. After all, these approaches have been researched, studied and generally worked over by some of the best brains in the business. So there must be some substance to the theory. Unfortunately, however, they don't work *all the time*. In fact, the hit rate on some of the more popular approaches is decidedly low. We have heard tales of 50% of TQM applications, for example, failing to reach managerial aspirations. And that's one of the better concepts. This shouldn't surprise us. We know now that most change programmes fail. The rate is quoted at anywhere between 80% (four in five programmes failing) to a staggering 93%. Stripping away the intellectual veneer and hype that surrounds most of these concepts, what we are left with is usually just another change programme – which have a tendency to fail!

♦ Second, they all cost – usually an arm and a leg! Some of the costs associated with these initiatives are huge, especially if they involve sizeable training programmes. After all, the gurus, consultants and learned academics who spawn these next good things have to make their turn, too. And rarely does such love and attention come cheap.

This is probably the most vexatious issue of all for the aspirant manager, especially those unfortunate enough to work in manufacturing or small businesses where there is rarely sufficient spare cash to allow the luxury of substantial discretionary spends. So, unless the boss actually thinks of doing it himself, the chances of the approach coming to fruition from elsewhere are often minimal.

♦ Third, and finally, most of these initiatives take a fair while to pay back their initial investment. It can be anywhere from two to possibly five years before the real benefits flow through to the organisation's coffers. Now, while it may be laudable to dismiss this as merely a consequence of sensibly taking a longer term view, the truth is that, for most decision-makers, this just ain't attractive. Given an average managerial tenure of three years, there is little incentive for Joe Average to take all the discomfort, hard work and risks inherent in embarking upon a long-term initiative if he's not going to be around to share in the glory. In these cash-starved days, most organisations have more than enough exposure to unavoidable long-term projects. Capital plans, facility investments and software programmes constitute enough on the average managerial plates without seeking more. Whether we like it or not, the pressure today is for paybacks that

can be measured in months, not years. And that, despite
predictable protestations to the contrary from obviously-vested
interests, rules out many of the currently fashionable management
approaches.

The purpose of this book is to introduce you to a concept that seems
too good to be true. A proposition that may seem like one of the
products of the earlier-mentioned snake-oil salesman but which, if
management execute it capably and sensibly:

1. Will cost you very little, except your time.

2. Is virtually guaranteed to improve significantly *every* single
   aspect of your business's performance quickly.

3. Has a very low risk of failure.

and

4. At the same time, is simple and logical.

Now the more discerning of readers already may have spotted the
carefully-inserted rider *if management execute it capably and sensibly.* This
is no throwaway comment; it is the single most important message in
the whole book.

Many organisations today could be described as dysfunctional. We
believe that the single most important causal factor behind that
dysfunctionality is usually the presence of a dysfunctional management
team or a dysfunctional leader. Accepting that weakness and doing
something about it is, in our opinion, the most powerful way of hitting
the bottom line hard. Without total and enthusiastic management
commitment to the general theme of 'employee engagement', your
endeavours inevitably will result in just another 'me-too' experience.
And the world is so full of mediocre, dispiriting and failed change
programmes that it doesn't need yet another one.

We cannot overestimate the simplicity of the concept either. Nothing
in this book will challenge you intellectually, although it will certainly
challenge the way you work. Rocket science this isn't, but therein lies
another major challenge. Sadly, over the years, we in management have
become intellectual snobs. We only take seriously those initiatives that
are complex, complicated and convoluted. The lack of sophistication can
itself, therefore, present a challenge. In so many organisations, we have

seen the principles here left to the whim of the personnel department or the quality function. And as a result, progress doesn't materialise, and initial enthusiasm simply withers on the vine.

The theory behind employee engagement has been rightly described as patent commonsense. In a traditional organisation, where the management ethos is lodged firmly in the 'command and control' category, not only key decisions are retained by the elite few. Creativity, imagination and innovation are also restricted to a limited number of influential managers, plus the odd boffin. From experience, we estimate that organisations like this tap into between 2% and 5% of the collective intellectual power of the company. If we were able to implement successfully radical levels of employee engagement, how much more would we generate? 100% may be a tad ambitious but, even if our targets are, say, a more modest 20% to 40%, just imagine the transformational capability that could realise.

It is too easy to dismiss this as fanciful or naïve. Over the years, we have interviewed scores of companies. Without doubt, the most alarming results come from the engineering or research departments of sizeable organisations. Here, we have highly-trained, highly-experienced and reasonably well-paid personnel generally left feeling demotivated, resentful and neglected. And yet, so often, when we have interviewed their counterparts in sales or marketing departments, we have found just the opposite. Those in sales who are allowed a degree of autonomy, by virtue of geography or customer base, are found to be more motivated, more engaged and more involved.

A lot of clients too easily dismiss this as being a mere consequence of the job. The very nature of the sales activity, with its greater freedom, independence and customer contact lends itself to improved satisfaction and motivation. Supplement that with theories of sales personnel being of a more optimistic bent, a dangerous assumption in our experience, and there you have it. Contrast their role with the much more restrictive one of an engineer constrained by geography, process and products and the reason for the difference becomes self-evident.

To us, this is a gross oversimplification of an eminently fixable problem. The root cause is management or, more specifically, people management. Sales directors in charge of autonomous workforces know instinctively that they have to motivate their sales force. They recognise that getting their reps to 'go the extra mile' routinely is the key to enhanced customer satisfaction, sales and margins. Senior sales management in these situations, aside from the odd exception, are selected in no small part due to their perceived ability in handling people.

Contrast this with our average Engineering Manager. He ('she' is all too rare here) almost certainly got the job through sheer technical ability. The best, most committed, and occasionally most opinionated, engineer usually wins the senior position. Whether they have any inherent talent in people management is pure coincidence. And if they haven't, which is so often the case, morale suffers and engineers become disenchanted.

The tragedy here is that most companies are dependent on their technical functions for the routine innovations, as well as product and process improvements, to keep them ahead of the competitive pack. Is it therefore so fanciful to imagine that better people management skills might lead to a more motivated workforce, which in turn might lead to better performance?

So why another book on the subject? After all, this offering follows very quickly on the heels of *The Team Enterprise Solution*,[1] written by one of the authors, which did very well.

The need arises from a closer inspection of the business marketplace. Most management books are written with the 'corporate' manager in mind, for convenience defined here as those employing a workforce greater than 250. However, the vast majority of managers, directors and proprietors do not have the luxury of working in such large establishments. In the UK, for example, 95% of companies employ less than 10 people; that's 3.7 million businesses with 51% of the total working population.

Engaging this element of the business community to a people-centred agenda has proven far more taxing than enticing their larger colleagues. Millions of pounds of well-intentioned Government funding has been poured into this area without any significant impact. The truth is that life for the average small business person is rarely easy nowadays. Already saddled with little in the way of administrative support, the weight of Government-inflicted red tape, legislation and general bureaucracy totally absorbs the working life of

---

1   Oliver, John J. (2001). *The Team Enterprise Solution: A Step-by-Step Guide to Business Transformation*, Cork: Oak Tree Press (ISBN 1860762255).

many in this sector. Their ability to focus on what they might consider to be *discretionary* activity is limited. Sadly, vital strategic planning is often placed in this category. Day-to-day operational duties are all encompassing. Most go along to the odd subsidised seminar, resigned to end with the inevitable conclusion – *"Nice idea, but where would I get the time?"*.

However, the business support industry cannot afford to leave it there. Productivity lags significantly behind national levels in many of our regions. And our national levels lie so substantially behind our continental and American cousins that it is probably too disheartening to point out the greater threat now emerging from the Far East.

The following may sound controversial but, in our minds, the great tragedy of successive attempts to improve the lot of small business has been its over-emphasis on *process* management. It is difficult to argue with the merits of a total quality ethos, of a balanced scorecard approach to business planning or the benefits of professional market planning. Unfortunately, the reality of life in small businesses is that, while these principles may be accepted as sensible, most managers do not believe they have the resources or the time to go down these paths. Merely staying alive is their most immediate challenge. Long-term planning is seen as academic, without a short-term future.

Nevertheless, what we see repeatedly in all businesses, big and small, is a profusion of wasted assets. Employees are simply not fully utilised. Each one brings to the workplace a whole raft of talents and expertise that rarely gets fully used on a daily basis. Were the small business manager able to tap into these hidden resources, then the ability to do lots of the good things exhorted by Government and the support infrastructure would become possible.

Our theme in this book is to introduce the reader to the real power of the optimal *culture*. In our mind, culture always comes before process. Get the former in shape and you will release progressively the potential for process improvement. Therefore, we seek a model that is as relevant to small business as it is to their larger equivalents. And while the following may appear simplistic or even commonsensical, we make no apology for precisely that. In our view, many businesses are damaged by the absence of those routine managerial disciplines so necessary to maintain employee morale and motivation. Management ego, in particular, has the capability of wounding any organisation, big or small. The difficulties in this approach lie not in the application of systems but in management's ability and willingness to respond to them. This is not a resource issue, but rather a function of personality. Without those 'character ethics' described so clearly by Covey,[2] management cannot extract the best of their people. Humility, fidelity, respect, honesty and a commitment to self-improvement seem to characterise all those successful in the world of radical employee engagement. These cost nothing, but generate plenty.

In this book, we also want to consider the lot of the middle manager. It is true that culture change has to come from the top. We have rarely seen success where this has not been the case. Senior management and owners not only have to understand the concepts involved but also have to embrace them actively. They have to be the conscience of employee engagement, exemplars and enthusiasts of this new, people-centred approach.

But what if you happen to be a middle or front line manager working for a senior team that is either ignorant of, or simply rejects, employee engagement? Do you have to conform to the more usual autocratic or micro-managerial stereotype?

We believe that there is much you can do here. Throughout the book, we will focus on how you can create an island of *excellence* in an otherwise barren desert. The impact on the business as a whole will obviously not be as profound, but it could do wonders for your department / section. And it may not do your career prospects any harm either!

However, all of this requires change and most of us don't like change, particularly that of a discretionary nature. We need a powerful incentive to tease us out of our nice little comfort zones. Is there sufficient here to do that? We believe there is, in spades.

In *The Team Enterprise Solution*, we examined a number of case studies to see how far organisations could progress by simply emphasising the need for a strong cultural foundation behind process excellence. It should be noted that none of the organisations cited in that book actually *abandoned* process improvement. Instead, they progressively built up their internal culture to *engage everybody* in

---

2   Covey, S.R. (2004). *The Seven Habits of Highly Effective People: Powerful Lessons in Personal Change*, London: Simon & Schuster (ISBN 0684858398).

wholesale development of their systems and procedures. Paradoxically, each of the case studies is now expert in process management. An untutored visitor to their doors might come away thinking that this was precisely the strength of the organisation, so evident are the signs of process excellence all around. Looking more closely, however, will soon reveal the real fabric, a solid underpinning of an engaged workforce – employees who give much more than the average and, as a consequence, are more motivated, more satisfied and have more self-esteem than the norm.

The benefits of employee engagement are manifold, both when measured as HARD Key Performance Indicators (KPIs) and the so-called SOFT ones. In fact, the dramatic potential offered on the latter indicators can be a problem itself. The most visible evidence of an engaged workforce is its greater harmony, contentment and commitment. As a consequence, many see this as the objective of the whole exercise. This is so dangerous. While we would be the last to knock this greater sense of well-being, we believe that sustainability can only be attained if the focus is placed on hard deliverables – for example, profitability, cash, efficiency and service excellence. To maintain the momentum for decades, we need to create the sense of being part of a high-performing team. Focusing on what is disparagingly termed 'social engineering' by the cynics is not a recipe for long-term sustainability. So as long as we understand the importance of continually measuring and discussing these soft issues, our main preoccupation should be on using employee engagement to deliver more effectively traditional measures of organisational success.

Taking the three examples where the authors have been involved directly, these hard deliverables have been seen to improve dramatically. It would not be too fanciful to say that each had been *transformed* by a greater focus on people. Of the three, only Business Link North & Western Lancashire actually qualifies as a small business, the object of this book. Nevertheless, a quick glance at the size and scale of the improvements in the other two will demonstrate emphatically the potential of employee engagement.

Without regurgitating the stories of Leyland Trucks and Runshaw College, already covered in *The Team Enterprise Solution*, a reminder of the statistics might be useful to emphasise the point.

LEYLAND TRUCKS

Leyland achieved the following results:

- Within two years, a 24% reduction in operating costs.
- Within two years, an annualised saving of £10,000,000 *per annum* against a total *cash* investment of £30,000.
- Within three years, a halving of break-even point.
- Within 30 months, a 35% reduction in warranty costs and an equivalent improvement in build quality.
- A significant reduction in absence levels from 8% to 2.5%.
- A reduction in customer overdues from around 250 days to an average of 10 to 20 days within five years.
- Much safer working environment, with Lost Time Accidents down from 65 *per annum* to single figures.
- Ideas per person increased from zero in 1991, to 14 in 1995, to 22 in 1997.
- A step-change in shop-floor attitudes and satisfaction levels.
- Build flexibility increased to best European practice, from a base of rigid demarcation.
- A positive and proactive representative structure.

However, this shows the picture in 1999, after the first 10 years of *Team Enterprise*, Leyland's term to describe employee engagement. One might think that the well would have been truly drunk dry, with little more to give. Nothing could be further from the truth.

Since then, an enterprising and farsighted young man by the name of Jim Sumner, Operations Director of Leyland, decided to use this cultural foundation to drive in new levels of process and product excellence. The techniques he used are very familiar to aficionados of *lean systems thinking*. However, this time, they were accompanied by an evangelical drive to sustain the emphasis on people and team-working. The end result is another transformation of the same order and magnitude as the first.

Cataloguing Leyland's achievements since 1999 would take far too much space; however, in the interest of record, they can be summarised as:

♦ A further improvement in build quality of 63%.

♦ An increase in inventory turn of 400%, from a level that the author thought to be at its theoretical maximum! (By 2005, Leyland had achieved 73).

♦ A reduction in build time per truck of 34%.

♦ An increase in trucks per year per employee of 22%.

And, if this doesn't sound impressive enough, the 1,000+ workforce generated cost savings of over £12,000,000 in a little over four years on bottom-up initiatives. Fifteen years on, the benefits of *Team Enterprise* continue to stream in. This truly emphasises that employee engagement is much more than a one-off initiative; it's a business philosophy for life.

RUNSHAW COLLEGE

Even more remarkable is the story of Runshaw College, a tertiary college stranded on a moss straddling the communities of South Ribble and Chorley. In *The Team Enterprise Solution*, we cited the following as indicators of the power of *The Runshaw Way*, the college's version of employee engagement:

1. In the period immediately post-incorporation ('privatisation'), the Further Education sector was riven by disputes, overtime bans, work to rules and generally abysmal labour relations as the Government pushed radical new contracts. These contracts were designed to eliminate both restrictive practices and demarcation, and to improve productivity by over 30 per cent in a very short timescale. In the midst of all this disruption, relationships at Runshaw remained cordial, supportive and co-operative.

2. A Level pass rates, originally at around 67% in 1984, rose to 95.7% in 1997 and 97.3% in 1999. At the same time, grades improved dramatically – so much so that the average point score rose from 16.4 in 1993 to over 23 in 1998, placing Runshaw as the No. 1 Further Education college in England for A Level results. It has retained that position up to the point of writing.

3. Vocational results also rose considerably. Advanced vocational pass rates rose to 95%, with distinctions rising to 23% and merits to 37% by 1999.

4. A rigorous inspection by the Further Education Funding Council in 1996 gave the college rarely-attained grade 1s on all cross-college management criteria. It commented:

   "... in a relatively short time, staff perceptions have been more positive and favourable. Morale is now generally high, staff feel the senior management is open, flexible and accessible."

   This transition took less than two years.

5. In 1995, the college was awarded Investors in People. The following year, it won the North-West Quality Award, administered by the British Quality Foundation, in a category that covered every public sector institution in the North-West of England. In 1997, it was 'Highly Commended' and described as a 'role model organisation' at the highly prestigious national UK Quality Awards. In 2000, it won the Millennium Award at the regional event in Manchester.

Since then, Runshaw has continued its phenomenal progress:

♦ A continuation of its exceptional academic performance with national leading out-turns on almost every course. In particular, its A Level results have continued their best-in-class progress for a further four years. It has been the nation's No.1 for nine years in a row. Interestingly, this defies conventional wisdom on getting the best out of 'A' levels. Current practice indicates that excellence is best achieved by student selection, small class sizes and small schools. Runshaw does not select, has perhaps some of the highest class sizes around and possesses the largest cohort of any Further Education establishment in England or Wales.

♦ Following on from the various honours cited earlier, in 2003 Runshaw won the coveted European Business Excellence Award (awarded by the European Foundation for Quality Management) in Helsinki for the *entire* public sector, not just the educational element. In addition, it was given a special award for 'Leadership and Constancy of Purpose'.

♦ As a consequence of its success, Runshaw was invited to write up its experiences and use them to mentor other colleges. *The Runshaw Way – Values Driven Management* was published[3] and circulated to all in the FE community. A more cogent and articulate declaration of the relationship between a strong culture and process excellence would be hard to find.

BUSINESS LINK NORTH & WESTERN LANCASHIRE

The third 'transformation' to be cited in this book as support for the power of employee engagement has not been written up elsewhere. Interestingly, Business Link North & Western Lancashire (BLNWL) is situated within a few miles of both Runshaw and Leyland. All three organisations fed off each other as they made their journey towards engagement. This mutual encouragement and swapping of experiences made the path so much easier. Both local authorities (Chorley and South Ribble) subsequently have done likewise. This atmosphere of support and assistance has proved invaluable to all the players. Kicking against tradition is hard, and often lonely. Finding others going in the same direction can be invaluable.

BLNWL was formed in 1999. Prior to that, the business support agencies in North & West Lancashire had something of a chequered history. Saddled with a cumbersome, bureaucratic and high-cost infrastructure, the original model was handicapped from the outset. Political and local bickering did not help either. As a consequence, it was of little surprise to anyone that, in 1999, all five not-for-profit companies were wound up and a fresh solution sought.

Out of the ashes of this calamity emerged one organisation: BLNWL. From the outset, it was determined that the overriding managerial philosophy of the new company would follow along similar lines to its academic and industrial cousins above. However, it had to recognise that there were other pressing priorities as well. The financial weaknesses of its predecessor organisations created an immediate problem of simple solvency. Mega changes in the

---

[3] Internal Runshaw College publication. Cited in O'Connell, B. (2005). *Creating an Outstanding College*, London: Nelson Thomas.

architecture of governmental business support, which seem nowadays to be a permanent feature of the trade, meant that much time had to be expended in simply getting to grips with its new role. Further distractions emerged in the need to apply for, and demonstrate its fitness for, a license to practice under the Small Business Service (SBS).

Fortunately, the management team was determined to create a much more radical management culture than had been seen elsewhere. They were amongst the first to adopt the 'Route Map' cited later in this book and, in many respects, pioneered key elements of it. The benefits are self-evident. Clive covers them in much detail in **Appendix 3**.

CONCLUSION

We could go on citing successes (and failures!) in this field but that is not the purpose of this book. The three examples quoted, from vastly different fields, demonstrate that radical employee engagement can be the safest, quickest and cheapest way of transforming your organisation. There are only two variables:

1. Understanding.
2. Management commitment.

Hopefully, we can provide the former here. Unfortunately for us, only you can supply the latter.

The three examples quoted above obviously represent real business transformations. Not every company achieves the same degree of success. However, the majority find the journey infinitely worthwhile. We have seen step-changes in efficiency, quality, employee morale and profitability in businesses ranging from local authorities right through to the smallest manufacturers. The more we learn about employee engagement, the greater we are convinced of its universality.

Which brings us to the final element in this introductory chapter. The title of the book, *Growing Your Own Heroes*, was used earlier by the Business Link and Learning Skills Council network to front its drive for employee engagement. The objective was to persuade organisations to focus more on employee skills as a means of improving overall business productivity. This campaign uncovered lots of stories, and even legends, about how such programmes tended to develop the most unlikely individual 'stars' – people who, frustrated and constrained by traditional autocratic regimes, found themselves for the first time with an opportunity to influence their own destinies. And that's exactly what happens. Individuals once considered unhelpful, uncooperative and perhaps even Luddite often find a positive voice and role within an engaged framework. We have seen the most unlikely of souls transformed in quick time into local champions of change.

The public relations and marketing fraternity cottoned on to this and christened such people 'heroes'. And, in many respects, they are. Not only have they had to overcome traditional management resistance in their battle to play a more productive role, often they have had to endure hostile and cynical peer pressure. We are not over-blessed in this country with a natural work-ethic. Employee engagement with its rewards of enhanced self-esteem, pride, job satisfaction and greater workplace harmony can help correct that deficiency. *Growing Your Own Heroes* is your key to greater organisational prosperity.

2
THE ROUTE MAP

The working title for this chapter was 'The Proven Path'. Our ambition was to develop a completely foolproof, step-by-step approach to get you from concept to execution. Sadly, upon reflection, that has not proved possible. In fact, to be honest, it's a completely *impossible* objective. No such plan exists, despite the claims of the many snake-oil salesmen in this business. As we said in **Chapter 1**, there are only two real variables in the game of employee engagement:

♦ Your understanding.

♦ Your commitment.

The 'Route Map' can aid your understanding, but your commitment is another matter altogether. It's for you.

Nevertheless, there is still huge merit in seeking to construct a guide to take you further into the mysteries of the world of employee motivation. Whether you choose to follow the signposts is largely a matter for yourself and your specific situation. However, should you decide to deviate from the recommended path, then please bear in mind that many have gone before, and most have fallen. All change programmes have a high mortality. Culture change programmes are no different, so why not use the pain and penalty incurred elsewhere to inform you on your journey? You don't have to make your own mistakes. Learn from others, it's cheaper and far less disruptive!

In *The Team Enterprise Solution*, we identified six common pitfalls. Four years and lots of experience on, we would not deviate from those conclusions, except perhaps to add a little emphasis. In summary, the reasons why organisations fail are:

♦ Employee engagement is a serious business.

♦ With employee engagement, you must think 70% culture, 30% structure.

- Perception is reality.
- Keep the atmosphere positive!
- Managers must manage.
- Once you've started, you can't get off!

PITFALL 1: EMPLOYEE ENGAGEMENT IS A SERIOUS BUSINESS

This is our pet frustration, the most common reason why organisations fail to see through change programmes. Management seems unable to grasp the importance of what they are trying to do. In essence, employee engagement requires a significant and permanent shift in the mind-set of the working population towards life at work. The extent of this shift varies from employee to employee. Those in management have to change the most. But experience tells us that the group most resistant to change is … management itself!

To illustrate this vital point, let's look at one of John's experiences. As he says:

> "A couple of years ago I was asked to speak at a high level conference attended by around 70 chief executives / senior director types. In order to make an impact, I sought the advice of a well-known speaker on the circuit and asked him for a few tips. He was very helpful and recommended that I concentrate on that very first impression. He argued that this was the key point in any presentation, as getting off to a sound start gave you a fighting chance of holding the audience's attention. He suggested that I should think of a question to which only a small minority could answer affirmatively. I could then use their smug self-satisfaction to embarrass the shamefaced majority who would then listen intently, in case I repeated the exercise!
>
> This seemed a lot more exciting than my usual, conventional introduction, so I decided to give it a try. Full of newly-found confidence, I bounded up to the lectern and declaimed, 'Let me ask you a question. At the last management meeting you attended, how many of you kicked off the session with a general review of what morale was like in your office, plant, factory, shop, school or whatever?'.

The response was definitely not the one I'd anticipated. Half the audience simply gazed at the floor. The other half looked at me as if I was speaking Swahili. The first signs of panic began to rise in my chest. I attempted to recover. 'OK, let me modify the question. How many of you AT ANY TIME during your last management meeting raised the issue of morale in your office, plant, factory, shop, school or whatever?'. Things got much worse. This time all 70 pairs of eyes were now firmly fixed on the floor. I was dying. The advice hadn't worked at all. I just wanted the ground to eat me up. In a hesitant, croaky voice, I managed to splutter out "OK, tell me, at ANY TIME DURING ANY MANAGEMENT MEETING THROUGHOUT THE WHOLE OF LAST YEAR, how many asked a question on what morale was like in your office, plant, factory, shop or whatever?'.

This time, four hands were raised, probably more in sympathy than enthusiasm. I suspect they were lying anyway.

I then asked how many companies represented in the room produced an annual report that included a phrase along the lines of 'people are our most precious asset'. Everybody raised their hands. I rudely asked how the hell they knew since they never bothered to find out. Heads returned to the floor."

But isn't this fairly typical of management in this country, in operations big and small. We pretend we understand the profound impact that general morale and motivation can have on the health of the organisation, but then clearly fail to do anything about it.

In our experience of examining numerous failed change programmes over the past 16 years, we discovered that most occurred because management, particularly senior management, failed to commit sufficiently. They either neglected to support the concept up-front or failed to follow it through. Is it any wonder that the expression *"we're good starters in our company but hopeless finishers"* figures in so many of our interviews? The root cause of this underperformance has to be senior management attention, commitment and enthusiasm. Or perhaps even courage.

PITFALL 2: EMPLOYEE ENGAGEMENT IS 70% CULTURE, 30% STRUCTURE

This statement is probably regarded as our most controversial. Increasingly, organisations are switching to the *systems thinking* approach pioneered by Deming and adopted by others. This preaches the benefits of sound, lean systems. It argues quite logically that most of the frustrations, hassles and hair-tearing moments in working life are caused by system inadequacy. Either the system is wrong or the organisation doesn't conform to it. Streamlining the system to ensure 100% conformance, total process capability and maximum real added value will eliminate at a stroke these stress points and restore motivation and morale.

We do not have a problem with this thinking. In fact, we whole-heartedly endorse the philosophy. But most of us start from a dysfunctional position. Managing and working in such chaotic circumstances has its impacts. Attitudes harden, positions are 'adopted'. The workforce becomes change-resistant. Mistrust breaks out between management and the managed. Blame cultures evolve. People become preoccupied by finding out *who* is to blame rather than *how* we can learn from the mistake. Sub-cultures become stronger than the corporate culture. Interdepartmental relationships disintegrate. Management attitudes become entrenched, reactionary and skewed. And that's just your normal, everyday, traditional company! Worse still, dear reader, it's probably yours!

Merely focusing on systems will not dig you out of this hole. Bitter experience tells us that your efforts here will be undermined by disbelief, hostility and sheer bloody-mindedness. So, first, fix the culture, the way you currently 'do things around here'. Eliminate some of the obvious weaknesses and, at the very least, try to persuade the *silent majority* that you understand their frustrations and are genuinely trying to do something about them.

PITFALL 3: PERCEPTION IS REALITY

We would strongly urge every key decision-maker to have this printed in large letters and stuck firmly on their bathroom mirrors! Each morning, as you clean your teeth, you could ponder on how management egos conspire continually to damage organisations whilst their owners bask in blissful ignorance. We manage not just on information but also on judgment, impression and perception. Sadly, much of this is biased or, worse still, plain wrong.

Figure 1 shows the so-called perception dilemma. Between you and your colleagues or subordinates lie barriers. These unseen barriers serve to distort the message both ways. As a consequence, what may seem to you to be normal management behaviour may well be represented to them as eccentric, damaging or even plain barmy. You need to identify these perceptions and face up to them. We will deal with the subject of perception and the impact of unconscious incompetence later on. In the meanwhile, just accept that, in our experience, this is the second biggest cause of failure after not taking the subject seriously (**Pitfall No. 1**).

Figure 1: The Perception Dilemma

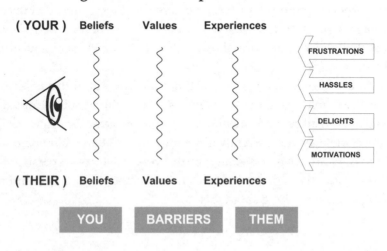

PITFALL 4: KEEP THE ATMOSPHERE POSITIVE

Every person who works for you comes through the door with a raft of inherent talents and expertise. It is rare for any organisation to exploit the potential fully here. Job definitions, departmental boundaries, burdensome procedures and management heavy-handedness all conspire to limit the contribution of our average employee. Incidentally, this applies at all levels in the organisational hierarchy, including the Board.

Many employees feel incapable of contributing creative, imaginative or innovative ideas. Peer pressure can be a major restrictive influence. As a consequence, you may be reliant entirely on your upper echelon for all your lateral thinking, those occasional out-of-the-box leaps that are so often needed to move the organisation onwards and upwards. An engaged workforce gets round this limitation and offers the prospect of access to much greater intellectual power.

However, if the prevailing ethos in your company is negative, caused through, for example, fear, apathy, complacency or mistrust, then the potential for accessing individual creativity diminishes. For employee engagement to be successful, you have to have a positive atmosphere. Management, in particular, need to be seen as constructive rather than as persistently critical. They need to be associated with success and celebration. Their language, demeanour and tone all have to strike a positive tone. You may have the most articulate mission and value statements in the world but, if your behaviour doesn't mirror these lofty intentions, then the whole package will be meaningless. Failure to acknowledge this will surely destroy any chance you might have of winning the hearts and minds of the workforce. And that's what this is all about.

PITFALL 5: MANAGERS MUST MANAGE

Earlier we said that, four years and lots of experience on, we would not deviate from our first conclusions on pitfalls *except perhaps to add a little emphasis*. In Pitfall 5, we need to do just that. If our empirical evidence from years of looking at culture change has any validity, then we would have to conclude that management everywhere has an almost infinitive capacity to ignore the blindingly obvious! The attractions of the new seem so readily to tempt them away from dull routine. In many respects, they seem like the student who decides to clean his room rather than revise for tomorrow's exam! As a consequence, they unconsciously send a signal to the organisation that routine is no longer important. Understandably, the organisation reacts likewise and also moves on. The good disciplines that underpin the new culture are forgotten or ignored, and the organisation goes backwards. One of the saddest aspects of working in this field has been witnessing companies make rapid progress and then suddenly fall back rapidly because the new cultural 'foundation' has been ignored or taken for granted. Employees feel the brunt worst. Being deprived of job satisfaction, pride and involvement can turn an enthusiastic workforce into a collection of Luddites.

Management must understand that they, and they alone, can initiate employee engagement successfully. They are also solely responsible for its continuation. Park your efforts for a few months or, in very small organisations, even for a few weeks, and your momentum will be lost. Recovering it will prove to be very, very time-consuming – if not impossible.

So do not go down this path unless you are totally *committed* and willing to be significantly and *personally* involved. Undertaking mechanistic endeavours like TQM, MRPII, BPR, Six Sigma, etc, etc is easy for your average managing director. All s/he has to do is sign the cheque! The rest of the work can be entrusted to a loyal, capable deputy, usually either the Quality or Human Resource specialist. However, with employee engagement, you have to be seen by the entire organisation, especially your direct reports, as being intimately associated with the philosophy. Only then will it gain the necessary credibility. This commitment has no shelf-life. Employee engagement is a permanent managerial philosophy. Once you sign up, you're in until retirement!

PITFALL 6: ONCE YOU'VE STARTED, YOU CAN'T GET OFF!

Continuing this theme of a permanent change in organisational mind-set, one has to recognise that enthusiasm doesn't last forever. You must regularly seek ways of refreshing the drive with new themes, new challenges and new approaches. The underlying foundation will be constant but we need to expand horizons continually to keep people interested, enthusiastic and energised. Runshaw College develops a different theme each year and uses engagement to drive for excellence in that particular area. The mainstay endeavours are not neglected, but the stimulus of using individual imagination, creativity and innovation to achieve really stretching goals is tremendous. This is actually not a difficult area, unlike some of the other pitfalls. But, as we said earlier, it is often these simple disciplines that management have a habit of forgetting!

Our advice is to remind yourself regularly of the mistakes that others have made. Employee engagement, particularly of a radical nature, is fortunately not yet a science. Its development at this stage is more akin to a black art. It is a commonsense approach to handling people and discovering what motivates them and what doesn't. There are no rules but there are guidelines. Ignore them at your peril.

Armed with this battery of warnings we now move to our recommended path, our 'Route Map'. The approach is designed to be followed sequentially, but there is no need to complete each stage before you move onto the next. This is a permanently iterative process. It is unlikely that you'll ever get any element Right First Time. You have to accept that employee engagement is a learning process and, hence, it is not unusual to be involved in several stages at once.

You might also find the path a little complicated or a little daunting at first sight. Don't let this put you off. In the same way as Roy Jenkins declaimed that you can't have a fair tax system that is also simple, detailed prescription inevitably looks difficult. But work through a stage at a time and all will become clear.

The principle of the recommended path is derived from the initial thoughts sent out in *The Team Enterprise Solution*. Its basic elements are shown in **Figure 2**.

Figure 2: The Route Map or Preferred Path

Step	
1	Understand your business
2	Identify the common crisis
3	Convince yourselves
4	Convince the rest of the management team
5	Establish the values
6	Find the perceived barriers / constraints as seen by the workforce
7	Construct the architecture
8	Go for the quick wins: Communication Recognition Management Style
9	Focus on the external customer : Going for customer delight
10	Focus on the internal customer : Learning to work together
11	Create the infrastructure: The right employee systems The right organisation structure
12	Enhance team-working and empowerment
13	Focus on the process
14	Start again

Steps 1 and 2 are all about understanding the business, where the threats and opportunities lie and how they should be tackled. We will discuss in detail later the determination of a 'common crisis', a mutually beneficial objective that will bind the interests of both management and the managed.

Steps 3 and 4 are fundamental. Throughout this book, the importance of overt management commitment will be repeatedly emphasised. Whilst it is not terribly important or even feasible to achieve wholesale conversion of management immediately, it is vital that, by the end of Step 6, they are sufficiently 'attuned' to the philosophy not to damage the process. It is too easy to reject or rationalise away the more critical employee perceptions. Aside from the obvious point that these perceptions are more often right than wrong, failure to be at least accepting of the possibility of *mea culpa* can flatten the new-found enthusiasm of your workforce. Saying 'Sorry' doesn't come easy to many in management, often because they lack the necessary self-confidence. Management must be mature, considered and prepared to display a little humility. Should you not be prepared to go that far, then employee engagement is just not for you. Stop here!

Steps 6 and 13 are all about *ownership*. Provided the process for identifying employee perceptions is independent, open and includes being fed back to all simultaneously, you have a fair chance of establishing *ownership of the problem*. In simple terms, this means that everybody is agreed on precisely what is wrong with the company. Most companies do not even get to this point because of different interpretations of underlying causality. Management thinks the workforce is at fault. The workforce becomes absolutely convinced it's 'them upstairs'. We are left with a stand-off. No-one can start resolving the matter because we cannot agree where to begin. Determining in a totally open and consultative fashion what employees are thinking, without any fear of management inserting its own biased editorial or spin, creates an understanding. The organisation can then move to do something about the issues ('Action Planning') without confusion, misunderstanding or disagreement.

In the same way as Step 6 was designed to gain *ownership of the problem*, Steps 7 to 13 are all about *ownership of solution*. Repeatedly, we find that solutions are best implemented successfully where a perception of local involvement exists. If, to this, we can add an element of local origination, then the traditional resistances to any change programme become considerably lessened. Experience tells us that solutions perceived to be generated 'bottom-up' can often be far more exciting, far more radical and far more enthusiastically embraced than those thought to be derived from senior management. The real power here is in designing a process that maximises this perceived involvement over a multitude of relevant issues and which is seen to be both genuine and well-intentioned.

You will by now have spotted the over-use of the adjective 'perceived'. It is difficult to discuss the issue without sounding Machiavellian or manipulative. However, our view is that the average workforce is sharper than most of us want to give credit. If they detect any insincerity or dodgy motives, the process will die on its feet. Nevertheless, it is vital that we recognise that the perception of involvement is as important as the reality. It is true that some issues may be too big, too sensitive or too complex to be totally delegated to junior staff. Allowing employees just to endorse the prevailing wisdom, as long as they have the opportunity to challenge, question or offer alternatives, can be sufficient to gain commitment. In finality, that is exactly what the process is about. By getting them involved with the solution, we increase the motivation to see it fulfilled. All the time, we must constantly remind ourselves that this is as much about *motivation* as it is about mere problem-solving.

In this book, our main objective is to create a step-by-step approach that is sufficiently prescriptive to maximise the chances of success and yet sufficiently flexible to allow for local circumstances. Benefits will be achieved by partial completion. However, *transformation* will only really become a possibility when the plan has been through several iterations. That is not to say you have to wait forever before the return justifies the benefits. Should your company be blighted by a negative atmosphere, change resistance or an adversarial climate between 'us and them', then, properly executed, you will see beneficial changes in a matter of weeks. Should your company be not quite as bad as this (and, therefore, in our experience, atypical!), the return may take a little longer. In any event, there are no downsides to 'having a go', save perhaps the danger of increasing employee expectations and then not delivering.

Clear? Never mind, it all will be soon!

3
TAKING THE PLUNGE

We are about to start a journey that will completely change the *culture* of your organisation. Before we do that, perhaps we need to discuss what exactly *culture* is. The word is used very frequently in all aspects of work and social activity. Public relations companies spend vast fortunes in projecting the right image for their clients. Simple sugared drinks beget a complete makeover when they become Coca-Cola, Pepsi-Cola, Dr. Pepper or even Irn-Bru! Likewise the humble hamburger assumes a much more complex image in our minds when associated with McDonald's, Burger King, Wimpy and so on.

The key word here is 'assumes'. By culture, we mean the attitudes, behaviour and values we associate with such organisations. It is a complex relationship between reality and image. However, we can never underestimate it. People want to work for companies that are perceived to have a strong culture, where stated and unspoken values and attributes make them attractive places of work. Our ambition in this book is to strengthen your company's perceived culture to such an extent that employees not only want to belong – they also want to be part of its ongoing development.

Adopting any culture change programme, especially one as far-reaching as this, is a daunting task. Employee engagement permeates the core of every single activity in the organisation. It is highly demanding on all management, not just those on the front line. Hopefully, it is the marked behavioural change in management that convinces the rest of the organisation of the seriousness of intent. Senior management, especially the proprietor or owner-manager, has to demonstrate not just that they understand the new game but also that they are prepared to change *personally*. Good practice demands that they become the exemplars of the new philosophy.

It is evident, therefore, that the senior decision-makers need more than an understanding of the structures and a simple appreciation of the likely benefits. They have to be ready for a permanent change in their behaviour, their thinking and their commitment to the cause. In many respects, some of the top team are going to have to become evangelists of employee engagement. Otherwise the first set-back, and there will be many, may knock them off-course or cause them to return to prior styles and behaviours. Senior management, therefore, must spend some time familiarising themselves with the total picture before they start. Staggeringly, few do. The temptation to leave it to others is often irresistible and invariably fatal.

STEP 1: UNDERSTAND YOUR BUSINESS

Step 1 seems a rather strange, if not insulting, request. Asking a senior manager whether he/she *really* understands his/her business is tantamount to inviting a sock to the jaw! However, this is truly an important stage that, if ignored, could lead to the company going down the wrong track, with potentially disastrous consequences. The two case studies that follow make the point.

Case Study 1

We were requested to visit a medium-sized operation by the site Operations Director. The factory had all the classic symptoms of a dysfunctional culture. Industrial relations were fraught, with unions seemingly in permanent confrontation with management. Departments suffered from chronic 'siloism', as they constantly fought and bickered amongst themselves. Morale, staff turnover and absenteeism were all problematic. At first glance, we saw this as an ideal fit for the 'Route Map'.

Two hours in the factory soon persuaded us otherwise. The factory was supposedly organised around discrete assembly lines. However, we couldn't see them! The entire shop-floor was strewn with work-in-progress, unfinished assemblies and component parts, much covered in dust. The attendant paperwork showed distinct signs of age. Further enquiries exposed massive inventories in products 'pulled ahead to keep the lads and lasses busy'.

The root cause of all this too-evident chaos soon became clear. The company relied on a rigid 'push' system for material and production planning, which was clearly inappropriate to such a dynamic and varied marketplace. It totally lacked process capability. No amount of goodwill, motivation or enlightened self-interest was going to solve this one. What they needed, as an immediate priority, was an effective logistics solution, based in all probability on a 'pull' system such as Kanban. Once identified and installed, the employee engagement approach could then be used to optimise implementation and final refinement. But without it, we would have been wasting their time as well as ours.

Case Study 2

Jim was the general manager of a hitherto successful operation in the textile business. He brought a group of managers, supervisors and team leaders along to us to hear about employee engagement. He was convinced that this was the right way forward. Our job, in his mind, was to persuade his colleagues to follow suit.

In the course of the initial discussions, it became clear that this previously profitable operation had suddenly lurched into considerable losses. When asked by his team how this could be so, as volumes had actually increased, he replied rather furtively that it was the 'mix'. Further questioning merely amplified, rather than resolved, the mystery. His subordinates seemed to be both uneasy and deeply suspicious.

An opportunity came up later in the day to examine this conundrum in a syndicate with Jim and his senior colleagues. Using our familiar technique of alternating simple questions with several *whys*, the weakness was identified. The company did not know the cost of anything, let alone product line profitability. Prices were struck on the basis of 'what the market could stand', quite dangerous considering the sales force were incentivised only on volume. As a consequence, products with similar cost structures had selling prices varying by up to 800%! Recently, volumes had come from the more demanding sections of the customer base, resulting in greater losses from greater throughput. Understandably, the junior management team were perplexed and found a major misfit between the perceived problem and Jim's solution of improving the culture.

We concluded that Jim's immediate challenge was not to pursue employee engagement. The urgency of the situation demanded a greater understanding of costs, revenues and margins. The sales force incentive scheme needed also to be changed urgently, to reflect margin rather than volume. Only when this was resolved, could the size of the problem be quantified. And then engagement could be used to crack it.

These are but two of many encounters we have had over the years. Radical employee engagement is not the immediate solution to every business ailment. True, it may not actually harm the organisation, but it could distract you from the really urgent. In the two examples above, the 'system thinkers' would have had much greater impact than the engagement advocates. We would speculate that this applies in about 25% of instances. Employee engagement will always be a useful tool if applied correctly, but it is not always the first port of call.

It is vital, therefore, that you understand your business to avoid making the same mistakes as Jim & Co. In **Figure 3**, we have two sets of questions, one about 'culture' and the other about 'process'. The way you respond should give you a clue about priority.

This is a deliberately crude questionnaire, designed not to give the right answer but to get you thinking holistically about your business. Should you register low marks on Questions 1 to 5, there is a strong possibility that radical employee engagement could really help you out. However, should you continue to register poorly on Questions 6 to 9, then there is a stronger possibility that there may be something wrong with one or more of the fundamentals of your business. You may be then best served either by favouring systems thinking here over engagement or doing both in parallel.

Whatever happens, we must never forget the basics of business. Employee engagement is an improvement tool. If the 'core of your business' is malfunctioning or below par, then in all probability you will have to look to this first.

STEP 2: IDENTIFYING THE COMMON CRISIS

Once convinced that the cultural route is suitable for your company, then you need to think about identifying a common purpose. We wish to 'engage' employees but their first response will be 'engage in what?'.

A simple definition of employee engagement was:

Empowered people working towards mutually beneficial objectives.

Figure 3: Employee Engagement Questionnaires

	CULTURE	Strongly Disagree	Disagree	Agree	Strongly Agree
Q1	People here tend to work well together.	1	2	3	4
Q2	There is mutual trust between management and subordinates.	1	2	3	4
Q3	We tend to plan our way out of trouble rather than firefight.	1	2	3	4
Q4	We are very successful at adopting new initiatives.	1	2	3	4
Q5	In general, people like working in our company.	1	2	3	4

	PROCESS	Strongly Disagree	Disagree	Agree	Strongly Agree
Q6	Our logistics systems are generally robust. Any failures tend to be due to application.	1	2	3	4
Q7	We generally understand the costs and margins of our products.	1	2	3	4
Q8	Our products are capable of being competitive.	1	2	3	4
Q9	With the right product at the right price, there is a viable market out there for our company.	1	2	3	4

As a senior director, proprietor or owner-manager in the private sector, it is highly likely that your personal objectives are something to do with wealth creation. This may be expressed as building up the saleable value of the business, a healthy dividend flow or one or more of the many Key Performance Indicators (KPIs) that purport to measure company performance. There is nothing at all wrong with this. In fact, any investor in your organisation would be quite alarmed if this was not the case. Business is sufficiently risky nowadays without having the senior decision-makers distracted by peripheral objectives.

Even those in the public or quasi-public sector have to conform to budgetary limitations. Their first priority is to deliver *within* those financial constraints. Hence measures on productivity, performance, customer satisfaction, efficiency or quality come to the fore. Employee engagement has the potential of delivering major improvements in all of these conventional parameters. However, to get employees interested motivated and committed, there has to be a reciprocal benefit that is both tangible and relevant.

You therefore need to search for this mutually beneficial objective. What is that common denominator that ties the interest of the employee to that of the employer? Can you identify one that will be instantly recognised by both parties? There are numerous possibilities here.

One area we would rule out immediately, and perhaps controversially, is anything to do with *financial gain*. We've seen over the years lots of so-called 'gainsharing' schemes where the financial performance of the business becomes inextricably linked to the remuneration of employees. At first sight, this seems both logical and fair. If the business prospers, then why should employees not benefit proportionately?

There are two major flaws in schemes of this nature. First, the prosperity of businesses, sadly, is not directly proportional to the *effort* of its employees. In fact, effort is well down the list of key business influences. Markets, legislation, products, macro-economic movements and sheer fortune probably come out far ahead of individual effort. It is illogical, therefore, to devise a payment system around a relationship that barely exists. This becomes much more relevant when we look at the second flaw.

Employees get used to pay levels and don't like them going down! Take a scenario where your business, due to enhanced market demand, prospers for a few years. Over this period, employees benefit likewise, because of the gainsharing arrangement and progressively adjust their standard of living to match their new incomes. Mortgages are increased, expensive holidays are taken and consumer durables are purchased, often on 'tick'. Then the honeymoon ends. The economy falters and your market with it. You now have to struggle to stay competitive. You are vulnerable.

At the point of your greatest fragility, when what you really need is everybody in the organisation redoubling their efforts, your employees are feeling the pinch personally as well. They are disgruntled and possibly very angry about this change in fortunes. And they may well blame management – wondering why you didn't see this coming and take action earlier to prevent these uncomfortable consequences? The arguments shift from understanding the real business situation to internal bickering and in-fighting.

In our experience, over many years of interviewing employees across a whole range of businesses, there is no positive correlation between employee morale and pay. Some of the most disaffected workforces we have ever encountered have been paid exceptionally well by competitive standards. It seems that management substituted money or reward for good managerial practice. People today need much more from the world of work than just a pay packet at the end of the week or month. They need an extension of society, a feeling of belonging, a sense of purpose and the opportunity of achieving a degree of satisfaction. The psychologists among you (they seem to be everywhere these days!) would probably have more to say on the subject. Sufficient for us to conclude here that there's more to working life than money. However, we will revisit the subject later.

In *The Team Enterprise Solution*, we coined the expression 'psychological gainsharing' to emphasise the complex nature of motivation in modern organisations. To quote:

> "Somehow, we must ensure that our employees perceive that they will use these newfound accountabilities, decision-making and responsibilities (as presented by employee engagement) ... to work towards objectives that not only satisfy the aims of the corporation or company but also meet the requirements of the individuals involved. We are looking for Win : Win; we are looking for that area of common interest which creates a

'psychological gainsharing' opportunity. The selection of the
mutually beneficial objective is all important."

For most of us in business, whether in public or private sectors, this
common purpose can be most readily identified by considering the
potential crises facing the company. Most of us have them and they
can be very useful in articulating a mutually beneficial mission. It has
been said, apparently by Tom Peters, that if you haven't got a crisis,
invent one!! This sounds terribly devious, but it conveys the point. If
you don't perceive you have a crisis, perhaps the true crisis is your
lack of appreciation of the real threats around the business! Companies
throughout the UK, whether in retail, agriculture, manufacturing or
whatever, face an ongoing challenge of generating the necessary
productivity and overhead cost structures to maintain international
competitiveness. For them, the crisis is sheer survival. Perhaps an
ambition to 'retain as many long-term secure jobs as possible' may
well fit the bill here. Should this be achieved, then the company would
benefit as obviously would its employees. If job security emerges as a
major issue in your Perception Barrier analysis (**Step 6**), you may have
to look no further.

Other organisations may find it better to focus on competitive
pressure. If you have a competitor or group of competitors posing a
threat recognisable to all the workforce, this might be the answer. You
could define the mutually beneficial objective by referring directly to
the competition. Or more generally, but equally effectively, as one
organisation declared:

> "In 10 years' time, it is confidently forecast that only FIVE UK
> companies will survive in our business. We want to be one of
> the five."

A far more difficult, but ultimately more beneficial, challenge is to
move away from the implied threat of a crisis and resort to the
motivating force of being part of a high-performing team. Success
breeds success. Getting individual employees at every level of the
organisation to feel that they have contributed significantly to success,
and will play an even bigger part in sustaining or even increasing it, is
as pure a common purpose as you are likely to see. It also fits very
sweetly into many of the other areas of employee engagement,

particularly with the so-called 'quick wins' seen in **Step 8** – *communication, recognition and management style.* However, it is extremely difficult to develop this from the outset in most traditional organisations. Cynicism, scepticism and plain mistrust, at the very least, will undermine it. So, unless you already start with a very balanced and switched-on workforce, our advice is simple. Start with your local definitions of the mutual crisis, expressed constructively, and eventually move towards a much more aspirational statement.

The foregoing may seem complicated, but it needn't be. Remember this is a two-way street. Both management and workforce have to be committed to make employee engagement really work. A little bit of enlightened self interest from the outset could be just the thing to provoke enthusiasm.

STEP 3: CONVINCE YOURSELVES!

If by now we haven't convinced you of the vital role that senior management play in the execution of successful employee engagement, then worry not. This theme will scream out of nearly every chapter in the remainder of the book! By now, you are probably more than familiar with the tremendous financial benefits bestowed when organisations get this concept right. Otherwise, you probably wouldn't have picked this book up. The rewards can be quite spectacular, perhaps transformational. Even the journey partwards towards implementation can be highly beneficial, whether measured financially or attitudinally. But the difference between success and failure will inevitably be either *your* understanding or *your* commitment, or both.

Therefore, you must spend some time beforehand with your senior colleagues or other key influencers understanding what this is all about and what it means for you personally. You need to be ready for the outcome of **Step 6**, the perception barrier analysis. You may be criticised personally. In fact, if you are the proprietor, owner-manager or managing director, you WILL be criticised personally! How will you react? How prepared are you to condition your behaviour as a consequence of receiving these criticisms? How capable are you of changing? Are you genuinely willing to acknowledge fundamental weaknesses in your business without resorting to blame?

In over 12 years of conducting these perception barrier exercises, we rarely have a problem with workforces. But we've had plenty with management teams! Most of these issues emerged through a lack of appreciation by management of their pivotal role in determining the culture of the organisation. Many simply find the price of personally changing too high to pay. They'd erroneously assumed that much of the consequent work downstream could be delegated. They themselves are now caught firmly in the headlights. This clashes with their egos, their self-perceptions and their hard earned 'images'. As a consequence, the momentum slows and the initiative is parked up. Nothing is said, but the signs are all there.

This is both a phenomenal waste of time and very damaging to workplace morale. More often than not, by the time the outcome of the perception analysis is reached, employees feel pretty 'teed up'. They are frequently astute enough to see the potential of engagement in improving both the physical and emotional lot of the organisation. Very frequently, we find employees becoming visibly excited at this stage. Seeing this new-found enthusiasm slowly evaporate is one of the most frustrating aspects of life in this area. Blighted expectations will damage the more positive in your workforce and feed the cynical and sceptical.

In terms of preparation, this stage will not be unduly onerous. We would suggest three simple steps:

♦ **Read about it:** Finish this book, read *The Team Enterprise Solution* or equivalent. Talk, if appropriate, to your local business support agency.

♦ **Visit somewhere where it works:** This is a very useful way of convincing you and your colleagues. If you pick the right location, the group will see at first hand how it works, how it fits together with more conventional initiatives and where difficulties are experienced.

♦ **Talk about it:** This is absolutely vital. Within the senior team, you are more than likely to have a range of opinions, from earnestly enthusiastic to downright sceptical. We have never yet, for example, found anybody from Information Technology or Finance who are natural champions of engagement! Engineering managers don't fill us full of hope either! However, the danger is that their views will not be articulated. Your challenge is to draw them out, getting them involved in open and honest debate. The results can be surprising. One die-hard sceptic admitted: "I don't even talk like this to the wife!".

In many organisations, there is another group of senior influencers who need to be involved here: the Board or equivalent. Elected officials in local authorities, for example, often exert tremendous leverage even at the executive level. Chairs of private and public companies can be short-termist in outlook. When profits drop or service levels shrink, they can often adopt quite a parochial and self-centred approach. Uneducated and unconvinced, they may perceive employee engagement as nothing more than a fashionable whim or sheer indulgence. Should you be in this unfortunate situation, it may pay to involve them from the outset. Better still, make them think it's their idea!

If there is one piece of advice in this entire book that is more likely than not to be ignored, it is this section. Provided you are open-minded and amenable to change, this may not in the end be problematic. But it is a risk, and an unnecessary one at that. So do make the effort, as you are going to have enough problems with the next step!

STEP 4: CONVINCE THE REST OF YOUR MANAGEMENT TEAM

Middle and front-line management are often cited as being one of the key areas of change resistance in any company. One organisation invented the term *middle management permafrost* to describe how well-intentioned initiatives have a habit of failing to permeate through this rigid block of ice-cold indifference. Having heard this theory so many times from less-than-perfect senior management makes one more than a little wary as to the true causal factor. Nevertheless, the point is taken. That middle rump of management between the board and the workplace is a highly influential group, which has the power to cause any change programme to fail. So, whether this represents half-a-dozen people in the smaller company to a whole battalion in their larger equivalents is largely immaterial. This is a group that must be carried along with genuine enthusiasm and belief if employee engagement is to be successful.

Having middle management as true owners of culture change can be highly beneficial in the longer term. There will be periods when senior management get distracted or diverted to other priorities. An engaged middle tier will maintain the momentum over these difficult periods to ensure that the organisation doesn't go backwards. Time spent in convincing and educating middle management in the principles and vagaries of culture change is rarely wasted.

Many organisations choose not to tackle this issue at this point. Instead they wait until the outcome of the Perception analysis, **Step 6**, is available. The power of subordinate criticism, delivered usually in quite an emphatic manner, is often sufficient to shock the entire management strata into acceptance. However, this is undoubtedly risky. A more natural reaction may be to reject or rationalise away these alleged weaknesses as ill-informed, prejudiced or mischievous. The less prepared management are for the outcome, the more likely they are to react adversely. As we indicated earlier, there is only a finite time between feedback, response and action before employee expectations begin to curdle. Our advice is to do something now to maximise your chance of success later.

Middle management attitudes, in reality, often mirror those of the organisation. However, for obvious reasons they are less likely to express their concerns vociferously, especially when their superiors are within earshot. But being the proverbial 'meat in the sandwich' can impose its own stresses and strains and result in a slightly cynical attitude towards top-down change. Most organisations claim to suffer from 'initiativitis', the infliction of unnecessary and ill-thought through change programmes that appear with every new management arrival or new corporate plan. Irrespective of the size of the operation, managers in this tier seem to feel threatened and disrupted by unnecessary change that rarely goes through to completion.

Resistance points from middle management include:

♦ The fact that they didn't invent or introduce the idea of employee engagement.

♦ An inevitable feeling of being threatened personally by the process.

- ◆ An attendant fear of the consequences of culture change.
- ◆ A fear of being personally exposed after the perception barrier analysis.
- ◆ A concern that they will not be able to adapt to a new participative style.
- ◆ A belief that this is yet another doomed initiative, just like all the others before.
- ◆ A lack of empathy with the sentiment, perhaps wrongly identified as another airy-fairy HR flavour of the month.
- ◆ A worry over the size and complexity of the task.
- ◆ Concerns over time absorption and competing initiatives.

All these are valid and cannot be ignored. In larger organisations with traditional structures, there will be a legitimate concern over 'management shrinkage'. As decisions are delegated and employees empowered, the need for expensive intermediate managerial slots diminishes. This reduction in old-fashioned, bureaucratic institutions could be as high as 30% to 50% as management added value spirals upwards. In a growing organisation, or one where the product offering can be enlarged, there is always the opportunity for transfer people to a new challenge. In a static or declining company, job losses may well be inevitable. This is an inescapable by-product of employee engagement which, whilst highly beneficial to the bottom line, can be both frightening and disruptive to middle management attitudes. It is best to have this out on the table from the start, otherwise the transparency and honesty of the entire initiative will be undermined.

By far the most effective mechanism for achieving this 'conviction and education' is internal communication and consultation. Better still, if members of the senior group become sufficiently 'expert' in the theory, they can act as trainers or facilitators to school the middle tier into adjusting to the demands of the new regime. External consultants can be used for basic awareness training and will undoubtedly be professional. However, there is nothing as powerful as internal advocates who demonstrate not just understanding but also belief and commitment. As we will see elsewhere, the 'real' values of the organisation are largely set by the behaviour and attitudes of the senior management group. Having them teach the principles will reinforce their overall credibility.

There is one final issue in this area that should not really create a problem but invariably does. This is the issue of 'overt status', those symbols of hierarchy so jealously guarded by their owners. However, they have the unwanted side effect of 'turning off' employees and reinforcing old stereotypes. If you are serious, they have to go! The most obvious 'trapping of power' is the reserved car parking place or the managing director's privilege of getting his/her car washed by the maintenance department. These can be powerful irritations to the workforce. Getting shot of them can be a clear signal that things are changing!

You must be on your guard against other demonstrations of demarcation. Our pet favourite has always been canteen facilities. Everybody has to eat so why do arrangements have to be different? Management seem to have an almost infinite capacity to delude themselves here. A couple of case studies illustrate the point.

Case Study 3

In 1978, John Oliver was asked to move a highly traditional operation into a brand new, greenfield facility just five miles away. Historically, the company had encouraged the development of whole tiers of canteens. Provision varied from the works canteen, the foremen's dining hall, the (two-off) managers' rooms and culminating in the splendid directors' emporium complete with liveried waitress service. A new factory seemed to be an ideal opportunity to break this ancient and needless tradition.

The new layouts for the factory were received with horror by management. "Where are we going to eat?" came well ahead of entry / egress, location of stores and disposition of machine shops! When told that there was only one dining facility for all, they immediately objected. There was a practical reason for their concern (there always is). It was pointed out that employees from the shop-floor might well use the facilities whilst still in their overalls. Machine oil would be splattered everywhere and ruin the day dress of 'staff'.

John offered a compromise. There would be two types of chair: red ones and blue ones. Anyone could sit on the red chair. However, anyone who preferred to remain in overalls had to use a blue one. Problem solved.

The canteen duly opened and was well attended by everyone except management. Most of the site management team preferred to jump in their cars and travel five miles back to the old site to revisit their familiar haunts. The only representatives of the senior hierarchy appeared to be limited to John and a very few others. Nevertheless, the arrangements were maintained and any attempt to re-introduce demarcation firmly resisted.

Sadly, there was an unexpected sequel. After about five or six weeks, a delegation of canteen representatives (yes, we had them as well!) trudged red-faced into John's office to ask him a favour. They had been approached by a number of their members to see if John would be good enough to personally stop eating in the canteen. They weren't used to seeing the boss in this way and it was putting them off their food!

Reluctantly, John agreed as the complaint was only addressed to him personally. However, it did demonstrate the huge gulf between management and the managed. How we could expect to get employee empathy, let alone engagement, against that backcloth defies belief. It is little wonder the UK automotive industry had such a bad time in the 60s and 70s.

Case Study 4

More recently, we were invited to visit the premises of a very large public sector organisation which, allegedly, was interested in empowerment and participation. We were taken on a tour of the very impressive facilities and listened to a very learned and erudite exposition of their ambitions in the area of culture change. We were mightily taken by their understanding and enthusiasm for the concepts. As the visit ended, our hosts asked whether we would like to stay for lunch. Aside from factory floors or big open-plan office areas, canteens are probably the best bellwether you can get of the prevailing culture. We quickly accepted.

However, disappointingly, we were led past the main canteen into an oak-lined room filled with leather chairs and settees. (I emphasise this is a public sector organisation!) Declining any alcoholic beverage on the grounds that this was hardly a good example to set to others back at our establishment, we settled into those big luxuriant chairs and listened to our hosts postulate further on the opportunities for genuine employee engagement.

A bell rang and we were summoned into a rather splendid dining room, grandly adorned by chandeliers and starched linen tablecloths. Our orders were taken by waitresses dressed in outfits last seen in black-and-white films from the 50s. Midway through the meal, we commented on the splendour of the setting and suggested politely that this would be the first thing to go if they had any hopes of participation, or partnership or whatever they were going to call it, actually working. Our host was dumbfounded. In all seriousness, he looked at us sternly and said "this place is very important to the culture of our organisation. People aspire to this. To take it away would deny everyone the ambition that, one day, they'd make it here".

Like the *News of the World* reporter, we made our excuses and left. With attitudes like that, they have no chance!

There are many examples of these 'humiliating systems' that emphasise differences between one group and another. How many managers for example use the same toilet facilities as the workers? Attendance controls are another area. Clocking may or not be a good idea. Some organisations might find it invaluable in support of their accounting systems, others may not see it useful at all. But what cannot be right is for one group to be obliged to 'clock on' and others, through some arbitrary distinction, allowed not to bother. Unconsciously, perhaps, we're sending a signal that one group matters more than another. This has to be a key obstacle to progress.

Those of us reared in a traditional business hierarchy often get used to these trappings. The metaphorical stripes on the sleeve or the pips on the shoulder give us a perceived status in a land where distinctions, however arbitrary, were important. Middle management need to get used to the idea that nothing really matters except behaviour and attitude. And these are best measured by subordinate perceptions.

STEP 5: ESTABLISH THE VALUES

Some commentators may find it surprising that we have inserted this element so early in the process. More logically, establishing values that drive the entire business ethos for management and managed alike probably belongs in the section on Management Style.

That is true, we will cover the whole concept of a Values Driven Culture much more intensively when we get down to Action Planning. However, before unleashing this on the organisation, senior management needs at least to reflect on where you're going and how far you wish to take it. Initially, we do not recommend a great deal of forethought here. But as the process goes through its second or third iterations, some key decisions need to be made.

On the basis that many of our readers are the key decision-makers in their organisations (owner-manager, proprietor or managing director), you will want to put your stamp on the company. Downstream, the values of the organisation may well be fixed in principle by others. You need to have a view on the subject so your colleagues don't come up with a model that jars against your personality, beliefs or philosophy.

No matter how much time is expended on the creation of a distinct set of values for a business, they all end looking broadly the same. For most, this is just a 'wallpaper' exercise, the creation of a series of bland statements that look good on the wall but mean nothing in practice. They seem like a clichéd collection of 'motherhood and apple pie' phrases half-hinched from last year's Christmas crackers. They are about as much use as a chocolate fireguard, up there with useless Mission Statements and Vision statements which nobody remembers or uses.

However, later we are going to try something different. We are going to attempt to create a set or sets of values that permeate through every interpersonal activity in your organisation. Not only are we going to construct these Values but we are going to learn how to use them to ensure that they are always reflected in the way we do business with each other. In short, we are going to create a blueprint for 'the way we do things around here'.

You need to reflect on whether you wish to impose any restrictions. Your views, opinions and behaviour are the key contributing elements to the ultimate culture. If you say one thing and do another, you are immediately going to undermine that culture. So think carefully here before the organisation commits itself to the undeliverable.

SUMMARY

And there we have it. The five preliminary steps in establishing the right culture for employee engagement. You will have the opportunity to return, for this is simply the first of many iterations. If employee engagement does become embedded into the organisational psyche, you will revisit Steps 1 to 5 many times, as this is a permanent change in management mind-set.

All five steps are appropriate to all businesses, big or small, public or private, community and volunteer. For a simple organisation, there may not be a lot to consider. But, nevertheless, the dangers of ignoring these fundamental issues are ever-present. Ignorance can never help!

These first five steps shouldn't take too long as they are 'launched' rather than completed first time. If you've been at it for more than eight weeks, then you're probably taking too long. Because in **Step 6**, things really begin to happen!

Figure 4: The Route Map updated 1

Step		
1	Understand your business	✓
2	Identify the common crisis	✓
3	Convince yourselves	✓
4	Convince the rest of the management team	✓
5	Establish the values	✓
6	Find the perceived barriers / constraints as seen by the workforce	
7	Construct the architecture	
8	Go for the quick wins: Communication Recognition Management Style	
9	Focus on the external customer : Going for customer delight	
10	Focus on the internal customer : Learning to work together	
11	Create the infrastructure: The right employee systems The right organisation structure	
12	Enhance team-working and empowerment	
13	Focus on the process	
14	Start again	

4

FIND OUT WHAT THE
BUGGERS THINK!

A little while ago, we were trying to explain to a rather forthright and old-fashioned Managing Director the need to understand employee perceptions. In those days, the term we used was 'Change Initiation', as that was the terminology used by the author of the original concept. Nowadays, we call this approach 'Perception Barrier Analysis' as it is self-explanatory, if a little longer.

This chap was having a great deal of difficulty with the principle of understanding employee perceptions, or more specifically why anyone should actually bother going to the trouble of finding out. As we increasingly and desperately rambled through the significance of unconscious competencies, barriers to mutual understanding, causal and symptomatic issues and the rest of the periphery that surrounds this essentially simple subject, a spark of recognition suddenly leapt into his eyes. It was as if someone had switched a light on. "Ah!", he said. "What you really want to do is *find out what the buggers think*!"

We blanched, thought about arguing and then tamely agreed. Anything for a quiet life. However, within that little vignette lie some of the key reasons why management fail so often in the area of culture change. We could, and should, have started with his reference to the workforce as 'buggers'. He would have dismissed the criticism outright as political correctness gone mad. He would claim that his people knew this to be just a bit of light-hearted banter, a joke. He would have argued that his boisterous management style was just part and parcel of a distinctive Northern culture. They understood he meant no harm and, in fact, enjoyed the blunt repartee. His men gave as good as they got.

We have witnessed this sort of behaviour and language on numerous occasions. The same justification, or dismissal, is always made by the manager involved. We are often accused of being oversensitive. However, we have a distinct advantage over the manager – we have the opportunity afterwards to talk discreetly and confidentially to the target of this 'banter'. And that always reveals a more complex situation.

True, the recipient rarely feels threatened or insulted. But although the barb might be seen good-naturedly, the sentiment left behind often does not. And repeated several times a week, a distinct legacy slowly develops. The continued use of such insulting language leaves people feeling inferior and under-valued. One manager used to jokingly refer to 'going back to the plantation' whenever he went out on the shop-floor. His witless attitude was quickly demolished when he realised that this merely reinforced the 'us and them' culture in the business by his incessant, unconscious references to a master-slave relationship.

The use of language in managing people is profoundly important. The words, tone and posture in which they are delivered send hundreds of signals, to most of which the speaker remains totally oblivious. To be an effective manager or leader, you need to find out.

Perception Barrier Analysis is definitely NOT about finding out what employees think. It's about holding a metaphorical mirror up to management and letting them see what they look like to others. It is rarely a pretty sight. Most managers think that they're fairly good, some perfect. They all appreciate and readily recognise weaknesses in others, but fail to, or chose not to, see the same flaws in their own profile. These *unconscious incompetencies* are common to us all. We all have them, in varying degrees of seriousness. However, generally, we also fail to recognise the consequences that this unconscious behaviour can have on subordinates and colleagues.

Let's examine a case study to illustrate the point.

Case Study 5

In 2002, we were asked to review an offshoot of a high-profile international operation. The factory and offices were ultra-modern and stylish. The place seemed professional and efficient. Above all, the management team and, in particular, the managing director, seemed approachable, open-minded and forward-thinking. We immediately felt that this was a company worth the effort.

To our great surprise, the Perception Barrier Analysis revealed some unexpected problems. Morale was not good, people didn't enjoy work and a fair few were looking elsewhere. Not what we'd expected at all.

We looked hard for some causal effect, some common flaw at the root of this general dismay. We eventually found it in a most unexpected area. The root cause behind all this general disharmony appeared to be the Managing Director. He was seen as rude, impersonal and arrogant. If this came as a surprise to us, it was a bigger one to him!

'Keith', for this was not his real name, struck us as thoughtful and quite charming. Nothing like the image portrayed by the workforce. But accepting the principle that 'Perception is Reality' (**Chapter 2**), we set forth to find out more.

We discovered a lot more about Keith, but nothing initially to explain this Jekyll and Hyde situation facing us. He was a workaholic in extreme. He was intensely shy, almost introverted. And his personal disciplines left a little to be desired.

His only contact with any of the workforce was every morning at 8.05 am precisely. Keith was inevitably late, which was a bit unfortunate as his reserved car parking spot was right outside the open-plan office block. Floor to ceiling one-way windows, as is the fashion nowadays, ensured that anyone within viewing distance would witness the following daily ritual.

Keith would tear up to his spot, brake hard and hurriedly try to exit the car and retrieve his briefcase at the same time. Invariably, this resulted in contortions or papers streaming left, right and centre. In foul weather, he also had a habit of wearing a very old, and very soiled, white mac, which was memorably described as 'one of Columbo's rejects'. Pulling this around his shoulders, he dashed into the building in a style reminiscent of a penguin with a limp.

To get to his office on the mezzanine floor, Keith had to endure the gaze of his entire office staff who occupied the space between the door and his destination. Befitting his introversion, he did this by rushing as fast as possible, eyes down, gaze averted. It was a relief to get into his own office. There he remained all day, except to venture occasionally into an adjoining conference room. In this domain, he felt confident, assured and in charge. The shop floor, rarely seeing him, christened him 'the cardboard cut-out'.

In the early days of the company, people would venture to speak to him as he scuttled across the office floor. Their cheery "Good mornings", "Hi Keith", or "How are you this morning?" were greeted with nothing. He galloped on, unseeing and unhearing.

In retrospect, you can see why people felt upset or offended. Unconsciously, Keith was demonstrating that he didn't care about his employees, that they simply didn't matter. Repeated exhibitions of the same behaviour over long periods created even worse perceptions, reinforced by local management criticisms such as "he's an odd one, Keith".

Keith also became a soft target for referential blame. Managers took the opportunity to lay every unpopular decision at his door when talking to subordinates. He was never likely to answer back or refute the accusation.

Once made aware of the severity of the problem, Keith changed. He disciplined himself to become more civil, more communicative and more approachable. It was difficult for him, but it paid off. Attitudes changed dramatically as employees began to see the 'real' Keith, not the image that he had so carelessly cultivated.

This whole concept of unconscious incompetence is at the root of most examples of organisation disharmony. Management do things in good faith and the workforce misinterprets their motives. The workforce, or their representatives, do something that management likewise perceives differently. And managers everywhere, unknown to themselves, go around displaying traits, habits or unsubtleties, creating perceptions that would horrify them – if they only knew about them.

Hopefully, it is fully accepted now that a 'good' culture will lead to improved performance. If unconscious incompetencies are preventing you from creating this good culture, then it stands to reason that you must find out what they are.

Your challenge, therefore, is to identify and to understand those managerial traits and behaviours which undermine the organisation. There are many ways of addressing this. For example, you could reflect on it yourself. However, you will tend in these situations to see what you want to see. Self–delusion is more common than not in this type of exercise.

You could employ expensive consultants to observe what is going on. However, this is often just as subjective as you doing it. They will also see what *they* want to see or try to fit behaviour patterns to 'standard' models they have seen elsewhere.

You could rely on the tried and tested 'employee survey'. If you do, however, you will have to overcome the general perception that these 'are questions posed by management for the benefit of management'. In terms of employee credibility, they often carry little weight. They are seen as partial, over-complex and subjective. Because they usually rely on a purely statistical format with no qualitative back-up, issues of priority can be quite distorted.

In one example we came across, a very high profile company came to the conclusion that the biggest issue in employees' minds was the way the organisation was perceived in the local community. Working for the company was seen as such a negative factor with one's friends and neighbours that it became a major demotivator. Vast sums on improving the public image were proposed to solve the problem.

Statistically one could not argue with this conclusion. The measure of the 'unsatisfied potential', whatever that might be, was twice any other question. Something had to be done, hadn't it?

Well, on further examination, the answer was no. Sure, people felt that working for the company did create negative influences in the community. But that, in their eyes, was a fact of life. The day they walked through the door, they knew and accepted it. Any scarce funds definitely should not be spent on public relations, but much more productively be diverted to process and facility investment. Had someone not shouted 'Stop – let's have a think about this!', the organisation could have ploughed on and wasted hard-earned cash on solving the wrong priority.

We believe emphatically in the power of 'subordinate appraisal'. The best way of finding out the consequences and severity of managerial ineptitude is to hold a mirror to the organisation and then look in at it. It is, as we said earlier, rarely a pretty sight! The face staring back at you will not be the same one you see in the shaving mirror every morning! Now you will see management in the eyes of its subordinates. Be prepared for the worst, as it more often than not emerges.

The process we are about to describe is not an exact science. We will seek to distinguish 'symptoms' from 'causes'. But that is not always possible. Adverse perceptions can be the consequence of responses to several generations of management. Our immediate objective is to establish a common understanding of the cultural downsides of the organisation. Once we all agree what the problem is, then the chances of resolution are that much greater. Our combined energies can be devoted to moving forward rather than wasting time and effort on debating whose fault it was.

Perception Barrier Analysis falls into six discrete stages as shown in **Figure 5**. Again, this looks complicated but it is relatively straight-forward. Once the model has been established, it can be used repeatedly thereafter. One of the key issues here is independent objectivity. It is always far more effective if you can use a third party seen by the organisation to be both neutral and even-handed. Here, the workforce is more likely to trust the outcomes with little fear of management distortion or selective editing. Unfortunately, most organisations have something of an 'us and them' barrier between management and managed. Without the independent honest broker, there is always likely to be an issue of credibility. We recommend, therefore, that you seek outside assistance to secure the sense of transparency and confidentiality.

Figure 5: Perception Barrier Analysis

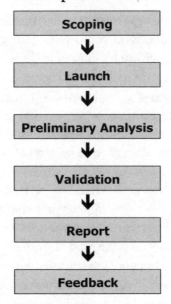

This could be achieved by:

♦ Using a consultant to undertake the process on your behalf. If you are going to the expense of actually paying someone to do this, make sure they are sufficiently skilled and experienced to be able to interpret the data and commentary.

- Seek assistance from your local business support agency. They may be able to assist, as programmes such as IIP (Investors in People) have close parallels with this form of employee engagement.

- Do a 'swap' with a neighbouring company where one of their managers acts as the facilitator for you. You then reciprocate, ensuring that both facilitators have a degree of 'people-sensitivity'.

- As a last resort, do it internally with the most neutral, acceptable and capable candidate you can find. You may have to delete the Validation stage due to obvious concerns on confidentiality and trust.

SCOPING

First, you have to decide how to split your organisation for analysis. In a very small organisation, you could have two groups: management and the rest. Note that we are looking at groups here, not individuals. The latter we can take care of later! In bigger organisations, it makes sense to look at functions / departments. We always recommend that the senior management team are separated. Occasionally, it may make sense to cut the organisation horizontally, although this does carry a major disadvantage in not relating to how most organisations actually work.

When the organisation is divided, ensure that every employee can easily identify which group s/he belongs in, otherwise confusion could reign. A typical example is shown in **Appendix 1**.

Second, a set of questions around the key pillars of culture are needed. **Appendix 2** gives you a starter. However, you need to make sure that the terminology involved, particularly job titles, is relevant to your establishment. Also add any additional questions that may better reflect the specific nature of your business. The questions are answered randomly, echoing strength of agreement. (**Appendix 2** shows them grouped in their final form for feedback). The groupings are:

- Communications.
- Employee Systems (Formal and Informal).
- Continuous Improvement.

- ◆ Internal Customer Focus.
- ◆ External Customer Focus.
- ◆ Organisation Structures.
- ◆ Management Style.
- ◆ Team-working.
- ◆ Empowerment.
- ◆ Working for the Organisation.

Finally, space needs to be left for employees to add their comments. We usually think this is best done by a 'SWOTF' analysis. Here, we simply ask employees to list their responses to the questions: *'What do you think are the key strengths / weaknesses / threats / opportunities facing our company?'*. We find that employees are more than willing to contribute to these requests, often offering long and detailed responses. However, when they are asked: *'What frustrates you about working in our company?'*, then the pen really does hit the paper! Of course, within this, there will be the usual pet moans, whinges, prejudices and the like. Nevertheless, taken collectively, you'll have more than a sporting chance of spotting recurring themes and issues that are worthy of further investigation.

LAUNCH

This is a key phase often neglected or given insufficient priority. Our objective within Perception Barrier Analysis is to create a *common ownership of the problem*. We want a general agreement that the outcome of this process really represents the issues facing the company. At the feedback stage, the presenter will end with the question: *'Does this present a fair picture of your company today?'*. Done properly, in our long experience, the answer will always be an emphatic yes. The reason why there is such general agreement is that employees genuinely TRUST the process. The foundation for that trust is laid down at the launch stage.

We recommend that the facilitator sees all employees in groups for a maximum of an hour. Group size will be dictated by availability and logistics. The bigger the size, the cheaper the launch!

The facilitator will give a detailed overview of the process along with a more general outline of the objectives of employee engagement. This is important: employees have to see the end game. Then s/he will give serious undertakings as to:

♦ **Confidentiality:** All individual inputs will be kept sufficiently confidential so that there is very little chance of personal identification.

♦ **Transparency:** The report will be shared by all at the feedback stage. No manager will contribute to, interfere with or edit the report. The reporting will be done entirely by the facilitator. There will only be one report, the one seen by all.

♦ **Simultaneous feedback:** Within the limits of logistics and availability, everyone will get the report at the same time. So if it takes one day to do the launch, then everybody will also be seen at feedback on one day. Management have the privilege, and the obligation, of seeing it first. However general dissemination follows immediately.

PRELIMINARY ANALYSIS

We recommend that the data is shown in a graphical form as in **Figure 6**. Here, we see that the answers to each question are shown for each group and that they indicate strength of agreement with the subject. Whilst there is no 'norm', we are looking for a greater than 50% response generally. Anything less than 35% to 40% agreement, unless the question is a reverse one, usually indicates a problem area.

VALIDATION

This stage is not essential, but it is useful in distinguishing causal factors from those that are merely symptomatic. The process is very simple. Armed with the initial conclusions from the graphs and the SWOTF summary, around 5% to 15% of the workforce are interviewed, either individually or in small peer groups. We always prefer to see managers by themselves, but others often prefer the security of colleagues alongside them.

Over a maximum of an hour, some of these initial conclusions are discussed. By 'drilling down' and seeking further evidence, the interviewer can often distinguish the serious from the frivolous.

Figure 6: Management Style

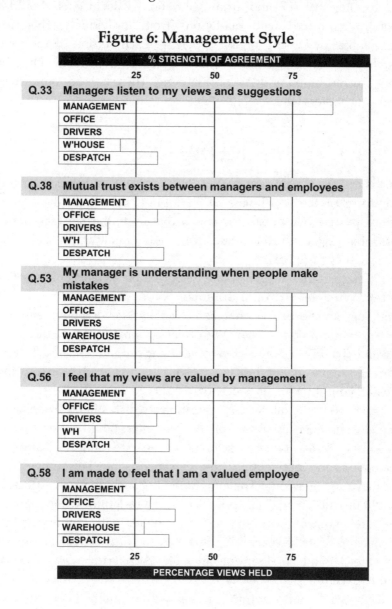

REPORT

A written report should then be prepared using the feedback from the graphs, the SWOTF and from validation. Conclusions should be liberally reinforced with quotations from individuals. This helps cement the 'ownership of the problem'. Each section of the report should end with an overall summary statement, accompanied by some ideas for resolution and Action Planning. These can be found in the relevant chapters later.

FEEDBACK

This is the most important part of the exercise. Having convinced the workforce of the worthiness of Perception Barrier Analysis at the launch process, we must now justify that faith. Further reassurances must be given on the issues of confidentiality, opticality and transparency raised earlier.

We suggest that the graphs are displayed on acetates or PowerPoint and that the report, or a summary of it, is given verbally. The groupings should be the same as in Feedback, everybody being seen for a maximum of one hour. We prefer a verbal report as there is no benefit in having lots of written copies lying around. The objective is to learn and move on. For the same reasons we do not advocate posting a copy on your intranet, or noticeboards, should you have either.

Time should be allowed for questions, which should be answered factually and honestly. Above all, the presenter should not try to attach unrealistic levels of accuracy here. We are simply dealing in perceptions and motivation. Those perceptions may be genuinely held but they may be wrong. The temptation to conclude may be great but should be resisted at all costs. Decisions can be left to Action Planning. For the moment, we should be content with simply gaining 'ownership of the problem'. To this end, the final statement from the presenter should be along the lines of: *'Does this represent a fair and accurate picture of your company?'.*

If you've done it right, the answer will inevitably be an emphatic yes from a substantial majority of the workforce. You will now know where to start.

SHORTCUTTING

The foregoing represents a tried and tested technique to understanding and agreeing employee perceptions. Having been involved in scores of similar exercises, we can express a high degree of confidence in its effectiveness. However, there may be occasions and situations where you simply don't have the time or resource to go through all this rigmarole. The choice is simple: a shortcut or no exercise?

This is one occasion when the end will always justify the means. If you can find a way of identifying what employees *really* feel about the key elements of organisational culture, then you're part way there. If you can get the workforce both to agree to and to identify with these conclusions, then you've achieved the objective. The key determining factors here are goodwill and trust rather than accuracy or statistical significance. This may offend the purveyors of employee surveys with all their pseudo-mathematical mumbo-jumbo but we have to realise that this is as much about motivation and belief as it is about problem-solving. Action planning will take care of the latter, as long as we define the tasks carefully and accurately.

You can shortcut this entire process simply by interviewing a cross-section of the workforce. The questionnaires can also be used in this process to augment the interviews, particularly in ensuring that the whole gamut of organisational culture is scrutinised. In smaller organisations, this may be highly practical and feasible. The critical factors here would be ensuring that:

♦ The interviewer is perceived to be sufficiently independent and objective.

♦ Sufficient information is gathered to draw broad conclusions.

♦ Those who attend the interviews have adequate peer acceptability.

And the most difficult bit of all, ensuring that:

♦ The purpose of the exercise is communicated extensively before starting and that its conclusions are conveyed to all with the same level of intensity as the formal process.

Our advice here is unambiguous. If you can adopt the formal process of Perception Barrier Analysis, then do it. It is tried and tested to give the organisation a balanced view of general perceptions. If you can't, then make the effort to get there anyway. Providing you are seen to be genuine, the fact that you have made the effort may be sufficient in many employees' eyes to gain the necessary credibility.

SHADOWS

There is never a 'right time' to gauge employee perceptions. Business is so volatile nowadays, especially in smaller organisations, that there is scarcely a clear period free from crisis. If there is, it is almost impossible to predict where and when it might be! As a consequence, the response to the survey might be 'coloured' by the prevailing situation. These 'shadows', as we call them, can dominate or even distort the response. Care needs to be taken to balance their impact on the survey as a whole. Today's crises are likely to be forgotten tomorrow. so we need to brace ourselves to discount them, if necessary.

Events that tend to cause these shadows include:

- ◆ **Redundancies:** This is one of the few occasions where we recommend postponing the survey until the redundancies have taken place. Otherwise, the emotions of the situation tend to direct attention to the departees rather than to the survivors. Without being cynical, it is the latter we need to focus on to take the organisation forward, to avoid repetition of such trauma.

- ◆ **Pay deals:** Emotions can run high during, or immediately after, a pay deal. Unless a strike is imminent or feelings are running unduly high, then we suggest you continue. Simply accept that questions on pay, conditions and related subjects are not going to be generously marked. These so-called 'protest votes' are not uncommon and should be handled maturely and honestly.

- ◆ **Major re-organisations:** All re-organisations have winners and losers. Feelings can run understandably very high, especially if the reasons for the change have been inadequately explained or if there has been inadequate consultation. Whilst this might be seen to distort the survey, nevertheless we strongly encourage companies to proceed with the exercise. Ideally, this should take place before the event so that the reorganisation can be used as a platform, a new starting point. In any event, letting people vent their spleens over the vexatious elements of the change can itself be quite therapeutic. At the very least, it should take the heat out of the situation and establish a common dialogue.

♦ **Single agenda organisations:** This happens occasionally when one issue totally dominates the response to the survey. Fears over longer job security, for example, can dominate the whole process. However, there are many benefits here. For a start, this skewed response probably reflects the reality of life in the organisation. If people are very much concerned over their future, it will dominate their thinking and influence their behaviour. Getting the issue out in the open and ensuring a constructive and healthy debate may not solve the problem but it can help hugely in getting people to face up to it. The only downside here is that other key issues may lie so far below the surface that a re-survey after a suitable dwell time (usually not less than six to nine months) may be the only answer.

♦ **Errant behaviour by one or more managers:** This is one of the more difficult areas to address in Perception Barrier Analysis. Ideally, what we are looking for are common managerial *traits* that are damaging the company. Unfortunately, in rare situations, you encounter *individuals* who exhibit such extreme behaviour that it is impossible not to become personal. This is very difficult to handle and demands subtlety and tact whilst never wavering from the fundamental honesty that underpins the exercise. Names should never be used, even if the guilty party is self-evident. Incidentally, the organisation at large will already know all about this. It is usually only management who are ignorant! Sufficient should be disclosed to indicate that the problem has been noted and will be addressed. Public flagellations are not recommended!

SUMMARY

Finding out 'what the buggers think' will strike a lot of busy, small-medium business managers as hard work. It is not, you will now agree, as simple as thinking up a few questions, sticking them in a survey and doing a bit of cursory analysis when the results come in. We have to develop a process that is seen to be fair, objective and confidential, without fear of managerial manipulation. Each of the six stages is therefore important but success impinges on how well you 'launch' and 'feedback'. These two stages will really determine whether you have the necessary ownership of the problem.

Why is all this so necessary? We believe that successful culture change has three vital ingredients:

♦ Top down commitment, belief and enthusiasm.

♦ A workable and transparent structure.

♦ Genuine bottom-up engagement.

With a traditional mistrusting or even cynical workforce, the last is difficult. You have to do something 'out-of-the-box' to demonstrate both the seriousness of the approach and its importance. Hanging management out to dry, as this process was once rather graphically described, will do just that!

Do you have to go through this rigamarole of you employ just a few people? Or perhaps if your resource is a small number of part-time volunteers? The answer is unequivocally 'Yes'! You simply must find out what people really think, if you are going to create a harmonious, and therefore ultimately, more productive, organisation.

Figure 7: The Route Map updated 2

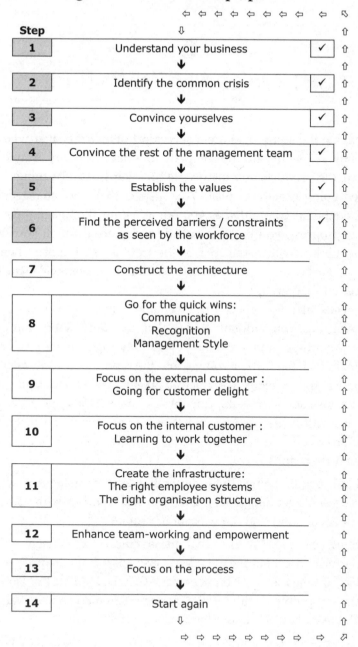

Step		
1	Understand your business	✓
2	Identify the common crisis	✓
3	Convince yourselves	✓
4	Convince the rest of the management team	✓
5	Establish the values	✓
6	Find the perceived barriers / constraints as seen by the workforce	✓
7	Construct the architecture	
8	Go for the quick wins: Communication Recognition Management Style	
9	Focus on the external customer : Going for customer delight	
10	Focus on the internal customer : Learning to work together	
11	Create the infrastructure: The right employee systems The right organisation structure	
12	Enhance team-working and empowerment	
13	Focus on the process	
14	Start again	

5
SETTING AN EXAMPLE

Just imagine the scene. You are a successful owner-manager who has over many years built up the company to what it is today. You know the place, the products and the people backwards. Lately, things have not been going exactly to plan. You suspect that your management team is neither as committed as you nor as astute at managing people. To make progress, you bring in outside assistance through your local Business Link to get to the root of the trouble. You expect them to support your frequent protestations to your management team that they need to sharpen up!

Six weeks later, the report is received and delivered. As you sit with your colleagues, you suddenly realise that, in a fairly subtle but quite evident way, these prats are telling everybody that *you* are part of the problem. In fact, the further you get into the report, you seem to be the *major* part of the problem. You micro-manage, instead of delegate, you harangue instead of consult, you nitpick instead of appreciate, you lecture instead of discuss and, worst of all, you instil fear instead of inspiration.

What do you do? Do you:

a) Look slightly pained but indicate that, as this catalogue of woes represents genuine perceptions, you will sit down with your colleagues and find out ways of improving.

b) Blow your top. Tell them that this is typical of their usual performance, blaming everybody else apart from themselves. Isn't it time they took on personal ACCOUNTABILITY? Isn't this the problem with middle management today – they want all the authority without the responsibility?

c) Accept their perceptions but emphasise that this is exactly what they are – just perceptions. In stressed organisations operating in volatile markets, this referential blame is commonplace. You are sure that much of this behaviour is unconscious, your colleagues probably genuinely believe the criticisms. Over the next few weeks, you will sit down with them to explore this well-known phenomenon of 'middle management permafrost'. After that, you believe you can really move on to getting them to accept OWNERSHIP AND ACCOUNTABILITY.

d) Say very little. Silently curse your foolishness in bringing these idiots in, pillocks who can't distinguish tittle-tattle from real issues. Vow to bury the report as soon as this purgatory is over.

e) Say nothing until you're on your own with the consultants. Then tell them that if they think they're getting paid for this rubbish, you'll see them in court!

f) Question the report intensively. Ask for statistical significance. Try to determine which individuals or areas made the criticisms. Generally make the consultants and your colleagues feel uncomfortable and embarrassed.

95% of you will no doubt say they would respond as (a). The other 5% will be telling the truth! Put down on paper like this, the answer is self-evident. Even the bit about 'looking pained' is logical. You can't really sit there like a Cheshire Cat after all this implicit, and occasionally explicit, criticism. That would frighten your subordinates even more!

However logical the first response may be, in practice this is rarely how managing directors respond. In about 50% to 60% of cases we encounter, there is severe subordinate criticism of the key decision-makers. The most common response is not the 'reasonable' one of (a) but probably the silent treatment indicated by (d). The second most common response is the frenetic interrogation of (f). Unless pre-warned, senior decision-makers are not very good at taking criticism. Statistically, therefore, dear reader, this probably means you – again!

Going through this time-consuming and often resource-intensive exercise is not easy for the average owner-manager or managing director. You are used to controlling everything. However, here you have entrusted a third-party, of whom you may know little, to come into your world and make value judgments. You are likely to feel uncomfortable, perhaps even threatened. Responses such as (b) to (f) are understandable, giving this juxtaposition of discomfort to potential discord.

However, you need to remind yourself before you go into that first debrief that this is, above all, an exercise in motivation. Experience tells us that having the opportunity, perhaps for the first time, to voice opinions confidentially on every aspect of organisational culture is a tremendously liberating experience for most employees. In particular, the use of quotations from peers to emphasise the occasional weakness can produce a tremendous empathy with the outcome. This is the real 'ownership of the problem' we identified earlier. As a consequence, people's expectations can increase enormously as a result of Perception Barrier Analysis. They expect change and they expect that they, or if not them, their close colleagues, will be involved in it.

The immediate response from senior management can have a profound effect on this newly-created goodwill. A positive and, to a degree, humble reaction will reinforce the belief that things are going to change for the better. An immediate rejection could cause permanent damage. Expectations will be flattened. The cynics and sceptics will have a field day, raising conspiracy theories by the dozen. You will have wasted your time, resource and energy.

One of the first practitioners in this field, Reg Hardy of HCH Associates, used to be so concerned about this first reaction that he would insist on addressing the issue with senior management well in advance of even starting the exercise. He constructed a 'Valley of Despond' (**Figure 8**) to illustrate the usual reactions to subordinate criticism of any intensity.

Initially, the manager might have a bit of an adrenaline rush as the criticisms came at him. After all, everybody likes a challenge! But then the realisation that perhaps he was a contributing factor to the general malaise cools things down. This intensifies, as the full consequence of his managerial inadequacies hit home. A new recognition that he is not, after all, near-perfect, leads to a despairing plunge in general morale and confidence. Hopefully, this does not last too long and the bottom is reached with an acceptance of the situation. Resignation eventually turns into determination. And once evidence of an improvement in workforce willingness comes through, often quite early in the process, management attitudes further stiffen towards Resolution.

Figure 8: The Valley of Despond

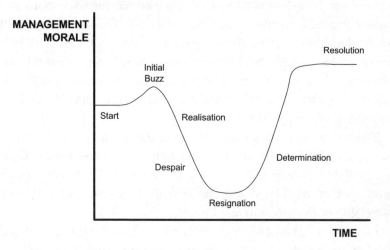

Now you might think you are strong enough, or thick-skinned enough, to avoid the perils of the Valley of Despond. Think again and prepare yourself. Both the authors have personally endured the process several times. On each occasion, we have been knocked back. Criticism on the second, third and subsequent cycles becomes progressively harder to take. Our advice is simple. If you can possibly manage it, have your debrief on a Friday afternoon. Then you can spend the weekend rubbing your bruises, rebuilding your ego and getting yourself in balance for Monday. Otherwise, the temptation might be to fire everyone in sight for such blatant insubordination!

The Valley of Despond is inevitable. Your task is to help your colleagues go through it. You need to minimise the depth of despond and its duration. Forewarned, you have every chance of getting through unscathed. Ill-prepared, you might have a much harder time.

The way you respond to the survey, therefore, is a key factor in its ultimate success. Accept that the emotional pattern described earlier will influence your behaviour. An immediate reaction is not advised, save to accept the findings and the distinct possibility that you might be a contributing factor. Reflect quietly for a few days, weighing up how best to build on any gains from the survey. In one survey undertaken in a small distribution outlet, the report was received by the assembled management in reverent, almost cathedral-like, silence. All eyes were firmly fixed on the General Manager, as a litany of complaints paraded before them. Morale was bad, managers weren't trusted, initiatives were strewn about like confetti but never finished. The list seemed endless but the facilitator took enormous care to ensure that a sense of balance prevailed. He thought he'd done a good job until the General Manager intervened. "Now, will you lot listen?", he loudly proclaimed, "I've been telling you exactly this for ages and it's taken an outsider to spell it out. What are you going to do about it?".

The sentiment may have been correct (it wasn't!) but that intemperate and badly thought-through interjection negated all the goodwill and benefit generated by the exercise. They were back to a 'who shot John?' blame culture in a flash. There was no common ownership of the problem any longer.

In another organisation, an otherwise OK-ish report contained a number of serious, but not earth-shattering, criticisms. The senior director immediately seized on one and proceeded to spout a torrent of statistics purporting to prove otherwise. One of his managers had the temerity to question his statistics and support the conclusion. She was lucky to retire with her head intact. With tears in her eyes, she physically shrunk in her seat. The remainder did likewise. At a stroke, ownership of the problem became a pipedream.

Over-enthusiasm can also be a problem if not thought-through. James, the owner, listened intensely to the perception feedback. At the end, he readily accepted all the criticisms directly and indirectly targeted at him. He promised to do better. So far, so good. But then he spoilt it by immediately leaping into action planning mode and appointing a very junior focus group to identify means of resolution. Whilst he didn't use the words, his actions sent out a very strong signal that the problem was everywhere in his company except the top!

Throughout this book, the importance of management behaviour in determining culture will be repeatedly emphasised. Nowhere is the point made stronger than at the point of feedback. Prepare yourselves, listen and get ready to eat humble pie. It'll taste good – eventually.

6
ACTION PLANNING: MOVING FROM AMBITION TO REALITY

The first two phases of an Employee Engagement programme – Education and Perception Barrier Analysis – are designed to establish a strong foundation for future progress. Significant benefits will be achieved directly here through a common 'ownership of the problem' and an all-round credibility in the process. However, by far the greatest return will be achieved in the final Action Planning Phase, where the role of external facilitators diminishes and the influence of internal champions and management takes over. It is reckoned that 80% of the benefits (as well as most of the hard work) will stem from a successful Action Planning phase, where efforts are made jointly to solve the bottlenecks, constraints and plain weaknesses identified earlier. It is crucial, therefore, that the structure of Action Planning becomes *permanently embedded* into managerial routine.

Unfortunately, most organisations completely underestimate the importance of this phase. Management often see the trauma of the Perception Barrier feedback process as an end in itself. Allowing the workforce to expose critically the weaknesses of their superiors is perceived to offer benefits in enhancing trust, engagement and improvements in motivation. Whilst this is indeed more often than not the case, any initial impact will quickly fade if not reinforced speedily with action.

There is no one *right way* to carry out Action Planning. Here we describe a path that has been used successfully elsewhere – although that is not to say it is the only route.

Nevertheless, departing from established practice carries with it risks. The objective of this chapter is to lay down the principles within which your particular architecture must conform. Each phase must be tested against these principles and where deviations are seen, then a high confidence is needed that they are both necessary and effective.

The principles of Action Planning are common to all organisations. However, how you actually apply them depends on your size. A company employing, say, 150 or more people may wish to adopt a formality that would not be appropriate in one employing 25. The key determinant is this expression: 'ownership of the solution'. Your challenge is to ensure people *feel* involved in the creation and implementation of solutions. Note the renewed emphasis on perception. Involving people is not enough. They must recognise that they've been involved.

There are four distinct phases in Action Planning that need to be followed consecutively, as shown in **Figure 9**.

Figure 9: Phases of Action Planning

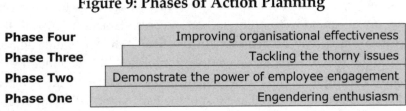

Phase Four	Improving organisational effectiveness
Phase Three	Tackling the thorny issues
Phase Two	Demonstrate the power of employee engagement
Phase One	Engendering enthusiasm

PHASE 1: ENGENDERING ENTHUSIASM

In most organisations, there is a natural cynicism within the workforce about management's willingness to respond effectively to the outcomes of the Perception Barrier process. In this first phase, we must both persuade people that, this time, this is for real and demonstrate that the only way forward is for them to get involved in helping to change things. This can be achieved by:

♦ Getting small groups of employees to reflect upon the issues facing the company.

♦ Creating a formal architecture that emphasises the use of multi-functional focus groups as the driving force behind problem-solving and continuous improvement. This sounds very grand, but really is just about putting a structure to this important phase.

♦ Constantly and effectively publicising the structures, the objectives and progress to all within the company. We strongly recommend a local bulletin-type communication here, preferably in hard-copy, if your workforce is greater than 100 people. Below that, direct communication may be more appropriate.

This concept of multi-functionalism is key to the success of Phase 1 and, indeed, to the remaining phases. Our end objective is to create a framework of continuous improvement processes, driven both top-down and bottom-up. Most organisational problems are rooted across departmental boundaries and necessitate cross-functional resolution. Focusing simply on addressing issues merely within one's own section or department can create major friction across service areas. A blame culture or a rigid silo mentality can often be the end product, to the detriment of all – but especially of the company. Phase 1, therefore, must encourage employees to work across functional divides.

Even in small companies, these departmental divisions can be most damaging. We need everybody attuned to the company view, not their own functional interests.

PHASE 2: DEMONSTRATING THE POWER OF EMPLOYEE ENGAGEMENT

Once the initial enthusiasm has been created, an early demonstration of the effectiveness of the approach is needed. This is best tackled by improvements in areas where there are obvious benefits to the employee. Whilst this should not be the exclusive emphasis, it is vital that employees see early impacts that reflect a managerial willingness to move in line with the aims and values of employee engagement.

This is usually achieved by concentrating initially on those areas which give immediate benefits and results, the so-called *quick-wins*. These include:

- ♦ Wholesale improvements in communication systems:
  - ◊ Huddles / *Hill St. Blues*-type meetings.
  - ◊ Effective team briefings.
  - ◊ Written, routine and regular communication on issues, opinions and views rather than mere facts.
  - ◊ 'Meet the Boss' / 'Bring a Butty'-type sessions.

◊   MBWA (Management by Walking About) – done properly!

♦ Introduction of low-key recognition systems:

◊   Thank-you cards.

◊   Tokens.

◊   Simple team recognition (not 'team of the month'!).

◊   Informal, private individual recognition.

♦ Acknowledgement of weaknesses in management style:

◊   Management style questionnaires.

◊   Greater visibility of senior management.

◊   Establishing codes of behaviour (managerial and reciprocal).

All these suggestions will be discussed in much more detail in the appropriate chapter.

Again, we must emphasise that projects should be appropriate in size and depth to the capability of the group. Junior groups should not be given major projects. Each group should be aided by internal skilled facilitators who can ensure proper teamwork, individual contribution and an outcome compatible with organisational interest. In small organisations, this facilitation may have to come from the 'top'.

PHASE 3: TACKLING THE THORNY ISSUES

Once the pattern of employee involvement has been established, it is then time to use the approach to tackle bigger issues within the organisation. The emphasis still needs to be very much on multi-functionalism, but a more senior level representation is likely to be more appropriate. Limited lower level representation can still be used to address concerns on opticality and relevance but, in general, the groups should be of a more senior status.

Issues to be addressed here usually include:

♦ Inter-departmental tensions.

♦ Pay and conditions.

♦ Appraisal systems / training needs analysis.

♦ Promotion and development.

The role of the facilitator becomes even more important here in ensuring the integrity of the team and in developing the 'art of the possible'. They must be particularly vigilant to ensure that the project is not hijacked in pursuit of self-interest.

PHASE 4: IMPROVING ORGANISATIONAL EFFECTIVENESS

This is the most important part of the entire process. A steady and effective build up through Phases 1 to 3 is essential in creating organisational familiarity, credibility and enthusiasm for the approach. Phase 4 is all about delivering the end product of employee engagement: significantly improved performance. Benefits will be obtained by the earlier three stages, but it is here that the potential for quantum improvements really exists. **A truly effective employee engagement will have all four phases going simultaneously on a permanent basis.**

There may be some argument at this stage in larger concerns (> 150 employees) for establishing a 'Strategic Improvement Committee', if this was not done at the outset. This committee must establish the following:

a) A comprehensive list of areas for improvement, usually derived from Key Performance Indicators (KPI) variances.

b) A Root Cause Analysis to establish those factors most likely to deliver KPI improvement.

c) Some form of prioritisation.

d) A Continuous Improvement (CI) architecture with a range of standard techniques such as BPR, Six Sigma, Kaizen, 5 Ss, Ideas Generation, etc.

(e) A best fit of (d) to (c).

We will discuss all of these in **Chapters 15** and **16**.

The committee should be charged with achieving aggressive and predetermined performance improvements through the medium of employee engagement. Communication and Recognition will be important in developing the necessary momentum here. Whilst the focus groups will always be multi-functional, their size, constituency and longevity will now be dictated by the project rather than the arbitrary rules laid down in the earlier phases.

Visibility of organisational KPIs and their aspirational targets is mandatory here. The process should not be constrained by conventional SMART objective-setting, but rather geared to more ambitious, stretching ('Hoshin') goals. We need to encourage employees to break out of comfort zones and to think on a bigger canvas. Again, this will be covered extensively later.

It should be very apparent that, even more so than in the earlier stages, company senior management (SMT) need to be actively involved here. If not physically participating in the groups, they need to be around for sponsorship, endorsement or even facilitation. If Phases 1 to 3 have been introduced successfully, then it is likely that a direct correlation exists here between SMT interest and enthusiasm and ultimate project success.

Perhaps also at this stage, consideration needs to be given to creating internal specialists in continuous improvement. The need to create an internal pool of facilitators has already been touched upon. The complexities of the various devices needed to create a genuine ethos of continuous improvement are such that a similar pool of CI 'technologists' will be necessary. It is emphasised that this is not intended as an excuse to recruit dedicated staff, merely to have people about who have specialist capabilities. An early decision on the appropriateness of the various standard techniques noted earlier (and others) would be advisable.

Phase 4 needs to be approached determinedly as a long-term proposition. Employee engagement has the capability of transforming the companies from average performance to Best Value in the sector. Within Phase 4 lies the potential for making that capability a reality.

TEMPO

It is strongly recommended that efforts are made from the outset to build up a steady pace or rhythm in Action Planning. Stop-start is a major threat as people can be readily disillusioned, become impatient or even turned off by an inability to maintain a steady tempo in all four phases.

Focus groups should be encouraged to work quickly to completion. New focus groups should be planned well in advance to enhance this feeling of continuity. Formal recognition events, albeit low key ones, should be arranged to routinely boost morale. Communication systems should be augmented to ensure that all employees are constantly aware of this new direction and how it impacts upon them.

Above all, the tempo should be regulated by senior management involvement. Their scrutiny, commitment and involvement can benefit more than any other factor in creating this organisational 'heartbeat'. They should be actively involved in:

♦ Encouraging the committees.

♦ Driving the focus groups.

♦ Maintaining the pace, particularly through the Phases.

♦ Identifying areas for Phase 4 exploration.

♦ Recognising.

♦ Communicating.

♦ Living the vision.

♦ Being seen to change themselves.

SMALL ORGANISATIONS

This book is targeted at the SME (Small-to-Medium Enterprise) sector, which is defined as having 1 to 250 employees. However, there is a major difference between a company employing 5 people and one employing 250. In fact, as organisations grow within this band, the characteristics of engagement will change probably every 25 employees. Whilst the principles are universal and unchanging, the way you apply them will differ considerably. Micro-companies, those with less than 10 to 15 employees, will be wondering whether this applies to them. The jargon and scope of some of these activities will be seen as totally foreign territory to many in this area.

However small companies hopefully have ambitions to grow into bigger ones so, at the very least, you will be prepared for what is in store in future! Nevertheless, adopt the principles but adapt the architecture to suit your own situation. For example, multi-functional focus groups will be irrelevant to micro-organisations, Here, simply ensure that everybody gets a shout at both 'owning' and 'solving' the problem. The same goes for most of the other concepts. Micro-organisations should adapt the spirit and philosophy behind the suggestions on a pragmatic basis, rather than incorporating slavishly the more rigid structures designed for their bigger cousins.

ACTION PLANNING ARCHITECTURE

Employee engagement is a permanent change in managerial philosophy, not a new 'initiative'. Accordingly, the management of employee engagement needs to reflect this permanence so it is not viewed simply as a 'project' or an 'exercise'.

A suggested architecture is described in **Figure 10**. It has three discrete elements, all of which are vital to the long-term success of the initiative:

♦ A senior management steering group (SMSG).

♦ A culture change committee (CCC).

♦ Multi-functional focus groups (MFFGs).

Figure 10: A Suggested Action Planning Architecture

Senior Management Steering Group

The Senior Management Steering Group (SMSG) is the driving force behind the whole programme. It is essential that each manager within the company SMT, at the very least, is fully committed to the ideals behind employee engagement. It is also vital that a minimum of two to three senior managers become 'champions' or evangelists of the process to demonstrate the seriousness of management intent. Whilst we are looking for proactive 'bottom-up' involvement as the key element in changing employee mind-sets towards the world of work, it will simply not happen without top-down commitment. This has to be visible, obvious and serious.

The SMSG demonstrates this commitment. Each week, as part of the usual senior management get-together, the first 30 to 60 minutes will be devoted to implementing, measuring, monitoring and auditing employee engagement within the company. Elsewhere, the practice of attendees pre-reading one chapter of a book like *Growing Your Own Heroes* and coming along prepared to discuss its relevance to their situation for the first half-hour has been seen to be very useful in catalysing the process.

The other key task of the SMSG is to publicise progress and recognise good practice.

The Culture Change Committee

The outcomes of the Perception Barrier analysis are likely to contain a mountain of weaknesses and suggestions for correction. To avoid indigestion, we suggest that a group or committee is formed to 'spread the load'.

In most small organisations, this will be the senior group plus the odd enthusiast from other ranks. It can be bolted on to existing meetings but, for focus and psychological emphasis, it should be taken as a discrete section. Otherwise, experience tells us that it will be subsumed by operational detail. Sadly, culture change is still regarded as discretionary, even by the most well-intentioned.

However, these weaknesses will split into three separate areas that may need specialist emphasis. The three are:

- Culture – for example:
  - ◊ Recognition.
  - ◊ Communication.
  - ◊ Management style.
- Employment development – for example:
  - ◊ Pay.

◊   Conditions.

◊   Gradings.

◊   Appraisals.

♦ Strategy – for example:

◊   Quality.

◊   Process conformance.

◊   Process capability.

◊   Product development.

◊   Process improvement.

You must ensure that your resources and efforts are balanced across all three elements. In the beginning, you will favour 'culture'. This is where the *quick wins*, the early returns, reside and, therefore, it makes sense to exploit them. Employee development issues can be thornier and take time to resolve and, therefore, longer to benefit the organisation. Be very tentative about this area unless you are sure that it is a significant and current bottleneck. 'Regrading' exercises, for example, have winners and losers. The latter can take a long time to come round.

Where you are eventually heading is in the area of 'hard' performance improvements – the third group. In some organisations, the temptation to stay in the 'culture' box has proved irresistible. Whilst this may yield a warm glow and a 'feel-good' atmosphere, your job is to improve effectiveness and efficiency. Quickly use the released goodwill and potential to zoom in on process and product constraints. Never forget your ultimate target is to create a high-performing team. The sooner the improved performance comes through, the better. Improved attitudes, job satisfaction and team-working are all important by-products, but they are only the means to the 'end'. The end is a step-change in the efficiency and cost effectiveness of the company.

Focus Groups

The Culture Change Committee (CCC) takes its list of challenges and prioritises them. For each prioritised challenge, a maximum of three at a time, it will nominate a focus group and give them a defined period to come back with a solution. The project will be clearly defined, guided, resourced, sponsored and given the necessary facilitation support to ensure that the group operates effectively.

After the defined period (usually a maximum of four to six weeks), the group will report back and the CCC then needs to decide whether to accept the recommendations, amend or seek further clarity / investigation.

The focus groups will be no more than five to seven members and be cross-functional and cross-hierarchical in constituency. Care should be taken to devise projects that are 'bite-size' in nature initially and that are appropriate to the group's capability. More complex projects need higher-powered focus groups. Initial emphasis should be placed on areas of quick wins. Frequently, actions can be recommended within much shorter periods, particularly if we are simply looking for ratification or are making a choice from limited alternatives. Groups here may only have to meet for a few hours. The key here is to be *seen* to be actively consulting, engaging and extracting opinions and views from all levels of the organisation. On occasions, this may need no more than one or two meetings.

It is also quite possible for management to establish their own focus group to more quickly resolve some of the more complex issues. Credibility here will be enhanced if the process is communicated at the start of deliberations and progress reports released on a regular basis.

SUMMARY

Once again, the foregoing may seem complicated to the uninitiated. However, it does embrace the essential principles so necessary for success here. We would strongly recommend the adoption of this formal approach. Action Planning can be enormously effective, but nothing comes free. Care and attention here will pay dividends.

Small organisations must distil the principles here and use them pragmatically. In essence, life for you is much easier. You have far fewer variables to worry about. Your ambition is 'practical engagement of the entire workforce'. Pick and choose whatever you need to achieve precisely that.

Figure 11: The Route Map updated 3

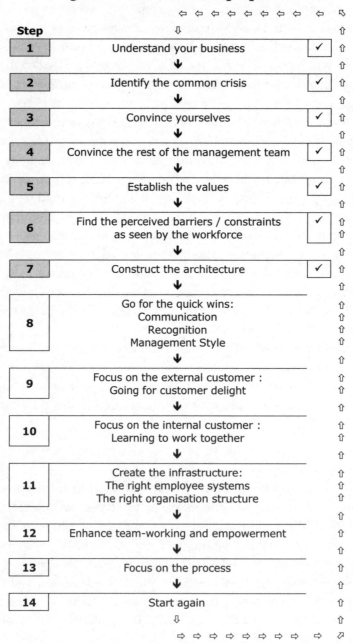

7
QUICK WINS I: COMMUNICATION

This is where it gets exciting! The hard work is now largely behind you, as is all the unpleasantness and pain of Perception Barrier Analysis. You now (nearly) understand the constraints and bottlenecks preventing your organisation from creating a healthy culture. The workforce will also be 'teed-up', ready and eager to embrace behavioural change. Inevitably, in their eyes, most of this change will revolve around the way the 'bosses', management, act in future. But the majority will readily acknowledge that there are also reciprocal obligations, requiring them too to alter their own behaviours and attitudes.

Many senior decision-makers find this last point difficult to believe. They sense danger here. They fear that the process downstream will be all one way, all take – no give. As a consequence, these first steps are taken timidly, almost reluctantly. This will totally undermine the initiative's credibility. A management team seemingly responding to criticism of their own weakness in a half-hearted, curmudgeonly way will quickly reverse out all the hard-earned goodwill and trust. You have to be positive, enthusiastic and trusting.

Being trusting is not a blind leap of faith. We have yet to encounter a workforce that has failed to respond to the momentum generated by Perception Barrier Analysis. Inevitably, in our experience, the biggest constraint will be management, not workforce, responsiveness. Employee engagement frequently fails through managerial inadequacy but rarely does it fail through any lack of willingness on the part of the workforce.

An example will help make the point.

Case Study 6

Paul was the managing director of a very traditional manufacturing operation dealing in high-value, machined goods. His background was exclusively finance, and he had been appointed to his position due to the continued failure of the organisation actually to make any money. He subsequently oversaw a series of redundancies, rationalisations and restructurings that left the company weak, vulnerable and extremely bruised. A business plan for survival was constructed, which certainly looked feasible. However, relationships between the workforce and management had deteriorated to such an extent that any attempt to change seemed to be doomed from the outset by chronic mistrust and negativity. Sensibly, Paul commissioned a Perception Barrier Analysis to try to understand the source of this severely dysfunctional culture.

It did not take long to get to the root of the problem. There was undoubtedly the odd 'bad apple' in the 70-strong workforce but, given the history of the place, that was understandable. Despite their protestations to the contrary, the real issue seemed to revolve around management behaviour. By a process of almost natural selection, and Paul's inexperience in people management, the majority of the management team left after the cuts were in the 'slash and burn' category. Autocrats to a man, they saw the workforce as predominantly lazy, negative and unhelpful, despite the long average length of service and the high individual skill level. Their response to this situation was to bully and cajole in an archetypal 'command and control' fashion.

Paul, when faced with the findings, quickly recognised the deficiency. His colleagues, despite the huge battery of evidence pointing to their failings, were much more grudging. They became defensive and rationalised away past behaviour, although they did apparently accept the need to change in the future. In keeping with the urgency of the situation, Paul swiftly went to the workforce and promised radical change. Management would now listen and involve. Communication would improve. Management style would shift from the autocratic to the consensual. Life would be very different in future.

Had Paul been a more visible and approachable leader, he might have gotten away with it. However, his comfort zone was quite definitely in the back room, away from all the muck and bullets at the sharp end. These changes, therefore, had to come from his direct reports, a group quite emphatically stuck in the first stages of the 'Valley of Despond' discussed in **Chapter 5**. Their mood varied from reflection to resignation. They themselves had little opportunity to discuss the situation, let alone undertake any training in these new and strange soft-skills. Unsurprisingly, the initiative failed abjectly. Within days, the workforce realised that Paul's promises were not deliverable and rancour returned, with each party vigorously blaming each other. The company folded shortly afterwards.

Paul's story tells us that the way management conducts itself in that first response phase is critical to the success of the initiative. It is absolutely vital that you 'hit the ground running'. Given the difficulty in getting management to emotionally adjust rapidly to this situation, we should not further add risk and complexity by selecting overcomplicated tasks initially. We are seeking simple solutions with fast returns that will also appeal to the rank and file. Fanciful? Fortunately not. The quick wins of *communication, recognition* and *management style* fit the bill admirably. In fact, many organisations stop after this phase, so pleased are they with the outcome. And that's a real pity. True transformation comes after the third or fourth iteration of the entire Route Map. We see employee engagement as a permanent journey in search of a utopian destination. You will never get there but every step on that journey continues to be very worthwhile.

The traditionalists amongst our readership will undoubtedly have a major problem with the proposition that simply focusing on those three basic issues will have such a profound impact on both organisational harmony and organisational performance. After all, we often see ourselves as already being more than proficient in all three areas. Who communicates badly? Who fails to recognise good behaviour? Who does not understand the linkage between management style and performance? One of the great mysteries facing practitioners in this field is how the majority of managers continually delude themselves on their capabilities in this area. The truth is that very few of us understand both the potency here and how to carry it out. It is much safer to start with the premise that you are deficient rather than exemplary when it comes to the quick wins.

Two case studies on communication may emphasise the point.

Case Study 7

In the 80s, Leyland Trucks prided itself in its ability to communicate – and it could prove that excellence. Its company videos were viewed nationally to be best in class. Its company newspaper, issued quarterly, likewise attracted countless awards. And it annually took the pulse of employee opinion by detailed employee surveys. To the outside world, Leyland was at the forefront of good practice in communication.

Take a look a little deeper. First, all of the foregoing were controlled and managed by the PR department, itself an offshoot of Central Personnel. The journalists employed in this area were superb professionals but their forte was in dealing with the external world, particularly the media. In essence, their ambition was to produce a product that met the acclaim of their peers. Unfortunately, this rarely corresponded with the needs and desires of the workforce. In the eyes of the latter, the information in the newspaper was either too late, irrelevant or sheer propaganda! Not exactly the ideal ingredients for motivational communication.

If anything, the video was worse. Once a year, people were herded into their local canteens where a large white screen would be set up in their midst. Seating and viewing arrangements were often far from ideal. The video would then start with something allegedly interesting from the world of truck or motor racing. This would fade out to allow a head shot of the latest Managing Director (we did have a lot!). He would spout very sincerely the same message delivered by his numerous predecessors. The impact was often negative.

We have discussed the weaknesses of standard employee surveys earlier (**Chapter 3**). Leyland made all the same mistakes. Few employees really identified with the objectives of the exercise. Nobody really got to grips with the myriad of statistics. And few people, other than management and trades union representatives, got involved in any downstream resolution. The end result was an expensive but futile exercise in ticking boxes.

Many large organisations delude themselves on the effectiveness of their communication systems. However, smaller companies can be just as guilty.

Case Study 8

Mark was the Manufacturing Director of a small high-precision engineering manufacturer employing 60 people. His factory was modern, well-equipped and carefully laid-out. Like everybody else in the UK manufacturing sector, his company struggled to make any money, mainly due to price competition from overseas. Mark felt that viability could be attained, providing the workforce took a 'more proactive attitude towards change'. He considered workplace apathy and resistance to be his biggest obstacles to creating a successful company.

Mark's eyes glazed over when we explained that the quick wins were as good a starting point as any. "We're already doing all of that. What I need is some form of wake-up call to the workforce".

Naturally, we were reluctant to leave it there, so we asked politely to see examples of good practice on communication. Mark enthusiastically leapt up off his seat and instructed us to "Come this way!". We followed him into the factory, where he proudly pointed us at the rear wall, the one that backed on to his offices. Along its full length was placed an array of bar charts, pie-charts, graphs, histograms and the like, all beautifully presented and crafted. Every single operating parameter was there, with current performance compared with both history and targets. It looked mightily impressive.

We then asked Mark what seemed to him to be a strange question: "Where do your employees enter the factory at the start of shift?". Looking puzzled, Mark turned around and pointed to the far left-hand side of the building. "And where are the toilets and rest-areas?". Mark then pointed to the far right-hand side "And how often do employees have to walk past THIS wall?". At this point, Mark reddened. It was obvious that the main beneficiaries of Mark's artistic endeavours were himself, his immediate reports and any visitors who might have strayed from the reception area. Nobody from the workforce or the offices actually had the opportunity, inclination or really the time to digest the complexity of this glorified Notice Board. This wasn't Communication; this was Information and not very useful information at that.

Mark is not alone here. Most of us in management do not grasp sufficiently the nature of good communication practice nor how to go about putting it right. We fail because either we neglect to think about it or we tend to see communication from a managerial standpoint rather than that of the individual worker. Three key points will help you improve your communications platform.

TELL THEM WHAT THEY WANT TO KNOW

First, we in management tend to communicate what WE consider important. This tends toward either bald performance statistics or PR 'puffs'.

Life in business now is wrapped up in statistics. As an owner-manager or key decision-maker, you will be faced with a myriad of business indicators upon which your performance will be judged. In the public or quasi-public sector, this can extend to ridiculous proportions. In the early days of the Business Links, for example, it was not unusual for companies with a turnover of little more than £3.5m a year to be subjected to over 150 KPIs! It is little wonder that we end up speaking in a completely new language, full of jargon, ratios and acronyms.

Because this becomes important to us, we convince ourselves that this should be important to everybody. As a consequence, our employee communications become littered with wild statistical references, which mean little to the rank and file. Just because you are turned on by performance statistics doesn't mean that everybody else is! Experience tells us that what employees value most in communication is that which gives them an insight into the broader aspects of working life. Most people like to have an holistic view of the world of work, not just the narrow confines of their immediate station. Work nowadays is an extension of society and, hence, the same rules apply. Employees are looking for a real comprehension of the key variables that determine the success or failure of the organisation. This information cannot be wrapped up exclusively in statistics; the workforce also needs access to the views and opinions of the main decision-makers in the business. If we really want employee engagement, then we have to demonstrate that it is worthwhile engaging in the business.

Your first challenge in establishing your communications platform is to devise a means of conveying these views and opinions in a clear, relevant and digestible fashion. The message must be a balanced one, neither over-negative nor unnecessarily optimistic. Spin or embellishment may work in the short-term, but will ultimately test the credibility of the messenger. You must communicate the position as you see it.

You must also paint a broad a picture as possible, bringing out the key external factors that impinge on the business. This includes macro-economic parameters, legislation, competition and market changes. Many question the wisdom of talking about issues that they cannot control. However, if a workforce suffers the consequences of one of these uncontrollable parameters and knows nothing about it, they will search for someone to blame. In the absence of any other likely target, they will default to blaming management. Your protestations will be too little and too late. Keeping employees informed about these external influences allows them to be prepared for the consequences. This can often take much of the emotion out of otherwise strained circumstances.

WHO'S GOING TO TELL THEM?

The second factor you need to consider when constructing your communications platform is the selection of the *messenger* to deliver the message. Different levels of management will be needed for different levels of information. Repeatedly, surveys of employees tell us that the preferred communication source for issues pertaining to *local* affairs is their immediate supervisor or line manager. These people have the advantage of familiarity with both individuals and circumstances. They can talk knowledgeably about the job, the targets and the immediate constraints. Dialogue here is most readily attuned to a two-way conversation. As long as local management conduct themselves in a non-autocratic and approachable fashion, communication at this level can be hugely effective and satisfying.

That's the theory, but it often falls down due to incapability or a lack of confidence on the part of the supervisor. Sheer disinterest can be a problem as well. Before you embark on any form of team briefing, you need to ensure that those charged with delivery have been adequately trained, have the confidence to speak publicly and are sufficiently aware of the importance of the task. Bad communication is often worse than no communication.

An example again to make the point.

Case Study 9

Charlie took over a position running a company in the food industry employing 130 people. Three years earlier, a formal Team Briefing System had been introduced to good effect. Employees had seemed to appreciate it. However, Charlie found that the situation had deteriorated appreciably, with the majority of comments now highly negative. He needed to find out why.

Investigation identified a number of problem areas. First, Team Briefing had been introduced as part of a major 'Participation' initiative devised by the then Plant Manager. The whole exercise had been so successful that its initiator was quickly promoted and whisked off to pastures new. Unfortunately, his replacement was a traditionalist. He had little empathy with these elusive concepts of empowerment and participation. However, he accepted the need to carry on with the Team Briefing. Politically, it would have proved difficult for him to do otherwise.

Progressively, and quickly, the 'oomph' behind the initiative faded. Local supervisors found themselves short of information or in a position where the system was being used to exhort and cajole, rather than inform or motivate. Confidence fell and many supervisors resorted to simply reading out the core message in a flat monotone, without inflexion and without supplement. In time, the entire system became simply another addition to bureaucratic ritual.

Team Briefing can be highly effective but it does require the right structure, the right senior level support and the right deliverers. However, it is rarely effective in conveying the 'big' messages about forthcoming change or major shifts in company policy or procedures. Here, only the key decision-makers are appropriate. They are seen to understand the full background and have the necessary insight into the nuances and subtleties of the issue. Familiarity with, and access to, the key decision-makers, therefore, is all important. There are major dangers in managing directors or their ilk simply emerging out of the ether to deliver complex and challenging messages at times of stress. The audience will not know their leader sufficiently well and might misread signals, inflexions or intonations, with negative consequences. The leaders in any business have a key and distinct role in communication and should therefore recognise and prepare for it.

IT'S HOW YOU TELL THEM, TOO

The final issue here is to consider the vital importance of both body language and tone. The words used in the message constitute only a small part in its potency. Of much greater impact are the signals sent out by these indirect contributors. We have witnessed, on many occasions, important presentations destroyed by often unconscious behaviour. Excessive confidence or evident nervousness can completely undermine the effectiveness of the exercise. If you are in a small business and have neither the time nor the money to be trained formally, we strongly recommend that you have someone assess your performance objectively until you get it right. Better still have the audience fill in a brief confidential questionnaire immediately after the event. It may not be pretty or complimentary but it will serve you well in the long term!

TECHNIQUES

There are many ways of communicating but rarely any means of detecting in advance which are going to work and which won't. A technique that works in one company may not be appropriate in another. Likewise, something that works in one department may not be as successful in another function. You really have to gauge the interrelationships of people, personalities, logistics and situations. However, we strongly counsel against 're-inventing wheels'. There is lots of good practice out there. By trial and error, other companies have arrived at models that seem to work. Sadly, many organisations become a little oversensitive here and avoid direct plagiarism. Recognise that this is 10 times more likely to be down to stubborn pride rather than the uniqueness of your own circumstances. By importing techniques well-tried and tested elsewhere, your confidence of success will be much greater and you will always have a reference point if things go wrong. This is the advice we give repeatedly to companies going down this path. Unfortunately, 75% choose to ignore it! It is so frustrating to stand by for many months and watch organisations struggle so unnecessarily.

Take the example of this book as your guide. There is hardly an original thought in it; its contents have been purloined unashamedly from the experience of many others over 30 years of struggling! Don't reinvent the wheel.

We will split the techniques into two categories, those for senior management and those for the more junior level.

SENIOR MANAGEMENT COMMUNICATIONS

Earlier, we discussed the importance of the workforce accessing the *views* and *opinions* of key decision-makers on those macro-factors that dictate company fortunes. It is obviously highly impractical for owners and directors to spend all their time wandering around the organisation wittering about the world in general. Inevitably, these people are the busiest in their companies and their time is very precious. We need to ensure that the effectiveness of any contact is maximised. One technique that has proved highly efficient in many organisations over the years is a weekly *Meet the Boss* or *Meet the Team*.

Meet the Boss / Meet the Team

The format here is relatively simple, the difference between the two approaches being that the former deals with individuals selected randomly from across the operation whilst the latter involves members of the same department.

A number of people are invited to attend a meeting with the Managing Director or other major decision-maker. The ideal size for effective dynamics seems to be between 12 and 16 people, although smaller firms may have to go lower.

Location is often important. If it is possible, the session should be held somewhere where the attendees feel comfortable, as long as the acoustics are acceptable and the seating not too painful! Employees often feel intimidated if dragged along to *your* boardroom or *your* conference room. It is vital that they can relax.

You, the Managing Director, are allowed to ask one question at the start of the session, which will be along the lines of *"What's troubling you today?"*. The audience sets the agenda and you need to respond to it without being defensive, overreacting or, heavens forbid, manipulating the session to suit your own ends. Your objective is to create an atmosphere of approachability, honesty and reflection.

In many traditional companies, the first attempts at this will probably be a trite uncomfortable for everybody. In all probability, over the initial months, there will be an over-emphasis on the 'hygiene' factors surrounding daily life. Pay, conditions, car parking, canteens, holidays, pensions and even the state of the toilets may dominate conversation. It is important to be patient and listen carefully at this stage. This may be the first time ever that individuals have had the opportunity to vent their spleens, to get their pet hates off their chests. However, we are not asking you to take personal ownership of all these questions. The right response may simply be to point the speaker in the correct direction, with an assurance that s/he can come back to you if unsatisfied. Above all, recognise that this phase is almost inevitable and reflects the dysfunctionality in your organisation's capability in managing people. These early months may be painful and bruising for you personally, but it is a necessary part of the cultural blood-letting.

Progressively thereafter, the mood will change, as will the subject matter. Questions of a strategic nature will creep slowly into the dialogue, reflecting a more holistic view of the world of work. Ultimately, if you do it routinely and correctly, the debate will mirror that of the boardroom. Subjects such as market expansion, competitive pressure, financial robustness and long term strategy will be commonplace, demonstrating that you are well down the path of real employee engagement.

We would strongly recommend that you seriously consider *Meet the Boss* and *Meet the Team*. For an investment of an hour or two a week, the return in goodwill and improved empathy will be considerable. In larger organisations, the load may need to be spread to other influential directors. Each employee needs to be seen a minimum of twice per year. For very little effort, a stream of benefits ensue. They include:

♦ Giving the boss a real perspective on workforce perceptions, priorities and concerns.

♦ Allowing regular access, at least twice per year, for every employee to the key decision-maker to discuss matters of importance.

- ◆ Establishing a greater understanding of each other's situation.
- ◆ Providing a routine safety valve on matters of potential controversy.

Many people resist this form of approach, claiming that such access bypasses middle and front line management. Our response to this is relatively straightforward; if you cannot handle this issue maturely and sensitively, then there's probably something very wrong with your people management capabilities! Employees need access to senior decision-makers. *Meet the Boss* ensures that this is done in an effective and controlled manner.

Here's a case study to show how it works in practice.

Case Study 10

Kurt is the Manufacturing Director of a sizeable manufacturing operation dealing in the retail industry. He inherited a shop-floor intensely hostile and suspicious of management behaviour. The gap between 'us and them' was as large as you were ever likely to encounter. Kurt was encouraged to introduce several initiatives to improve employee engagement, including *Meet the Boss*.

Four weeks into the meetings, Kurt is at an absolute loss. He followed the framework exactly, apart from asking for volunteers rather than inviting randomly-selected individuals. There is an obvious danger here, as the chances of attracting the negative, the barrack-room lawyers and the mouthy Luddites are far greater! Despite that, Kurt was still shocked at the hostility, the aggravation and the sheer negativity. As he said, *"There's blood everywhere and most of it's mine!"*.

However, he persevered week after week. By the end of the first quarter, admittedly a long time to be facing all this flak, things began to change. People started to appreciate the effort, patience and courage that Kurt was exhibiting. The tenor changed subtly from outright whingeing into a more positive *"How can we go forward?"*. Several years on, Kurt never misses a session.

Managing by Walking About

The most conventional means of familiarising employees with senior management is the practice of 'Managing by Walking About' (MBWA). Here the idea is that the owner-manager or managing director takes anything up to an hour a few times a week, simply strolling around talking to people at random. The opportunity also exists for employees holding particular issues or grievances to tackle their ultimate boss directly.

In principle, this is a very laudable endeavour. Theoretically, it humanises the face of the boardroom, allows access to the otherwise untouchable and, at the very least, enables the boss to 'take the temperature' of the establishment. S/he can therefore decide for themselves what's hot and what's not. All very sensible – in theory.

Practice, however, falls far short of this utopian ideal. There are five obvious weaknesses that we see repeatedly:

♦ Most managers feel inhibited about this unstructured meandering, particularly those not possessing an extrovert nature. Likewise, most employees feel at least a little discomforted about the 'big gaffer' suddenly appearing at their work station. Dialogue is likely to be halting and stilted. It is not a natural process.

♦ The ones who really value the opportunity of meeting the head honcho are those at the lower end of the positivity tree – the loudmouths, moaners and generally disaffected. As a consequence, we get this 'paradox of management attention', where management spend a completely disproportionate amount of time with the bottom 20% attitudinally. This can lead to the more positive 80% becoming quite disaffected, as they misinterpret management behaviour: *"You have to be a pillock to be noticed in this place!"*.

♦ Many managers use MBWA as an inspection process rather than a means of improving mutual understanding. The practice then disintegrates into 'fault-finding' where the managing director uses the daily perambulations to 'nitpick' and generally 'keep people on their toes'. This will certainly not aid communication and mutual understanding.

♦ Some managers eschew the subject of work when doing the rounds and focus exclusively on the social life of their employees and mutual shared interests. The occasional use of such references can be very useful in breaking down barriers and establishing affinities. Unfortunately, excessive chit-chat can undermine the whole point of the exercise. We visited one organisation where the Finance Director was very proud of his ability to interact with his subordinates. However, they had a different view: *"All he wants to talk about is bloody Sheffield United! Doesn't he ever think about work!"*.

♦ Finally, our pet hate. Those managers who still believe that information is power, leftovers from the bad old days of command and control. They slink around the establishment finding weaknesses in colleagues for use over the boardroom table. Often, they do likewise with intermediate management levels. The end result is people being 'warned-off' with dire consequences for speaking out of turn to the boss, in case they drop their immediate manager in it!

Case Study 11

John was an aggressive manager who prowled, rather than walked, the floor. His particular technique was to interrogate each junior manager intensively until he found a weakness. Then he would action the unfortunate to resolve the matter within 24 hours, before moving on to the next victim. After a while, his subordinates wised up. They would 'plant' weaknesses that could quickly be resolved. In fact, this led them to creating problems or even delaying fixes until the boss had spotted them. Life for them became much easier. John never cottoned on.

Management by Walking About is to be recommended. However, it is not an instinctive process and needs to be planned, reviewed and measured like any other management activity.

Written Briefs

Sometimes, it is not possible to communicate complex issues through routine verbal channels. Some messages, particularly those highlighting impending change, may need constant repetition. In these circumstances, consideration should be given to some form of written document. Certainly if your organisation swells to more than 75 employees, or you have a smaller number on a multi-site operation, the benefits in making your communications platform robust will be considerable.

Before you resort to developing such an instrument, you need to focus very clearly in your own mind on what it's all about. We despair at so many companies' efforts in this direction. The temptation to become sidetracked, to elaborate and to mimic the worst excesses of the tabloid industry seem irresistible. Some rules:

♦ This is a routine communications device. Full stop.

♦ You do not need photographs, icons, computer-generated graphics or pseudo-magazine formats. Glossy paper is forbidden!

♦ Keep it simple. The best examples we have seen are desktop-published. A plain A4 sheet is folded in half, giving four pages. Three are for management information. The fourth is a social page.

♦ The document is for employees, not customers. Do not confuse the two. It is also not about public relations. Mix the two and you will be accused of 'spin' and management propaganda.

♦ As before, focus on management views and opinions. Statistics should kept to a minimum. Hectoring and lecturing will turn people off.

♦ Decide on a frequency and keep strictly to it. If you say it will be issued at 9.00 am on the first Monday of each month, remember that 11.00 am is too late. Reliability breeds credibility.

Writing the brief can be a fairly onerous challenge for one person. We would strongly recommend a rota, calendarised in advance for the next 12 months. Managers would have plenty of notice to come up with subjects relevant to the publication. For those not particularly skilled when it comes to grammar, spelling or sentence construction, assistance should be given with editing. Articles should be clear, relevant, written in plain English and, if possible, touched with a little humour. Those technophiles amongst you should also question whether distribution through e-mail adds the right gravitas. Our belief is that whilst you *might* get away with it with regular users of PCs, hard copies may well be better for those with limited access. In any event, routinely audit and measure its impact. The workforce will tell you whether you are getting it right.

State of the Nation

Most organisations tend to have an annual or six-monthly 'State of the Nation' presentation where the principal director stands in front of the workforce and presents the status of the company. Frequently, the Finance Director is roped in to given an overview of profitability, cash and balance sheet movements. In theory, again, this is a very good thing. It offers the opportunity metaphorically to take every employee up in the helicopter and give them a birds-eye view of their firm. Just as powerfully, employees can look into the eyes of their key decision-makers and make up their own minds about the bosses' competency, trustworthiness, honest and integrity. As a showcase for these two objectives, there could scarcely be a more useful platform.

Sadly, organisations have a habit of cocking this up as well. Whilst about half of these events tend to be viewed moderately favourably and upwards, an equal share leave the workforce dissatisfied, confused and demotivated. If you are going to conduct a 'State of the Nation', make sure you do it correctly.

Common faults include:

♦ Using the event as a 'wind-up' for other issues. We hesitate to use the expression *hidden agenda* here, as there is rarely anything hidden about it. Employees tend to be far more astute than management gives them credit. The objective of the exercise is simply to give an overview of the business. If there are likely to be any subsequent unfavourable consequences, then that should be the subject of a *separate* communication. Otherwise the whole concept becomes discredited.

♦ Many managers use the process as a means of criticising, frightening or plain bullying. Our experience in this situation is that people simply switch off or perhaps not bother to turn up. It is difficult, even with a well managed event, to get a decent two-way communication flow. In this sort of atmosphere, only the lunatic fringe or the organisational creeps are likely to stick their heads above the parapet. That's of no benefit to anybody.

♦ Over-focussing on negative messages. People like to feel part of a successful team. Even in your worst situations, there are likely to be a host of successful accomplishments. It is always beneficial to introduce liberally examples of positive achievements whilst, at the same time, maintaining a sense of balance.

◆ Using obscure terminology is the most common fault of all. For a presentation to a general workforce, there is little point in referring to complex financial terms or obscure performance ratios. We in management may be more than comfortable with inventory turns, debtor days, provisions and the rest of the 'egg-box' indicators of organisational health. However, most employees are unfamiliar with the terminology and, more importantly, their implications. Keep the language simple and focus only on a few parameters to demonstrate your point. Trying to educate everybody on Profit & Loss accounts, reading a balance sheet and the rest of the management accounting system is, in our experience, usually a complete waste of effort. By the time people come along to the next State of the Nation, they'll have probably forgotten it all!

◆ And finally, something so self-evident that we feel guilty raising it. But experience tells us that this problem happens all too often. If you are going to communicate to all and sundry, make sure that first they can hear you, second they can see any visual aids you use and third they are in a position to understand you comfortably. Having people hanging from rafters in a cold, gloomy warehouse is hardly likely to aid comprehension!

Case Study 12

Derek was very proud of his 'State of the Nation'. He spent weeks in preparation for this annual event and carefully ensured that the script and the accompanying PowerPoint presentation met all the criteria of relevance, succinctness and clarity. Due to the size of the workforce and his view that everybody should hear the message simultaneously, Derek delivered to the non-manufacturing population, whilst his colleague Malcolm spoke to manufacturing.

At a subsequent Perception Barrier Analysis, Derek was mortified to discover that the workforce had very mixed feelings about his pride and joy. The non-manufacturing sector spoke very favourably, mentioning Derek's sincerity and detail consciousness. On the other hand, manufacturing were cynical, disbelieving and occasionally hostile.

It turned out that Malcolm didn't share Derek's enthusiasm for communication. His delivery was characterised by simply reading out Derek's script in a flat monotone, accompanied by a body language that was scarcely less than aggressive. Occasionally, he would break off and harangue the audience on a particular theme of his. As someone commented, *"Malcolm delivers the message as though he's got a nasty taste in his mouth and he wants to get rid of it".* Malcolm broke every rule and, frankly, didn't care. His view was that the more his subordinates knew, the more they were likely to give him trouble.

Trade Unions / Employee Representation

Many small organisations find it difficult to establish an effective and efficient role for employee representation. This is often down to inexperience but, quite frequently, also due to a fear of the potential disruption that representative bodies can create. Memories of the 60s and 70s will take a long time to fade. However, the relationship between senior management and any representative committee must not be allowed to undermine the need to communicate properly.

Even in these enlightened 21st century days, too often we see management concede responsibility for vital communications platforms to union representatives. This is unfair on the company, its employees and, indeed, the representatives themselves.

Employees, as we said earlier, want information from those who they consider to be proactive in the decision-making process that affects their future. They do not want routine company communication routed through shop stewards because:

♦ Representatives do not carry the same authority.

♦ Representatives do not have the same informed outlook.
and

♦ Representatives cannot be assumed to be able to convey the necessary nuances and subtleties of the *management* message.

The average shop steward / representative is not selected or elected primarily on their ability to communicate. They are much more likely to get there through dint of personality or negotiating skills. To expect them to convey the routine day-to-day detail of workaday life, much of which may be of little interest to them, is folly of the highest order.

The first prerequisite of an effective shop steward is to have a high level of credibility with their constituents. This will not happen if they are perceived to be management lackeys. To be effective, they must distance themselves from management to a degree and be seen to be taking an impartial line. In times of disagreement, they must show the workforce that they will convey their concerns with passion and commitment. Using your representatives regularly to persuade employees of the merits of a company approach or to sell specific management policies is never going to be effective in the long-term. Management have to accept that the only channel of communication between the company and its workforce on matters pertaining to the organisation is management itself. This is not an anti-union stance. In the longer term, this will help representatives by allowing them to focus on what they do best and what they've been elected for.

Meeting Disciplines

Before we leave senior management communications, a few words must be said about the general standards of meeting disciplines in firms, big and small. One might expect larger organisations to be a bit more sophisticated than their SME colleagues but, sadly, this does not seem to be the case. Most companies could improve the effectiveness of their staff and support areas by at least 5% if they simply focussed a little attention in this area. It is not difficult. Readers of a certain generation will have seen the John Cleese *Meetings, Bloody Meetings* video (Video Arts). Despite its age, the message is still as relevant today as ever. Most management meetings are over-long, over-populated, mis-directed and mis-managed. That's a fair old indictment, considering many of you spend perhaps the majority of your working day in them!

It is not the role of this book to get into meeting skills in any great detail. There is plenty of literature out on the subject. A few bullet points will suffice:

♦ Identify with your colleagues the problems that they encounter with meeting disciplines in your organisation. Whilst they won't be experts in the subject, you can almost guarantee that they'll get 90% of the way there. Criticism from 'within the kirk' is so much more telling than getting it from a book.

♦ Set guidelines for all meetings in your company. These should be posted in all the conference / meeting rooms.

♦ As part of this exercise, review various acceptable and unacceptable behavioural traits to ensure that attendees are aware of what can go on. Examples include:

  ◊ Proposing – Summarising.

  ◊ Building – Bringing in.

  ◊ Supporting – Shutting out.

  ◊ Disagreeing – Defending / Attacking.

  ◊ Open – Cross-talking

  ◊ Closed – Not listening.

  ◊ Testing understanding – Interrupting.

  ◊ Seeing information – Blocking.

  ◊ Giving information – Going off on a tangent.

  ◊ Gossiping.

♦ Understand what a chairperson needs to do. It is not the chairperson's task to batter everybody into submission but many ignore this point! In brief, chairing a meeting is about:

  ◊ Planning the meeting – prepare an agenda.

  ◊ Setting objectives for the meeting.

  ◊ Introducing and setting out the purposes of the meeting.

  ◊ Reviewing action points from the last meeting.

  ◊ Seeking participation.

  ◊ Controlling both the time and the people.

  ◊ Summarising the discussion.

  ◊ Stating conclusions and allocating action points.

  ◊ Managing the administration – sending minutes out.

  It sounds straight forward but, sadly, theory rarely matches practice.

♦ Ensure that the meeting is only as long as it needs to be. An attendee involved for, say, only five minutes in a two-hour meeting is likely to be pretty bored. Many in this situation will seek to deflect the debate, either mischievously or through sheer ennui, to something of relevance to them. It is much more effective to release these individuals once they have fulfilled their purpose. A radical, but interesting, device here is to remove the chairs from the room. Stand-up meetings guarantee brevity!

MIDDLE / FRONT LINE COMMUNICATIONS

There are many techniques available for routine communication between management and the workforce, too many for a book of this nature. The challenge for you is to find one that best fits the characteristics of your operation. Factors to consider include shift working, multi-site logistics, geography, supervisor / subordinate ratios, flexible hours and employee availability. Below we will touch upon a few systems that have been seen to work elsewhere.

Hill St. Blues

These early morning 'huddles' are named after an American police show popular some years ago. The idea is that, at the very start of shift, members of the team come together for a rapid five-minute get-together. One individual, normally the leader, welcomes everybody and conveys the latest situation and the priorities of the day in a rapid, bullet-point fashion. Others will add concerns, challenges or contributions to help understand how the team is going to achieve its daily objectives. There is no gossip, no chit-chat and certainly no intellectual contemplation. The idea is to get everyone together for an extremely short period, to exchange immediate issues and to highlight any challenges. As a by-product, it also builds teamwork and does wonders for curing lateness!

Case Study 13

Sheila ran the logistics department of a small distribution company. This was a stressful job with a wide range of responsibilities spread over her nine subordinates. Friction was never too far from the surface and arguments would frequently break out. At times, she felt her job was more a referee than a logistics manager. In time, the department split into three cliques, with a distinct frostiness between rival factions. In Sheila's opinion, most of these differences arose more from misunderstanding than malice.

Sheila then adopted the practice of getting everybody together at 8.30am for a five minute huddle. Due to flexible working patterns, this was the first opportunity for all to be present. She kept the agenda tight and gradually opened up the forum to others to contribute. The breakthrough came when someone voiced concerns about their particular load that day. To Sheila's surprise, another from a rival clique volunteered to help out as she had a 'bit of spare time'. Within weeks, the atmosphere in the office changed remarkably and peace broke out. Longstanding irritations such as lateness, holiday cover and temporary work imbalances seemed, as she said, 'to disappear'.

We heartily recommend this huddle-type approach, but it does have its limitations. It is not suited, for example, to big departments. Here, you may have to fragment, which could itself be problematic. It is also far more suited to areas with a high frequency of decision-making. Long-term project management may, for instance, be too slow to achieve any real benefit. Here, perhaps the weekly staff meeting may be better suited.

Staff Meetings

In areas where the advantages of an early morning huddle are not so apparent, then a simple staff meeting may suffice. There are many versions of this but, to be successful, experience indicates:

- ♦ An optimal size, probably best 10 to 12 people, but no greater than 16.
- ♦ Management contribution kept to a minimum and limited to highlighting issues and explaining strategies.
- ♦ An extensive opportunity for two-way communication and a peer exchange of views.
- ♦ No longer than 45 to 60 minutes maximum.
- ♦ Brief, action points taken at the end of each meeting.

Case Study 14

Jim ran a busy purchasing function, where the benefits of the early morning huddle did not seem attractive. In particular, he felt that some issues required more attention on a regular basis than the five-minute session would allow. Accordingly, he instituted a weekly one-hour staff meeting where all staff could attend. Initially, he set the agenda and acted as chair. After a few meetings, he felt confident enough to allow the chair to rotate across the department. Each nominee would set the agenda for the following week, ensure that action points were followed up and that everybody with something to say got the opportunity to say it.

The end result was a considerable success both in information gathering and distribution and in teambuilding.

Cascade Briefings

Cascade Briefings, or Team Briefings, are a very common device to routinely get key management messages across to the shop-floor or workplace. Despite protestations to the contrary, they are rarely 'two-way', although dialogue occasionally takes place at the sharp end of the cascade. They are also notoriously difficult to get absolutely right, although this shouldn't deter us from trying.

Cascade briefings are a simple concept that take a lot of maintenance. Most organisations fail because they put considerable effort in up-front, often so much that it tends to raise unrealistic expectations. They then omit to provide the necessary attention on a daily or weekly basis. 'Doing the routine things routinely' is a mantra that suits most management initiatives. Sadly most of us ignore it, preferring the shock of the new. Keep to a few simple rules:

♦ Determine a mechanism for creating the 'core' senior management messages. This is the series of statements that provides the bedrock for your daily or weekly team briefing. If the exercise is to be conducted weekly, then you can take a fairly leisurely, albeit still disciplined, approach to constructing the core message. If it is daily, then you have to be quite dynamic and reactive.

♦ Determine the parameters for onward communication. Decide on topic areas, frequencies and level of detail. Do not be tempted to communicate key strategic issues through the team briefings. These are likely to be too complex and far-reaching for this vehicle. You should signal the coming debate and address it through one of the devices discussed earlier that involve senior management directly. If there is no information to be conveyed that particular day or week, say so. Do not resort to 'fillers', as they will simply discredit the process.

♦ Determine a timetable and stick to it religiously.

♦ Ensure that each individual involved at each stage in the cascade is sufficiently adept in this process. Measure 'customer' responsiveness by frequent (twice a year?) and simple questionnaires.

SUMMARY

Communication is the lubricant of organisational efficiency. People often baulk at the time and effort required to do it right, but the costs of NOT communicating are likely to be far higher. Others often worry about the consequences of over-communicating.

We wouldn't be unduly concerned about this. First, if you limit downward communication by focussing on strategy and key issues rather than facts and figures, then you will struggle to saturate the system. Second, if, as recommended, you constantly measure the effectiveness of your communication system, you will find out very quickly if you're overdoing it in some areas. Simple, informal questionnaires will again suffice here.

The real threat of over-communication comes from an excess of meetings. In nearly every company we have encountered, employees raise the issue of either too many meetings or poor meeting disciplines or both. Again, you can identify whether you have a problem by issuing occasional questionnaires asking attendees to comment on the meeting they've just attended.

Above all, be flexible. Life is changing all the time and your communications platform needs to reflect that change. Doing it the way you've always done it can never be right.

Many of the structures here may not be appropriate for micro-organisations. However, the challenge is still there. Take what you want from this chapter to ensure a healthy, two-way dialogue throughout your fledgling empire.

8
QUICK WINS II: RECOGNITION

OK, let's start this chapter with a question:

> "How many of our readers work for companies that have a **written** Recognition process?"

Oh dear. Well, perhaps that was too difficult. Another one then:

> "How many of our readers work for companies that (honestly!) have a generally understood, but not yet written down, Recognition procedure?"

Oh dear, again. A final question:

> "How many of our readers work for companies that accept that they are not very good at Recognition?"

Now you're kidding yourself!

After scores of conferences and seminars where we have posed the questions above, 90% and upwards of respondents answer in the negative to all three! They do NOT have a written recognition procedure, they do NOT have a clearly understood routine and yet they all believe that they are far from unacceptable when it comes to recognising employees! However, when we measure the same perception from an *employee's* standpoint, usually a far more accurate barometer of reality, the vast majority of organisations are not seen to recognise at all well.

We believe the above not to be a matter of shame but of huge opportunity. This entire book is based on the now widely-accepted premise that employee motivation can be a major contributor to organisational success. One of the best ways of motivating employees is to regularly recognise their contributions to the organisation, to make them feel valuable, useful and appreciated. If we accept both of these propositions, then it is not too great an intellectual leap to equate good recognition practice with good performance. And the great news is that Recognition is easy, fun, time-efficient and usually very effective. Providing a few simple rules are followed, then there is often no reason why your organisation should not be an exemplar in these practices in a matter of months. Once this level of sophistication is reached, the benefits in motivation and attitude are usually followed in quick succession by improved performance and a greater acceptance of ongoing change. Recognition systems are one of the most powerful, and least used, tools in the management armoury. Statistically, it is unlikely that your competitors have realised this, so you still have time!

INDIVIDUAL & TEAM RECOGNITION

To understand the power of Recognition, we must first distinguish between INDIVIDUAL and TEAM appreciation. We recommend that two entirely different approaches are adopted here. With individuals, we suggest that you are circumspect and confidential. However, when it comes to recognising Teams, you can let your hair down a little more, but don't go daft. Now this approach could differ from books and theories you may have encountered elsewhere. Practices that seem to work exceedingly well in the US, for example, often disintegrate into cynicism and rejection in the UK. Longstanding and successful Japanese variants are dismissed likewise as merely patronising when launched into a British culture. Many may criticise the approach proffered in this book as being unadventurous or unambitious. They might be right. But we strongly suggest that you create a solid foundation of these admittedly conservative techniques before venturing into the more exotic. Going off too far and too fast is a guaranteed recipe for failure. The enemies of effective recognition are cynicism, mistrust and Machiavellian management. Sadly most organisations in the UK carry the baggage of all three impediments from the past, if not the present. If you are saddled with that background, it may take *you* several years, not months, to get into that elusive exemplar category. You must resist the inclination to be too readily disheartened here and persevere. The rewards are simply too great for you to contemplate failure. Good recognition practice is one of the finest attributes any management team can exhibit.

Before you start to consider which techniques to adopt, you need to spend a little time reviewing the challenges to good practice. In essence, this simply means taking a hard and honest look at the culture of your organisation. Ask yourself and your team the following:

♦ Is morale in the general workforce negative?

♦ Is there a pronounced 'us and them' attitude in your organisation?

♦ Is your organisation's predominant management style verging towards the autocratic?

♦ Do you have a history of resistant or confrontational relationships with your representative body?

♦ Have you a history of ongoing, but unfinished, change initiatives (so-called 'initiativitis'!)?

♦ Is your management team resistant to new ideas, particularly those associated with the 'softer' management techniques?

If you answer affirmatively to any of the above, you are likely to encounter resistance to recognition practice. This could come in many forms, ranging from disbelief and rejection on the part of the workforce to cynicism and dismissal in the management ranks. You have to be prepared for this and appreciate that your journey inevitably will be longer than the ideal. Set out with this in mind and you are far less likely to be discouraged. A couple of examples may help.

Case Study 15

When John Oliver attempted to introduce some of these techniques into Leyland Trucks in the early '90s, he encountered huge suspicion of management motivation. Coupled with a resentment bordering on rejection by some managers more used to a 'natural' autocratic style, the opportunities for quickly launching recognition into the company were seen to be very limited. Accordingly, a very gentle process of slowly drip-feeding initiatives was adopted. It took a good three to four years before 'maturity' was established.

In retrospect, perhaps the process could have moved a little faster, but this would have increased the chances of total failure. Despite the slow pace, each stage in the process resulted in modest but progressive improvements in the motivation so vital to the company's fortunes.

As the organisation's starting point was so bad, these admittedly minor changes had perhaps a disproportionate benefit when compared with other companies. Recognition eventually became an integral and valuable part of the culture.

Case Study 16

The virtues of recognition were being explained to a medium-sized retail outlet employing around 45 to 50 people. The audience of eight managers / supervisors listened patiently, if somewhat nervously, until the subject of 'Thank You cards' (see later) was raised. For some reason, this provoked a sharp interruption from one agitated female middle manager. If she had given a Thank You card to any of her staff, she claimed, she would have been told, to paraphrase, to depart elsewhere and insert it vigorously into a part of her lower anatomy!

Interestingly, upon further discussion with both her and her colleagues, it was conceded that the greatest discomfort here would be endured not by the workforce but by management themselves. For years, the prevailing management style had been distant, impersonal and often sarcastic. Some of them simply could not see how they could handle the apparent formality of acknowledging good performance. Instead, they preferred to rely on a passing "Ta" for the odd occasion where it was felt absolutely necessary to express any form of appreciation! When told that this was hardly likely to trigger a change in attitude, morale and motivation, some of the group became visibly nervous. They really failed to comprehend that **their** behaviour in the past was probably a key contributor to the total absence of employee engagement in the company.

Many of our readers, particularly those in the retail or hospitality industries, will have an *Employee of the Month*. Here, after internal or (occasionally) customer nominations, some poor soul is acclaimed to be the best worker in the company for the previous calendar month. They then suffer the indignity of having their photograph plastered all over the reception area for everybody, friend, foe or stranger, to see. This, to these companies, is recognition.

Or is it? Recognition, by now we hopefully all agree, is about motivation of individuals or groups. The immediate response to this 'acknowledgement of exceptional contribution' should be a feeling of pride, achievement and self-satisfaction. The muzzy, warm glow of success. There should also be an appreciation, by those around the anointed one, that the plaudits are justified, deserved and fair. After all, what we are trying to create is a general aspiration to repeat the behaviour that we are recognising.

Late in 2004, we visited a smallish hotel employing 14 people in the North-East of Scotland. As we entered the foyer, we spied the usual *Employee of the Month* board, adorned with a photograph of November's nominee. Interestingly, no-one had managed to repeat the victory. January to November all had different winners. December would no doubt be someone else.

What does this tell us of employees' feelings towards *Employee of the Month*? First, that it will have no credibility at all. The expression often used in this sort of arena is 'Buggins' turn'. In other words, your turn will come to take the laurel wreath – as long as you keep your nose clean! No merit, no reflection of performance and hence no motivation.

Second, what about the few who fail to get their mugshots on this Hall of Fame? Their emotions are likely to waver from anxiety to bitterness and then to cynicism. Hardly a recipe for employee engagement, is it?

We have spoken to many hotel managers about this iniquitous practice. Half of them argue vigorously that, in their situation, the award really is motivational. Their employees enthusiastically aspire to the monthly acclaim. In their hotel, there is no jealousy, envy or cynicism. Subsequent conversations with employees are usually brief, but inevitably accompanied by a wry smile. In our experience, these managers are simply deluding themselves, a not uncommon skill in the profession!

The other half are honest and concede it is not a workforce thing but more a matter of customer relations. There is apparently a certain reassurance when a guest or prospective guest enters the foyer and sees these visible examples of excellence adorning the walls. Recognising these individuals when they encounter them in the restaurant or in reception also creates a certain comfort. Hence, the nominees are usually those with some form of face-to-face contact with guests.

There is nothing at all wrong with this. This is good, effective public relations. However, it needs to be seen as precisely that and employees need to be 'in on the game' as well. Otherwise, the marginal benefit in customer satisfaction will be swamped by the negative consequences of a potentially demoralised workforce.

It is therefore very easy to get Recognition wrong and to end up damaging the organisation rather than benefiting it. Fortunately, it is just as easy to ensure that you get it right. All you have to do is review not just the structure of recognition but its impact on the workforce. And if you're not sure how to do that, just ask them. A simple, confidential 10-point questionnaire will suffice. The following case study demonstrates another way that companies get this highly straightforward concept so wrong. Again the problem is that they do not really reflect upon the impact on individual employees and produce another example of the 'bread and circus' motivational style typical of so many managers.

Case Study 17

Len is a self-made man, running his successful insurance company, which had grown from 'one man and a dog', as he put it, to 70 employees in a little over five years. He is proud of his achievements and equally confident of the efficacy of his blunt, no nonsense management style. He firmly believes that the success of his operation is down to his motivational skills. We were invited along to his 'glittering awards evening' to see this at first hand.

The ceremony took place in a local, plush hotel with all employees in attendance, but no partners. A Master of Ceremonies was hired for the evening, who, after a sumptuous meal, invited Len to give his annual address. Interestingly, Len sat with his direct reports all evening and made no attempt to converse with anybody else. After his speech, received in silence with only polite applause at the end, a series of awards were made. Each nomination was received with a cacophonous acclaim, the rowdiness best explained by the amount of alcohol imbibed rather than the popularity of the nominee. The entire evening was hugely enjoyable, with the participants obviously having a whale of a time. Len was delighted. *"This"*, he shouted over the noise *"is what it's all about"*. In his mind, an expensive gesture but one well worth the effort.

But was it? Chatting to the award winners and some of the other attendees cast a different light. The 'employee of the year' was very modest about his achievements. He explained that Len had been very keen on expanding the business into critical illness cover that year, his personal speciality. He felt the award had more to do with Len's subliminal message to the organisation rather than his own personal merit. Another group of winners, nominated by a peer group, explained that this was simply a return of favour. The previous year they had nominated them successfully and now it was their turn. Given the limited eligibility for each award, this was relatively easy to do.

Many commented how the smiling persona projected by Len on his 'night of nights' didn't reflect his usual daytime behaviour. As one said, *"Len's great quality is that he's always right and he makes sure you know it".*

Regardless of the entertainment value of the evening, we came away feeling highly disappointed. In truth, Len was not only wasting his money but he was also guilty of grossly wasting his energy. Len was an exceptional businessman but his success was based on drive, technical knowledge and an abundant energy. His people skills were limited to old-fashioned autocracy. Whether the latter was sustainable in the long-term, particularly as his business expanded, was questionable. However, we were absolutely certain that his attempts at Recognition were damaging rather than supporting his prospects. And all because he failed to ask the simple questions that would have led him to understand the real nature of Recognition.

INDIVIDUAL RECOGNITION

Given the propensity of management to get things so wrong in this area, it is probably wise to lay down a few rules about individual recognition. These have been developed by experience over many years in successful practice.

Individual Recognition SHOULD:

♦ Be sincere, genuine and appreciated as such.

♦ Be free-flowing.

♦ Be responsive, live and active.

♦ Be spontaneous, don't miss the moment.

♦ Be flexible.

♦ Reflect and promote the desired culture and organisational aims.

♦ Be reasonably confidential, private.

and

♦ Be routinely measured for effectiveness.

The best form of recognition is a simple, spontaneous 'thank you' delivered verbally at the appropriate time in a manner that is seen to be heartfelt. It costs absolutely nothing and yet can have such a profound impact on subordinate motivation. Regardless of what follows in the rest of this chapter, you must never lose sight of this simple fact. When you come to write down your 'official' Recognition procedure (which you must do, otherwise you'll forget about it), this should be the top of the list for everyone.

Sadly few, if any, companies manage to do this right. Even in the simplest of unions, marriage, we have to rely on other gestures to make each partner feel appreciated. Birthday and anniversary cards, gifts and moments of spontaneous affection are all seen as vital in even the strongest of relationships. To imagine we can get away with none of these accoutrements in social interactions as complex and convoluted as those found in business or commerce is sheer folly.

Here we list some of the techniques that have been seen to work elsewhere. Do not think for one moment that you have to adopt all of them. It is much better to take on one or two and really embed them into the organisation. We have, for example, included a section on Suggestion Schemes and described one that is known to work. But developing and, more importantly maintaining, a system for collecting employee ideas is notoriously difficult. If you feel you have to have one, then adopt the 'proven' practice here. But most organisations will benefit from placing their energies and efforts elsewhere. Life is too short for unnecessary bureaucracy!

Recognising People Exist!

Perhaps even before 'Thank You', comes 'Hello'. In all organisations, irrespective of nature, employees like to be treated as individuals. There are few things worse than working for a company where you feel 'part of the furniture', where your value is perceived to be on a par with the fixtures and fittings. Work, as we said earlier, is an extension of society in our modern, developed world. As we've seen in **Chapter 4**, the consequences of people feeling routinely and deliberately ignored can be quite devastating. You must ensure that all your managers practice basic interpersonal skills. The oft-heard excuse of being 'too busy' is both unforgivable and totally unacceptable in a modern manager. Not recognising that your employees exist and have the same social needs as managers themselves will lead to a corrosive grapevine and to corrupted perceptions. Establishing a healthy rapport between manager and the managed can obviate the need for many more 'artificial' devices.

We recommend that you approach this from three directions:

♦ Incorporate such disciplines and demands into management training. If you don't train or induct new management routinely, ensure that the expectation is made absolutely clear from the outset.

♦ Senior management should set an example in their 'managing by walking about' and in their setting of formal organisational values.

♦ Measurement.

We strongly advise the use of suitable subordinate questionnaires here, an issue we will revisit in detail in the next chapter. However, a cheap and cheerful confidential survey on this one topic may well be sufficient.

Informal, Individual Recognition Tokens

As will have become obvious throughout this entire section, the most effective recognition is that done spontaneously and informally. Unfortunately, the vast majority of organisations cannot rely on spontaneity and informality. It simply does not happen. Managers everywhere tend to be too operationally focussed to keep this soft issue as a priority. The day-to-day demands of business are such that 'optional' activities get parked up until 'important' transactions are completed. Initially, recognition becomes that optional extra. Very quickly, it becomes forgotten and is resurrected only when conscience, or the HR department, pricks.

Managers innately respond to *tasks* so, to get them into the good habits of recognition, you may have to take a structured approach. Some organisations do this successfully by introducing a limited number of 'recognition tokens'. These are low value items given to those employees who are perceived to have done something 'above and beyond the call of duty'. Examples we have seen include 'Green Shield' stamps, pens, pencils, travel alarms, T-shirts, clocks and so on.

One of the more effective was a rather garishly-coloured Parker Vector pen upon which was transcribed a single word, 'Thanks'.

As you do not want to flood the organisation with your new tokens, you limit each manager to a proportion of his / her headcount. A good starting point may be 25% of the workforce to be recognised over the next 12 months. This is an exceedingly modest target, as it only reflects your ambition to kickstart a general movement in this direction. Hopefully, the success of the token will encourage your managers to move progressively to less artificial measures.

Two general points here that apply to all forms of individual recognition:

♦ Unless you belong to an unusually mature organisation, always conduct individual recognition privately and confidentially. Despite many learned management academics suggesting otherwise, the idea of being singled out and praised in front of your peers is absolutely anathematical to most people. Now some might think this is a bit strong, after all the (Chambers) dictionary definition of anathema is: *"a solemn ecclesiastical curse or denunciation involving excommunication, a curse or execration; an object of abhorrence"*.

However, we have seen many examples where the people involved have felt just as strongly as that! A traditional, brownfield organisation characterised by marked dislocation between management and the managed can be extremely difficult culturally. The last thing many employees want or need is to be singled out by management, for fear of being labelled 'a blue-eyed boy', an 'Uncle Tom' or, worst of all a 'creep'. The culture of some workplaces can be very hostile and there is nothing to be gained by making the lives of your best employees a misery.

So, except for those exceptional situations where you feel confident that the recipient of your praise will escape such venom, we suggest that all individual recognition is done quickly, confidentially and privately. In any event, doing it this way makes it easier to convey sincerity and helps the employee to feel 'special'.

♦ Never, ever, confuse recognition with financial reward. If a significant monetary value is associated with any form of recognition, it immediately devalues it in the eyes of the workforce. Your objective is to harness pride, self-esteem and a feeling of achievement in individuals, whilst hopefully stimulating others to do likewise. Money tends to create envy and unrequited expectation. The envy will come from those who do not receive the token. The unrequited expectation will come when the perceived value of the token fails to match the aspirations of the recipient. Throwing money at recognition, or indeed anything else in management is a cop-out of the worst form. It is unnecessary and counterproductive.

The 'Thank You' Card

A neat aid to recognition, first seen at Milliken Carpets, is the 'Thank You' card. This is a purpose-designed greetings card that has a bold 'Thank You' on the front and inside has space to say whom it's to, who it's from and why it's been sent.

Initially, these should be used by management to help introduce the concept of recognition into the organisation. Eventually, this can be extended to all employees to encourage peer appreciation. There is a certain novelty value here as one often sees a flurry of activity followed quite shortly by less frequent use. This is natural. Having them clearly available helps enormously in reminding the organisation that good teamwork necessitates the occasional acknowledgement.

Suggestion Schemes

We would prefer it if most readers would skip this section and move on to the next item. Suggestion schemes have been seen as the panacea for disaffected employees for at least the last 50 years. In principle, the logic and the idea appear sound. In practice, they rarely work. In fact, suggestion schemes contribute more to creating *poor* morale than they do in improving it.

They appear to have many flaws, the two most significant being:

♦ **Bureaucracy:** The most common scheme 20 years ago was the Suggestion Box. Here an employee took an entry form and filled in the triplicate carbon copy before depositing the top two copies in the appropriate boxes scattered around the workplace. Occasionally, they would have to get a signature from a supervisor before entry. At the end of the next quarter (not exactly the most dynamic of schemes), the Box would be emptied by the poor sap given the job of administering the scheme. Having discarded the fag ends, sweet papers and associated detritus which also found its way into the receptacle, s/he would collect together all the submissions. These would then be evaluated and those worthy of further consideration sent to the appropriate department. Several weeks later, after numerous reminders, the reviewing department would come back with a 'yes', 'no' or 'needs further investigation'. As the suggestion scheme was scarcely a major priority, the proportion in the last category was often by far the largest!

Those suggestions eventually finding favour would be earmarked for introduction. After a suitable time to test both the feasibility and the benefits of the proposal, a report would be sent to the Suggestions Committee, which met quarterly. As a consequence, it could take many months before the originator knew whether his idea was a) successful and b) worthy of a financial reward. The net result of all this bureaucracy would be that ultimately *everybody* would be totally disenchanted. From the disillusioned originator, through the disinterested intermediaries, right through to the distracted committee, the whole circus would carry on for one reason and one reason only: senior management thought it was a jolly good idea!

♦ **Demotivation:** Imagine the day. You have found out at last that the suggestion you raised some nine months ago, and had assumed to be dead, is now eligible for a cash prize. In fact, you have picked up the third prize worth £500. Are you elated, are you motivated? Well, not quite. You were pleased initially, but then you saw the first two ideas and, to be honest, they weren't a patch on yours. In your mind, you haven't won £500, you've been robbed of the £1,000 first prize. You're not motivated at all. You've lost five hundred quid!

You're not motivated. And neither are the others whose suggestions were not deemed good enough. Come to think of it, neither are the bulk of employees who didn't bother to contribute because no-one listens anyway. *"Why do I have to communicate with a box when I want to make a suggestion?"* was one telling and somewhat insightful comment we have heard.

The end result of this annual jamboree is, perhaps, one or two people feeling pretty pleased with themselves and the rest totally hacked off. Not the ideal recipe for attitude development!

Our advice is pretty unequivocal: leave the concept alone. You've enough to do elsewhere and plenty of more productive opportunities to develop ideas generation without spending your time on such a high-risk and high-maintenance endeavour.

However, many of you apparently find the concept irresistible. If you do, and if we can't persuade you to look elsewhere, this next is probably as good a scheme as any.

Every Little Counts

Employees are asked to think of ideas to improve their own area. You are not, within this process, looking for *their* ideas on how others can improve. You are looking for self-development or team-development of some part of the process the employee is intimately involved in.

They fill in an Every Little Counts (ELC) form, printed in duplicate. The essence of the document is simplicity – a minimum of reportage and a maximum of detail (of the idea).

This is then submitted to their immediate manager. S/he immediately judges whether the idea has been submitted in good faith and is a positive suggestion, as opposed to a negative criticism. Note the perceived *benefit* is of no consequence at this stage but the perceived *intention* is.

If s/he deems it to be a constructive offering, s/he then hands over a token of appreciation, for example a £1 Argos or Marks & Spencer voucher. The £1 value of the token is incidental; it is just a means of expressing gratitude. Going above £1 could completely undermine the spirit of the scheme.

The idea is either:

♦ Given back to the initiator who is told to investigate it further or simply get on with it, or

♦ Given back to the initiator alongside support for further investigation or implementation, or

♦ Reasons are given as to why the idea is impractical.

This first response should be given within 48 hours.

There are lots of variations to support such a scheme. You could have a central, workplace-based committee charged with managing the scheme and maintaining its popularity. You could have a reward system, judged by peers, for the best ideas in a quarter or a year. Caution is needed here, for reasons explained before. You have to be absolutely certain that such embellishments meet the approval of the majority. We do not want pockets of envy or jealousy emerging.

Every Little Matters

A version of Every Little Counts, which we love, despite having no personal experience of it. It does, however, seem an ideal fit to a truly engaged workforce and we are assured by its originator that 'it really does work'. It does so, as follows:

♦ Employees or groups of employees are invited to submit local process improvements that they have self-generated and, more importantly, implemented. These are called ELMs, Every Little Matters.

♦ Each ELM is evaluated by the local line manager against a predetermined set of criteria. The majority will result in a visit by the manager to thank them personally and to present them with a simple certificate. This is usually conducted during a rest break and accompanied by a free sandwich or 'cookie'.

♦ Exceptional ELMs are diverted into the Team Recognition scheme (see later) for a higher level of recognition.

A simple process that nevertheless seems to get to the heart of what employee engagement is all about – employee ownership, enthusiasm and autonomous action.

Other Ideas

There are no limits to the opportunities for recognising individual performance. As long as it meets the stipulations made earlier, including acceptance by the majority, then the only constraint is your imagination. We have seen flowers sent to the homes of employees' partners, meals and scores of other local initiatives that significantly improved employee identification with the company. The key is to emphasise the sentiment, not the value.

Frequency of Recognition

People often ask how often should they recognise. After all, going around madly congratulating everybody in sight is not only counterproductive, it is often quite irritating. This, incidentally, frequently happens after the management conscience has been severely pricked by a Perception Analysis. The key determinant is the need to be seen to be genuine, something that over-use can erode.

There are, however, no fixed rules. As a rule of thumb with no scientific rationale whatsoever, we estimate that, on average, each employee in an engaged environment would do something worthy of recognition about eight times a year. So, if like us, you feel the need to discipline yourself and diarise your commitment, each month you should recognise approximately:

$$\frac{\text{No. of monthly}}{\text{recognitions}} = \frac{\text{The number of your}}{\text{subordinates}} \times \frac{2}{3}$$

If you manage a department of 12 people, this means that eight should be recognised in some form each month. These 'recognitions' will be spread across thank you cards, recognition tokens, letters or simple verbal acknowledgements. The latter will probably predominate, but set yourself little targets for the more structured approaches.

If you manage a department of 120 employees, then obviously 80 recognitions per month seems at first sight to be more demanding. But there will be others in the chain beneath you who are also obliged to do likewise. So determine an 'acceptable' target, split into the various modes at your disposal. And then work from there, adjusting through experience and observation. If it doesn't feel comfortable, then alter the frequency and mix. The means doesn't matter, only the end. When your audit and measurement scores demonstrate you've got it right, stick with it.

In summary, informal recognition is the acknowledgement of individual presence, role and contribution. As such it is a vital part of a good manager's toolkit. Remember to make sure it is done genuinely and is perceived as such. Celebrating what you want to see more of is a proven way of seeing your wishes fulfilled.

TEAM RECOGNITION

You will be relieved to hear that team Recognition is much less complicated than individual Recognition. All the same rules apply except that, for reasons still mysterious to the authors, public recognition for teams does not carry anything like the same level of risk as for individuals. Perhaps the security of being in a group overcomes the personal concerns of being 'exposed' individually.

The characteristics of good Team Recognition differ slightly from their individual equivalent. **Figure 12** shows the pre-requisites defined in one organisation we dealt with.

Figure 12: Team Recognition

Good Team Recognition demands:

◆ A robust, coherent structure.
◆ Consistency.
◆ Clearly defined guidelines or targets.
◆ A genuine reflection of team effort.
◆ A reflection of organisational values.
◆ Ongoing audit and measurement.

If you have followed the recommendations in the earlier chapter on Action Planning (**Chapter 6**), ultimately you will have an organisation characterised by lots of multi-functional teams. Some will be spontaneous, others planned. Some will be highly structured, some loose, temporary affiliations. Some will tackle big projects over long periods, others will be short-term, task focussed. However, what they all have in common is a need for recognition and it is vital you do it well.

As the guidelines say, it is important that you have a formal structure that operates consistently. We do not recommend that your recognition process distinguishes one group from another. We've had our fills of *Teams of the Month*. They only serve to downrate the efforts of the majority. However, it is important that you have a defined set of criteria that determines eligibility for recognition. Our advice is to broaden the scope as much as possible – the more, the merrier. But some companies prefer not to recognise teams for simply doing their jobs well. There are arguments both ways. You must decide and stick to that decision.

One of the key pre-requisites is that the team in question actually perceives itself as a team. If you want a multi-functional team focus as your principal *modus operandi* for problem-solving and continuous improvement, then teams should conform to minimum standards. Having ill-disciplined, loose affiliations may be a short-term expedient but could be problematic in the longer term. Again *celebrate what you want to see more of*.

Our recommended approach to Team Recognition is as follows:

♦ Form a small Recognition Committee chaired by the organisation principal (CEO, MD, owner-manager, proprietor or site manager). Keep the numbers low (2 to 4 people).

♦ Define the qualifying criteria for team recognition. We would recommend some or all of:

◊ Clear objectives and agreed goals.

◊ Clear evidence of achievements.

◊ Multi-functional involvement.

◊ The use of company prescribed problem-solving techniques, if appropriate.

◊ Team-working within the group.

◊ Indicators of behaviour 'above and beyond the call of duty'.

◊ Supportive of company value statements.

♦ Define the qualifying criteria for a team. Issues you might want to occasionally, but not always, support include:

◊ Evidence of formal interaction.

◊ Evidence of external facilitation or management sponsorship.

◊   Efforts to include relevant departments.

◊   Good communication across departments.

◊   Recognition of peripheral involvement.

♦ Once a quarter, ask for nominations from the management
group of teams that have exceeded the usual bounds of duty and
achieved an exceptional outcome. As the process matures, you
can call on peer nominations. Ensure that you get sufficient
suggestions. If you really want to create a team-based
organisation, this is a highly effective means of encouraging it.
As a guide, we suggest the following minima:

No. of Employees	No. of Groups Recognised Each Quarter
<50	2
<100	3
<150	4
<250	5

If you suffer from a shortage of nominations, then it is good
practice to go out and find them yourself. You rarely have to
do this more than twice! Your subordinates will be extremely
thick-skinned if they don't take the hint.

♦ Having received the nominations, the next stage is to approve
them. This is not a difficult process as we are not going to rate,
compare or assess them in any manner. Our only objectives are,
first, to ensure validity and, second, to familiarise ourselves with
the width and depth of efforts within the organisation to
improve – bottom-up.

♦ Recognition itself should be a formal, but low key, process. We
strongly recommend:

◊   That all groups are brought together. Lunchtime over
sandwiches is ideal if funds permit.

◊   The organisation principal thanks everybody for coming and
briefly summarises each submission.

◊   Each group comes up in turn to receive a simple certificate
acknowledging performance. A photograph is taken.

◊ Copies of the photographs are posted later on a special board. You will find this eventually to be one of the most visited noticeboards in the establishment.

◊ Use the company communications media, as discussed in **Chapter 7**, to broadcast these achievements.

And that is all we would do on Team Recognition. No big prizes. No cash payments based on savings. No flash company parties. No fuss. Just routinely, formally, and enthusiastically praising good practice and thereby encouraging more of it.

SUMMARY

There are probably many other aspects of recognition systems that we haven't covered in this brief review. The foregoing is designed to construct a solid foundation with a minimum of effort and a maximum chance of success. In time, you will encounter good practices elsewhere. Once you have this foundation in place, try them. Take such suggestions and adopt them without modification, lock, stock and barrel. But do not re-invent wheels. There is no need to replicate the mistakes of others. And never lose sight that you are dealing here with motivation, pure and simple. Neglect that and you'll lose the plot completely.

This is a very important chapter in the book. In some respects, it is second only to the next one on Management Style. Ironically, Recognition is one of the most neglected areas in most companies, big and small, in the UK today. And therein, as we said earlier, lies a huge opportunity. Be serious about recognition.

And just because you work in a small organisation doesn't excuse you. As Colin Potter demonstrates in **Chapter 17**, recognition is a key to building co-operation and understanding – in any size of organisation, Work on it!

9
QUICK WINS III: MANAGEMENT STYLE

This is the most important chapter in the book. Employee engagement depends entirely on constructing a suitably supportive *culture*. In turn, creating this culture is largely dependent on the way management conducts itself, consciously and unconsciously. Improving management behaviour is the single most powerful element in developing employee motivation, morale and attitude.

The study of management alone, however, could fill many libraries. Every aspect of management science, from strategic to operational management and back again, has been covered copiously in the past and will be done again many times in the future. It is not our intention to summarise or to generate new theories. Here, we will focus exclusively on those areas that appear through experience to support and accelerate employee engagement. Whilst we will not be extensively searching for academic reinforcement, we do recommend that you read up this vital topic. The more you know, the better you'll be!

In **Figure 13**, we examine what a leading academic, Schein, considers to be the major factors influencing an organisation's culture. This really is a fascinating area. When you ask management teams to decide what they believe are the underlying drivers determining the unique culture of their company, you can end up going down some really fanciful avenues. On one exercise with a company from Liverpool, for example, votes were cast for two cathedrals, two football teams, Scouse comics (Ken Dodd and Jimmy Tarbuck *inter alia*), the Beatles, Gerry and the Pacemakers, the Mersey and the stereotypical 'Scouseness' portrayed so distortedly by the media! All very interesting, but sadly misplaced. When you examine Schein below, there is none of this peripheral causality. Stripping it down to the bare bones, we can see that the only common denominator to ALL the key influences is the behaviour of organisational 'Leaders'.

Figure 13: How Culture is Determined in an Organisation

1. What Leaders pay attention to, measure and control on a regular basis.
2. How Leaders react to critical incidents and organisational crises.
3. Observed criteria by which Leaders allocate scarce resources.
4. Deliberate role modelling, teaching and coaching by leaders.
5. Observed criteria by which Leaders allocate rewards and status.
6. Observed criteria by which Leaders recruit, select, promote etc.

Source: Schein, E. (1992). *Organizational Culture & Leadership*, San Francisco, CA: Jossey-Bass.

Who are these organisational 'Leaders'? We would speculate that they could be any of:

♦ Intrusive shareholders and non-executives.

♦ Elected officials on public bodies.

♦ Representatives.

♦ Management.

♦ Influential technical staff.

For the vast majority of organisations however, leadership will be mostly delivered by 'management'. Accordingly, if you really want to develop employee engagement, you will have to focus on the conscious and unconscious behaviour of your management team. All levels of management will exert an influence. In terms of the total organisation, the higher you are, the bigger your leverage will be an organisational culture. However, at a team, department or function level, the influence exerted by a local supervisor can be highly significant. It all depends on the visibility, access and intrusion of more senior players. To summarise, the greatest influencing factor by a country mile in any organisation is the behaviour of its management. As we noted earlier, a dysfunctional culture could be said to stem from a dysfunctional management team. Perhaps we in management get the culture we deserve.

Case Study 18

Andrew was the young Manufacturing Director of a fairly sizeable operation dealing in bulky consumer goods. His outlook was very much that of a modern manager and his views on participation, empowerment and local democracy shared by his immediate assistant, Garry. The processes in the organisation were highly complex, with many customer streams, many product types and multiplicity of manufacturing methods. The 'art' of maintaining continuity was believed to rest at the start of the production chain and, hence, most of Andrew and Garry's time was spent with sales liaison, production planning and material control. Along with a constant overview of throughputs and efficiencies in the supporting machine shops, this virtually occupied all of their personal resources. Fortunately, in charge of final assembly was Frank, a long-serving, highly-knowledgeable and streetwise Production Manager. Unsurprisingly, Andrew and Garry were content, by and large, to leave this difficult and fractious area to the loyal and highly capable Frank.

Try as they might, they could not get the operation to work effectively. Frank was being continually let down by support from all areas, internally and externally. Even his patience and temperament was being sorely tested. Andrew and Garry tried even harder to knock these functions into line.

Eventually, they resorted to a Perception Barrier Analysis to identify some of the cultural barriers preventing a smoother manufacturing flow. The outcome was quite shocking, a veritable litany of 'siloism', interdepartmental bickering, blame culture, initiative fatigue and a total distrust of management. And the common denominator at the root of all this dysfunction was ... Frank, their loyal and trusted lieutenant.

In the presence of Andrew and Garry, Frank was dependable, reasonable, honest and conscientious. To his subordinates and peers, Frank was a monster, bad tempered and totally unhelpful. He ran his operation with a series of unofficial cliques and clans supporting his ultra-autocratic iron rule. He was feared as both a bully and a manipulator. Little of this reached the ears of Andrew and Garry. They knew he had arguments with other functions, for example, but that was 'because they're always letting him down'. The fact that he had probably created most of the problems had escaped them.

This was not the only time we have encountered more junior management exerting a bigger influence than their more senior equivalents. It happens very frequently in multi-site, multi-shift and geographically-dispersed operations. It can also occur in small companies as well, where the key principals are remote from the operational minutiae. The message from Schein is clear. If we really want to change direction, we have to understand cogently the influential power of every manager and supervisor in the system.

The model of Blake and Mouton, the aptly-named 'Management Grid', may help us here (**Figure 14**). Looking at the qualities of managers who run businesses, they attempt to relate *concern for people* with *concern for the process*. Going back to our insurance man, Len, in the previous chapter, we can see that he was firmly in the bottom right corner (9.1). His autocratic, bullying stance reflected not just his egotism but a genuine belief that only he knew best. Ultimately, and time alone will tell, his workforce will 'play' the necessary obedient game in his presence but elsewhere will be spending much more time subverting it. Denied the opportunity to use their talent, imagination and creativity to work the system, they will be equally ingenious in working against it.

Figure 14: The Blake / Mouton Management Grid

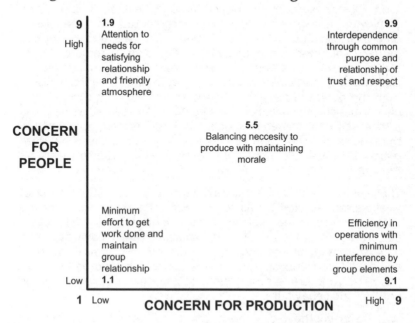

In many respects, the top left-hand manager (1.9) is just as bad. These 'anything for a quiet life' advocates often come to the fore when initiatives such as employee engagement are introduced. To him or her, acceptance by subordinates is much more important than the achievement of production goals. Their need to be liked often prevents them exerting the necessary pressure on the one element that dictates their livelihoods – company performance. These people are dangerous.

Effective employee engagement depends on your management team being well into the upper right quadrant, away from the process and people 'geeks'. Unfortunately, it is often extremely difficult to self-analyse yourself here. We have encountered many autocrats who believe they have exemplary people skills because their subordinates keep telling them so! When we use the famous Mandy Rice-Davies riposte, *"Well they would, wouldn't they?"*, the significance often passes them by. We will visit a technique for self-knowledge later in the chapter but, first, a case study concerning one of the authors to illustrate the point.

Case Study 19

John Oliver's success in turning around Leyland Trucks using employee engagement is well documented in *The Team Enterprise Solution* (Oak Tree Press). The idea was to replace former confrontational relationships caused by a remote, rather than autocratic, management style with one characterised by involvement, participation and empowerment. John recognised, from the outset, that he had to set an example but thought that his normal consensual style would suffice. All seemed to be going rather well until someone suggested a subordinate appraisal. As the man at the top, John volunteered to go first. Given his close relationship with his immediate peers, he had little to fear – he thought.

The results were far from complimentary with a whole array of weaknesses paraded for all to see. But, at the very head of the criticisms was a general view that John was ... well, er ... autocratic. To say that John was shocked would have been the understatement of the century. He did not see himself as such and asked for clarification (in a very consensual and participative manner!). One brave soul volunteered to give an example of his problematic behaviour ...

"Whenever you have a problem, and need a meeting, you always ensure that the right people come along to discuss it. No-one ever feels left out. When they get to the meeting, you always take great pains to ensure that the terms of reference and objectives of the session are clearly defined at the outset. No-one ever feels confused about why they're there. And then you make sure that everybody has a chance to speak. If anybody's quiet, you draw them in by asking their opinion ..."

"Hang on", said John. "This seems right to me, this sounds highly democratic".

"So far, so good", came the reply, "but then you reach your threshold of boredom and your nervous tick comes out."

At this point, everybody falls about laughing, except for John who looks increasingly bemused.

"You reach a point in the meeting where you've obviously had enough. Automatically, your right hand goes up and then down in a guillotine motion and you say, 'Right', signalling the end of the debate. And then you come out with the conclusion that everybody knew you walked in with at the start of the meeting. This isn't democracy, this is closet autocracy!"

Interestingly, although John accepted the account as fact (he could hardly do otherwise with so many witnesses present!), he claimed he was totally unaware of the habit. This wasn't a conscious manoeuvre to get his own way. However, his team remained unconvinced. John did it so often and so consistently that it had, in their minds, to be a deliberate element in his management style.

This concept of unconscious incompetence, or even occasionally unconscious competence, is a vital one to all in management. Over the many years of examining barriers to employee engagement, the failure of senior staff to recognise the severity of the damage that these unknowing signals have on workplace morale seems to be everywhere. And perhaps that's not surprising. By its very definition, it's not obvious and, without a tool to spot it, remaining in the dark seems the most obvious outcome.

There are any number of ways of attempting to extract these dark secrets. Facilitated away-day events where peer and subordinate perceptions are painfully extracted and debated can be very effective. 360-degree feedback is another feasible tool, providing you can guarantee unbiased, honest and fearless contributions from the participants. You could always get yourself 'psyched'. A psychological profile may reveal your tendencies, if not your actual behaviour.

However, we prefer a very simple, cheap and straightforward technique called the Management Style Questionnaire (MSQ). The great beauty of the MSQ is that it can be done so quickly that you can repeat the exercise a further once or twice a year. By doing it often, you can gauge trends in your behaviour until your weaknesses settle down or, preferably, disappear.

The MSQ consists of about 20 questions on management behaviour. These are not fixed in stone; you can add or delete for depth or width. **Figure 15** shows an example that can be readily adapted to any organisation, big or small. You can use it as follows:

- ◆ Twice a year, a suitable questionnaire is sent to each of your direct reports. (Note: You really need a minimum of six to eight people to ensure objectivity. You may therefore wish to extend the circulation to others who perhaps don't work directly for you – dotted line contacts, for example. Alternatively, you may wish to consider including key peer contacts). All recipients are told that it is confidential, unattributed and the outcome will be shared with them. The objective is stated clearly as an evaluation of the boss's performance in the eyes of his/her subordinates.

- ◆ Each recipient completes the report, marking satisfaction on a suitable scale. No other markings or comments are allowed to protect confidentiality.

- ◆ The reports are collected by an independent third party, whose sole task is to collate the responses and to work out a mean and a range for each question.

- ◆ The consolidated report is returned to the subject under review. They should study it first alongside any previous reports to look for improvements, deteriorations or new findings. Copies are then sent to the participants.

Figure 15: Management & Leadership Style Questionnaire

My Manager (Name):	LOW								HIGH	
	1	2	3	4	5	6	7	8	9	10
1 Encourages me to go 'the extra mile' and leads by example.										
2 Motivates me to achieve the team's and my own objectives.										
3 Involves me in improvement activities (for example, Kaizen, Six Sigma, or other general CI activity).										
4 Encourages me to come up with ideas for improvement.										
5 Welcomes and responds to my ideas.										
6 Helps to ensure that the processes and procedures we use achieve results of the required quality.										
7 Ensures that we have regular team meetings.										
8 Encourages effective team-working.										
9 Organises regular 'face to face' communication with our team on company or department / team issues.										
10 Communicates effectively on day-to-day issues that arise.										
11 Makes sure that I have a PDP at least once a year.										

My Manager (Name):	LOW 1	2	3	4	5	6	7	8	9	HIGH 10
12 Ensures that, if we agree training needs in my PDP, I do get the training.										
13 Recognises and celebrates success and good work.										
14 Shows me respect and consideration.										
15 Gives me credit for good work.										
16 Gives me support on work where I need it.										
17 Delegates to me effectively on jobs where I am confident and experienced.										
18 Helps create an enjoyable working environment.										
19 Encourages me to maintain a safe and tidy working environment.										
20 Involves me in decision-making, where appropriate.										
21 Encourages good working relationships with other functions.										

Please mark your answers by placing an 'X' in the appropriate scoring box for each question.

What you do next is really down to you. You could resolve merely to do better and wait for the next survey to see whether you've made a difference. Alternatively, you could call everybody together and invite them to comment. However, this may be difficult if your unconscious behaviour really has a serious consequence on the organisation. A trusted intermediary may be better suited to interviewing participants on your specific area of weakness and exploring further.

Progressively, all management, right down to front line supervisory level, should be encouraged to do likewise. Disclosure of results upwards is really a matter for debate. Ideally, we see this as a self-development review, confidential to the subject and their direct reports. Sharing the information amongst facilitated peer groups could also be beneficial. We have always been nervous about unilaterally allowing senior management access to subordinate ratings. No matter how many times you tell people that you cannot compare the absolute ratings of one individual with another, they choose to ignore it. A manager with an average rating of 94% over the 20 questions may not be a superior people manager to one with, say, 82%. It may simply reflect the generosity of ratings by his or her group. Staff areas, for example Human Resources and Sales, tend to mark higher than Engineering or Production. Whilst, possibly, there may be a certain validity in some comparisons, it really is too difficult to call. You should leave it as a self-development tool and, only by exception, when other evidence indicates a colleague could have a serious and ongoing problem, should senior management demand access.

Of far more importance is the way managers react to the survey. We have covered this area extensively in **Chapter 4** and the same rules apply. Considered reflection with an acute awareness of your likely impact on your subordinates when you respond is always a good idea. We strongly commend the Management Style Questionnaire to you. Both authors have benefited enormously from it over the years, although that may be because both had a lot to improve!

STYLES OF MANAGEMENT

For years, we have debated the merits of various management styles. Academically, we could point favourably to interpretations based on quadrant 9.9 in Blake and Mouton's Management Grid, shown earlier in **Figure 14**. However, on a more pragmatic level, such is the diversity of management styles across apparently successful practitioners that it seems impossible to be totally prescriptive about what's right and what's wrong.

In the past, we have ducked the issue and come up with a dynamic model:

> The best management style is ... one that is continually assessed and challenged by one's subordinates and which is constantly modified according to circumstances and perceptions.

In other words, we simply adjust our behaviour to suit the situation, taking into account the reactions of the people who work for us. In the end, however, we are responsible for our own behaviour and the only real test is the subsequent performance of the business. We senior decision-makers are all realistic enough to know that, at the top, the subject of fairness is largely academic. If the business does well, we succeed. If it fails, regardless of causality, effort and attitude, we fall. The best we can do is to understand the parameters and, like a chameleon, adjust to suit the circumstances.

The rigid demarcation between autocracy and consensus is largely academic. To manage a business in these complex times demands that we alternate between the two according to the situation. **Figure 16** explains. The horizontal line is used to denote *urgency*. Very urgent situations lie to the left, more leisurely situations to the right. The left hand vertical indicates the level of *autocracy*, whilst the right refers to consensus.

We have to accept that, in certain situations, an autocratic response may be essential. If a manager sees flames, then it is hardly sensible to initiate a debate on the wisdom or otherwise of vacating the premises! At the other extreme, a decision on whether to have chicken or fish for lunch would seem to be highly suitable for consensus.

Figure 16: The Preferred Range of Management Styles

In between the two extremes come a range of behaviours. Next down from autocracy is *persuasion*, where we attempt to convince people that the management line is right. Beyond that, we attempt to *consult* with our subordinates, hearing what they have to say before we decide. We may go further and *jointly decide*, but giving a greater weight to management than the workforce, à la the old union 'block vote'.

The important thing here to recognise is that the effective manager will have the whole range of these styles at their disposal. S/he can use them according to circumstances and situations. Whilst this may seem sensible and reasonable, unfortunately many managers choose to major on one particular area all the time. Ironically, it would seem that the higher the position the manager holds, the greater propensity there is to become unidirectional. We might speculate that this is something to do with management egos (autocracy) or insecurities (excessive emphasis on consensus). However, we'll leave that to the psychologists to explain. Here, we will deal with the *consequences*.

Autocratic, Participative & Laissez Faire Styles

For clarity, we think of management styles as being on a continuum:

Autocratic ←→ Participative ←→ Laissez Faire

A 'participative' style is one that promotes maximum employee engagement. On the other hand, a 'laissez faire' style is usually associated with a weak or lazy manager who avoids difficult decisions and relies on the organisation making them for him, if at all.

Imagine you are a competent manager faced with the opportunity of transforming a failing organisation. Your immediate challenge is to improve its relative competitive performance from 'poor' to 'average'. Which management style do you adopt as your dominant characteristic in the early days? Autocratic? Participative? Laissez faire?

It is far too easy to say that the dominant characteristic of any manager in any situation automatically should be participative. Look at **Figure 17**, which examines the speed of impact.

Figure 17: The Impact of Management Style

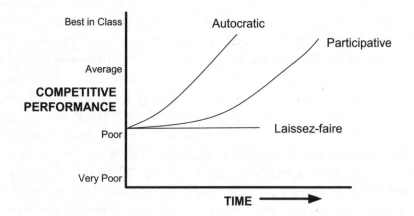

Very frequently, we can see that, in this situation, adopting a predominantly autocratic style is actually much faster at getting immediate results than a participative approach. In failing situations where employees have a low self-esteem, you may encounter cynicism, mistrust of management and outright hostility. Persuading people of your sincerity, honesty and, most importantly, your capability, will take time. You will get there, but perhaps you would have arrived at your objective quicker if you had merely adopted a *"We're in trouble, we have to do something, this is what we're going to do,*

follow me or else" campaign. We're assuming here, of course, that you actually know the answers at the start of your journey!

However, let us cast our sights a great deal higher. Our target is not the mediocrity of being 'average', we want to be the 'best'! How do the different styles fare then? Well, as **Figure 18**, demonstrates, laissez faire continues to do nothing. Autocracy continues to improve a little, but then peters out as the workforce reacts to their restricted role. Participation, however, has the best capability of moving onwards and upwards, by harnessing effectively the talents, goodwill and enthusiasm of a greater proportion of other managers and their subordinates.

Figure 18: The Impact of Management Style 2

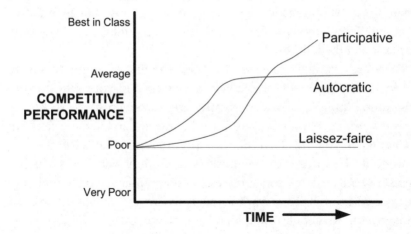

The common denominator in nearly all Best Value operations is that, somehow, they manage to extract more than dutiful conscientiousness out of their employees. They are able to tap into the initiative, imagination and creativity of a high proportion of their workforce. Autocracy signally fails to do this in most situations, unless the leader is exceptionally charismatic. Sadly, few of us fit into this category!

In summary, a participative style gives you the best chance of success. However, there are risks, there are no guarantees. You have to constantly work at it and avoid the ever present trap of falling into laissez faire. Hopefully the Route Map, along with constant measurement and audit, will keep you on the right track.

Values-driven Management

One of the great challenges associated with any culture change programme is knowing *how* to manage. What seems to be the utmost commonsense in the classroom, or in the text book, often seems far from clear at the sharp end. Different managers understandably place different interpretations on issues, depending on personality, understanding and commitment. The workforce can become quite perplexed at inconsistent application across functions and departments.

This is an ever-present danger in every organisation undergoing culture change. Many simply fall by the wayside, as disputes turn to rancour, positive enthusiasm into negative cynicism. As we said earlier, the most optimistic view on the success of any change initiative is about 20%. Inconsistent application accounts for a goodly proportion of the failures.

There are two ways to lessen the risk. The first is simply to ensure that senior management takes a very strong hold of your introductory programme and, equally importantly, are perceived to do so by the general working population. By introducing the architecture laid out in **Chapter 6**, you will have more than a fighting chance of working through it. However, in complex organisations, and this doesn't necessarily mean *large* concerns, even senior management vigilance may not be enough. They can't be everywhere and must rely on local management to get it right. Here a concept called 'Values-driven Management' could help.

Like many Human Resources-based initiatives in recent years, there has been a tendency to overcomplicate this essentially simple idea. Whilst the approach detailed below will inevitably incur the opprobrium of those expensive consultants who make their living helping you install these elaborate edifices, it is important to retain a sense of balance. Like lots of these apparently good ideas, the real value comes from the spirit, enthusiasm and honesty with which they are introduced. There is little point in installing hugely complicated structures if they lack this emotional underpinning. After all, we are dealing in motivation, not brain surgery.

Both authors have been strongly influenced and impressed by the work of a further education establishment, Runshaw College, in this area. Using 'Values-driven Behaviour' (their terminology), Runshaw became the 'nation's No. 1' for nine years in a row and is still counting. In 2003, it was awarded the European Excellence Award for the Public Sector (EFQM), as well as the Special Award for Leadership and Constancy of Purpose. Their story was written up in *The Runshaw Way: Values-driven Behaviour* and circulated to educational establishments throughout the UK. **Chapter 1** described their achievements in more detail.

The following draws heavily on the Runshaw approach.

Why Values?

Work means different things to different people. However, what we increasingly recognise in these modern, competitive times is that social demands of the workplace are infinitely greater than even 20 years ago. If we as management fail to recognise and meet these emerging needs, then, at best, our workforce will be dissatisfied. At worst, they may simply walk away and find jobs elsewhere that do meet them. If they can't do that and subsequently feel 'trapped', the consequent alienation could be quite damaging all round. The traditional 'autocratic' manager responds to this either by throwing money at the problem or by seeking greater and even greater levels of control. Throughout the 70s and 80s, the UK automotive industry tackled its emerging 'industrial relations' problems by investing heavily in systemised industrial engineering, finance and personnel practices. The decline of so many famous marques and names speaks volumes for its lack of impact, another example of 'command and control' hitting the wrong target.

We do not wish to burden the reader with too many academic references in this text but the work of Dr. Frederick Herzberg is worthy of introduction here. Herzberg attempted to identify 'events' that resulted in *high morale* in the world of work as well as others that created a *grievance*. The former became known as his 'motivators'. Amongst the top motivating factors were in *descending* order:

- Sense of Achievement (1).
- Recognition of Ability (2).

- ◆ Interesting Work (3).
- ◆ Responsibility (4).
- ◆ Promotion (5).

Interestingly, earnings figured only at the margin.

Among the 'hygiene' factors that created a sense of grievance, he noted, in *ascending* order:

- ◆ Earnings (5).
- ◆ Boss's attitude (4).
- ◆ Work conditions (3).
- ◆ Boss's technical skills (2).
- ◆ Policies, administration and communication (1).

Perhaps surprisingly, the key 'hygiene' factor Herzberg found at the head of this list was 'policies, administration and communication'. These are key frustrators for employees, as they often create a sense of inequity and confusion. If through our values-driven culture, we can construct a sense of common ownership of these important instruments of management and control, then perhaps, at the same time, we can reduce their demotivational aspects as well.

More contentious is the finding on 'earnings'. Contrary to popular wisdom, Herzberg didn't actually say that money was *never* motivational. He simply concluded that, whilst a lack of money was extremely *demotivational*, its power as a motivator was limited to both its symbolic measurement of achievement and progress and as a yardstick of recognition of our abilities. **Figure 19** is our attempt to describe this, although undoubtedly many will still dispute this perennial point of argument.

Where employees are paid well below a level they perceive to be fair, the 'Felt-Fair' vertical line, money will be an acutely demotivational factor. Once this level is passed, then other issues come further into consideration, and the rate of change slows or even stops. In extreme cases, there is often negative correlation between high pay and morale (the dotted line). This is not as absurdly illogical as it may seem. Very frequently, because organisations remunerate very well, management feels able to pay far less attention to the other social needs of their employees. If problems arise, the management response is to give the workforce more money. Thus, we find that the end product is a dissatisfied workforce, totally 'cocooned' from the realities of working life elsewhere. And all management seem to come up with is, *"This lot don't know they're born!"*. We will revisit this point under Employee Systems (**Chapter 13**).

Figure 19: Remuneration & Motivation

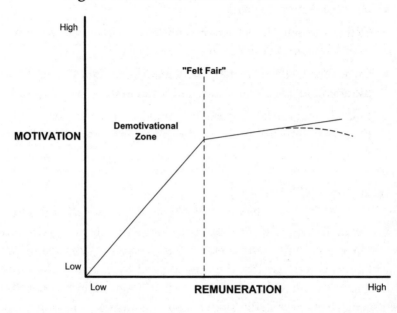

The objective of a values-driven culture, therefore, is to ensure that your organisation clearly maximises the benefit of Herzberg's motivating factors. By clearly extracting an agreed position on what the company stands for, we hope to negate two key dissatisfiers – a lack of ownership and a lack of clarity.

Companies often tackle this by Mission Statements and Vision Statements. Experience demonstrates that these rarely work in isolation, as they are too distant, too remote from the average employee. Meaningless exhortations adorning the office or factory walls, at best, will be ignored; at worst, seen as objects of cynicism and rejection. Similarly, avoid like the plague those frightful 'motivational' pictures which litter so many organisations nowadays. Rubbish like *"there's no 'i' in team"* alongside a picture of rowing eight may ring some bells in the advertising studio but does little for workplace attitudes. Over years of being exposed to these admittedly imaginative little offerings, neither author has ever encountered any hint of stimulation, aside from the bright spark who had the idea of buying them. In areas where morale is less than ideal, they can often even become negative cannon fodder for the disaffected.

There are four distinct steps in developing a values-driven culture:

- ◆ Establish your core values.

- ◆ Define and agree those personal qualities that individuals and managers need to display to achieve these core values.

- ◆ Create one UNITED management team behind these values and the attendant beliefs, attitudes and behaviour.

- ◆ Embed these values progressively into every element of working life to ensure this becomes a living philosophy not a 'wish list on the wall'.

Establish your Core Values

You have already had advance warning of this in Step 5 of the Route Map – 'Establish the Values' – but now is the time to crystallise those initial thoughts into more concrete objectives. Once again, it is important to emphasise that there is no need to re-invent any wheels here. One of the more frustrating aspects of working in this field is to see organisations repeatedly spend huge amounts of time and money on brainstorming, consultation events, steering committees and benchmarking groups to come up with – exactly the same as everybody else. Working with company syndicate groups at all levels has demonstrated to us that you can get 90% of the way there within a couple of hours. Why organisations want to spend days on the subject is beyond our understanding.

The other aspect of this 'predictability' is the 'motherhood and apple-pie' content of the final product. It may look clichéd, it may also look rather cheesy. To some, it will be a statement of the 'fairly bleeding obvious'. It will also look suspiciously similar to the Mission Statements / Vision Statements that we unceremoniously rubbished earlier. That is not surprising, we are effectively pursuing the same objective. The difference here is that we want to use this as a starting point, not merely an end in itself.

It may be of interest to look at Runshaw's core values. The world of education may differ markedly from the majority of our readership but it does provide a useful counterpoint.

Figure 20: The Core Values of a Further Education College

1. Teaching and Learning is our first priority.

2. Valuing the Individual
Our student centredness, our prioritisation of the learner coming first, our recognition that every individual has unique needs, that it is our task to fulfil their maximum potential and our fundamental belief in treating people with respect and dignity.

3. Opportunities For All
The college serves to be comprehensive, with open access to people of all abilities and all ages post-16, for lifelong learning.

4. Striving for Excellence
Our culture of high expectations, rigour, continuous improvement and constant search for best practice as a learning organisation.

5. Working Together and with Others
Our 'team culture' and our wish to collaborate in partnership with those outside the college.

6. Putting Ethos into Action
Our talk about values is empty rhetoric unless we implement the systems and processes which make these values reality. These processes empower staff by letting them know exactly what is expected of them and how they go about implementing these values. It follows that if we believe this and if we believe in our processes, then non-compliance is not an option because it would undermine our values and the efforts of our colleagues.

(Source: Runshaw College)

At first sight, you may think that this is all very interesting but hardly relevant to your situation. However, it could be more useful than it first appears.

Let us assume, for argument, that your company is small to medium-sized, private sector and operating in a highly competitive, low margin business. Your ultimate ambition is to grow and expand.

Value 1

Your prime core value is to make money. By making sufficient money, you can grow the business, pay a decent wage, reward the shareholders and reinforce job security. At this stage, there is no need to quote numbers, this is not a business planning tool. We have encountered examples where this has been done – for example:

> *"Our first priority is to make a 6% annual return on sales, a 20%+ return on our capital and a positive cash flow over each working three year period."*

However, we do not think the numbers add any great benefit and the absence of an underlying reason behind the value could be distracting. Accordingly, perhaps your first value should read:

Value 1: Profitable Trading

Our top priority is to generate sufficient profit and cash in the business to enable us to grow, to fulfil the ambitions of both shareholders and employees and to maximise the prospects of long term job security.

Value 2

The volatility of the market in which you operate could be an issue. Many newish companies manage to do reasonably well in a buoyant market but suffer, or even fail, in a recession. Planning for a downturn is often done too late, with businesses overexposed at the bank and saddled with a fixed cost-structure suitable only for better times. A second value could read:

Value 2: Surviving Recession

Our ambition is to survive in bad times, as well as good. We must always be ready for unexpected and severe downturns in our market to ensure the viability of the operation.

Value 3

The college majored initially on the learner, their *customer*. In your operation, you must place similar emphasis on your key external customers to ensure that the market progressively takes more and more of your product. Value 3 could read:

Value 3: Customer Delight

We intend to become our customers' first choice as a supplier. We will achieve this by constantly developing our products and service to attain a delighted, not just satisfied, customer.

Value 4

Given that the route to organisational success is now seen to be radical employee engagement, then our Values must reflect this clearly and significantly. We must make it clear to all in the company that we aspire to a cultural climate which maximises their contribution. This is a particularly important statement as it dictates much of the downstream direction. Perhaps:

Value 4: Valuing the Individual

We believe that all of our colleagues possess a raft of talents and expertise of which only a proportion is accessed in the world of work. It is our ambition to create a platform that maximises the opportunities for employees to use these talents, within a stimulating and satisfying general ambience, in pursuit of the key goals of the company.

Value 5

Examination of most successful companies reveals that, invariably, they have an intense focus on best practice. Usually, a strong cultural foundation supports an intensive and restless scrutiny of added value, waste and process integrity. Unless you declare from the outset that your ambition for radical employee engagement is to use it to drive best in class systems, then there is a danger that the 'social' attributes of the approach may dominate. This 'social engineering' may have some benefits, but it may never deliver the competitive edge required. Accordingly, state from the outset your ultimate goals. Perhaps:

Value 5: Striving for Excellence

Our culture of involvement and empowerment is designed to lead to a best in class operation where the imagination, creativity and talents of all of our colleagues will lead to an operation characterised by maximum added value, minimum waste, maximum process conformance and total process integrity.

Value 6

Most organisations have issues with cross-functional working. Likewise many also struggle with relationships with key external stakeholders – for example, suppliers, partners and others. This can result in much wasted time and effort, which will both frustrate and lead to a failure to achieve Value 5. Accordingly a straightforward transplant of the Runshaw equivalent may suffice:

Value 6: Working Together and with Others

Our strong internal team culture will be developed and improved alongside similar relationships externally with those who we 'partner' both commercially and administratively.

Value 7

All the foregoing will be simply fine words if we fail to make it happen both by convincing our colleagues of the validity of the approach and by embedding the philosophy into real actions. Runshaw's final value should be mandatory for all companies.

Value 7: Putting our Ethos into Action

Talk about values is empty rhetoric unless we implement the systems and processes that make these values reality. These processes empower staff by letting them know exactly what is expected from them and how they go about implementing these values. It follows that, if we believe this, and if we believe in our processes, then non-compliance is not an option because it would undermine our values and the efforts of colleagues.

Your first pass at generating a set of Core Values can be done, therefore, very quickly if you are so inclined. The cautious amongst you may baulk at this expedition but, as long as there is nothing fundamentally wrong with your first pass, you can always return to it later on. Of course, you should try to get it as right first-time as you can, but this is an iterative process. Your values will subtly change over the years as you mature in your thinking, your understanding and, indeed, in your business. We strongly recommend you resist the temptation of intellectual mastication here. Procrastination often evolves into bureaucratic overcomplexity. Instead, move quickly.

Once agreed by the board or senior management team, these values should be released to the organisation for discussion, debate and amendment. If employee engagement, under whatever title you choose to use, is new to the workforce, you may have also to explain your new philosophy. **Figure 21** may be useful here. It is Runshaw's attempt to highlight the differences between the new world of engagement and a traditional command and control approach.

Figure 21: Why Values First

Values-driven	Hierarchy-driven
◆ Employees work because they want to. Because it is worthwhile. They are motivated or even inspired.	◆ Employees work because they have to.
◆ Autonomous action to realise values.	◆ Directed activity to avoid negative aspects of non-compliance.
◆ Sense or purpose, identity and belonging.	◆ Resentment at being controlled.
◆ Creative striving.	◆ Creative non-compliance.

Define Personal & Leadership Qualities

This is always a very enjoyable part of the process. The objective here is to get the organisation to establish which qualities, behaviours and attitudes the average employee should exhibit in support of your new culture. Again, the temptation to spend aeons on this should be firmly resisted. You will find that nearly every organisation comes up with virtually the same result, so why waste too much time in simply confirming that conclusion?

We recommend that you set up two or three mixed groups of employees to demonstrate consultation and involvement. Each group meets for a short while, perhaps examining examples of other companies adopting personal behavioural characteristics and then deciding what they consider to be appropriate for your organisation.

Senior management receives the results and produces a consolidated response, which is then circulated to the workforce for commentary. After a suitable period, you publish your final conclusions. You may wish to wrap this up and define it as the desired qualities of your '(Company Name) Person' – for example, an IBM person or a BBC person. An example (based again on Runshaw) is shown in **Figure 22**.

Figure 22: Distinct Attributes of a 'Runshaw Person'

◆ Positive ◆ Caring ◆ Energetic ◆ Team Player ◆ Initiative	◆ Enthusiastic ◆ Friendly ◆ Optimistic ◆ Rigorous ◆ Respectful	◆ Committed to ongoing change ◆ Committed to Excellence

In addition, you may wish to get the groups to consider what additional qualities *managers* in your organisation are expected to exhibit. Note that every employee, irrespective of status, is expected to display the qualities shown in **Figure 22**. Managers are, however, expected to do more – as shown in **Figure 23**.

Figure 23: Additional Qualities of a 'Runshaw Manager'

◆ Create Team Spirit ◆ Good Communicator ◆ Good Listener ◆ Involving	◆ Coaching ◆ Informing ◆ Creating Frameworks ◆ Managing Change
Plus: ◆ Have the integrity and courage to challenge inaccurate or unfair perceptions of staff. ◆ To effectively manage poor performance, non-compliance, absence and negative or destructive behaviour.	

The final elements of **Figure 23** (the 'plus' items) are absolutely vital. When challenged on what sort of behaviour employees want to see from their management, the expression 'firm but fair' always emerges. There is nothing more exasperating or frustrating for the average conscientious employee to see their peers 'knocking the system' and getting away with it. Even in traditional, highly autocratic structures, we have seen major subordinate criticism of managers for failing to sort out the 'wasters, shirkers and bad eggs'. Very few managers get the balance right here, with the majority seemingly inadequate when it comes to tackling organisational miscreants. A clear statement of the need to do that raises expectations in the workforce and steers a firm course for all levels of management.

Create One United Team

It is easy to underestimate the extent to which values-driven behaviour can change an organisation. Even in traditional enterprises, carrying the baggage of getting it wrong for so long, the responsiveness and eagerness from the bulk of the workforce can be overwhelming. As elsewhere, the key determinant of success or failure is management's ability to manage this enthusiasm. Employees will be constantly scrutinising the words, deeds and behaviours of management to see whether there is a genuine commitment on the part of their superiors. Any hint of inconsistency, or lip service, will completely undermine the initiative. As with every other change programme, support is needed from one united management team on the issue.

You need to establish ground rules to set the standards for your colleagues. Runshaw's list included:

♦ **Collective ownership**: All members of the team agreeing that, once a decision is reached, everyone must promote it as their own.

♦ **Cabinet responsibility**.

♦ **Disciplined communication**: To eliminate the leaks and premature communication that can create destructive rumours and erroneous assumptions.

♦ **Team cohesiveness**: All members of the team to be mutually supportive, never undermining each other.

♦ **Behaviour at meetings**: Punctuality, being prepared, no moral high ground and no aggression.

♦ **Self-regulation**: Our own behaviour, setting 'soft' targets for management style and behaviour, as well as 'hard' performance targets.

From time to time, review this list with your colleagues and ask yourself whether they believe they are united and are perceived to be united. Better still, use the Management Style Questionnaire format highlighted earlier to get the direct reports of the Senior Management Team to express their opinions. You could be in for a surprise.

Embedding the Values

This is the part that really determines whether your values-driven culture is a real change or simply one more in a long list of failed initiatives. A good idea that merely faded away!

Embedding these values is not difficult. Areas where they can be used include:

♦ Recruitment of new employees.

♦ Recruitment of new managers.

♦ Appraisal systems.

♦ Management style questionnaires.

♦ Culture surveys.

♦ Communication.

♦ Recognition.

♦ Management focus.

None of the foregoing is difficult. Runshaw regularly refers to its Value culture not just internally, but also when it presents itself to the outside world. It constantly exposes the philosophy to external scrutiny *via* EFQM, OFSTED and IIP (European Foundation for Quality Management, Educational Inspection and Investors in People, respectively). Each year, with its employees, it revisits the subject and challenges itself rigorously over the extent and integrity of the application. At the same time, it annually refines the content of its statements and ambitions. By this constant refreshment, it can keep the approach fresh, challenging and ambitious.

In time, all employees in your organisation will develop a profound understanding of, and commitment to, the values that underpin the rationale for management decision-making. This enables them to link their required behaviours to shared values. By progressively understanding and internalising these core values, you will achieve the 'Holy Grail' of employee engagement: common ownership of both the problem and the solution. And then you'll really see the difference!

Figure 24: The Route Map updated 4

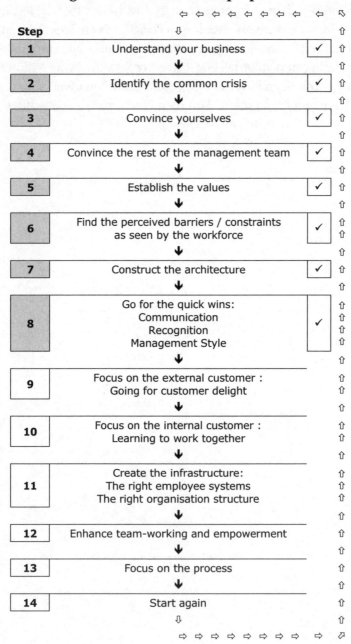

10
SUMMARISING THE QUICK WINS

A considerable proportion of this book has been devoted to discussing and developing the three *quick wins* of Communication, Recognition and Management Style. These three really are at the heart of effective employee engagement. Whilst there is a lot more you can do to exploit the concept further, many will be content to stop at this point and really embed the lessons deep into their daily life.

There is a lot to be said for this approach. So far we have incurred little in the way of risk and even less to upset the most Luddite in your management ranks. No-one is going to argue against good communication, fair recognition and a more approachable management style. Few are going to find anything unwelcome in either the core values or the behavioural attributes required of all, aside from the small minority who might see management's increasing obligation to challenge poor performance as something of a threat! And the commonsense of it all so far is going to placate those who fear being overburdened by initiatives. So taking stock for a while may make sense.

In addition, there is also a strong possibility that many of the approaches recommended in the rest of the book might evolve quite naturally. Inter-departmental tensions, for example, frequently abate in the face of values-driven management. One organisation experienced a 20% improvement in quality standards in the first 18 months of this approach, without management doing anything specifically about process or product quality. After the event, they were able to explain the change in terms of *employees* unilaterally taking ownership of the many small quality issues that bedevil organisations. And then solving them without fuss or publicity, aside from the odd Recognition event.

The temptation to race headlong and complete the Route Map may also be very strong. In particular, many organisations are so keen on

Continuous Improvement that they even start there. However, to do so is to increase the risks of failure significantly. Continuous Improvement tends to be about processes and procedures. Without the necessary foundation stone of employee engagement, there is a distinct possibility of another 'flavour of the month' failure.

Therefore, we do encourage you to take time out after Step 8. By all means, study, plan and train for the remaining stages, but expend your greatest energies on making sure the quick wins are both bedded in and paying dividends. Many people ask us how they will know when the quick wins are working. Our answer is that, if you have to ask the question, you haven't got it right! The impact is so profound that you'll really see something different is happening. Attitudes change and performances improve, significantly.

In essence, what you are seeking is to move the organisational mind-set from Reactive towards Proactive, as in **Figure 25**.

Figure 25: Improving the Organisational Mind-set

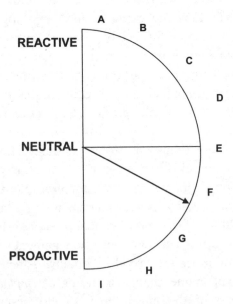

In the majority of companies, even in these more enlightened times, the 'average employee mind-set' is at the top. People are naturally 're-active'. They come to work for the money and work to job descriptions. Demarcations between individuals and between departments are legion. 'Getting away with it' or 'bucking the system' is fair game. There is no natural affinity between the company and the employee.

Employee engagement works on the principle that, in the 21st century, such companies will be soon out of business. The aggressive competitiveness of all markets will expose those dinosaurs as being too slow, too predictable and too inflexible to survive. What is needed is a much more proactive workforce, where the *status quo* is challenged routinely by everybody.

How do you gauge where you are on the journey to pro-activity? A colleague of ours, David Graham, uses this model to help companies gain a broad understanding of their status, as shown in **Figure 26**.

Figure 26: Improving the Organisational Mind-set 2

Position	Characteristic
A	Open hostility at certain levels, crisis, disputes, high turnover, total change resistance, stagnating performance. Customer cancellations.
B	'Us and them', very low morale, chronic negativity, delays, opposition, incompetence. Customer complaints.
C	Reluctant conformance, 'Us and them', poor morale, top down communication only. Poor performance.
D	Cynicism and exaggerated grievances, little dialogue, failure to embrace change. Negative elements vociferous. Average performance.
E	Neutrality
F	Increasing trust between management and managed, good communication and recognition. Negative elements no longer vociferous. Performance improving in steps. Customer satisfaction.
G	Sense of partnership. Emergence of positive peer presence. Successful adoption of effective continuous improvement hierarchy. Low turnover/absence. Competitive Performance.
H	Change constant and accepted. Pride in company. Most performances approaching Best in Class. High morale and personal sense of achievement. Customer delight.
I	Best in Class – and you know it.

Going from one segment to another need not be a complex business. You have to really assess what initiatives within the quick wins can really make a difference for you. This might help:

Case Study 20

Arthur runs a small, longstanding family firm in the printing, publishing and packaging business, employing around 40 people. Competition has been severe over many years, necessitating management changes, rejection of marginal products and some structural change. Performance Barrier Analysis revealed poor morale, a dislocation between senior management and the rest, no real continuous improvement and a distinct lack of enthusiasm for the end-customer. After careful consideration of the circumstances and challenges, Action Planning was fixed as:

1. Architecture ˉ

The senior management team, which met daily, would become the 'Culture Club'. They would devote one hour per fortnight to overseeing the employee engagement initiative at a dedicated, diarised and action-minuted session. *Ad hoc* invitations would be made as required to other key influencers. Their key task was to ensure measurement, audit and review.

2. Communication

a) The introduction of twice-weekly *Meet the Boss* sessions alternating between the Chief Executive and one other.

b) The introduction of five-minute 'huddles' at the start of shift for all departments and sub-departments.

c) A *State of the Nation* twice a year.

d) A Written Brief, detailing the views and opinions of key decision-makers, issued six times a year.

3. Recognition

a) Each manager to record how many times they formally recognised employees. Target to be the formula used in **Chapter 8**.

b) Thank you cards to be developed for management and then, within four to six months, for all.

c) A team-based Recognition system to be developed, with a minimum target of three groups per quarter.

4. Management Style

a) Immediate introduction of the Management Style Questionnaire for the CEO. Then progressively cascaded down to all managers / supervisors.

b) In six months time, a values statement to be developed as specified in **Chapter 9**.

c) A progressive introduction of one-hour one-to-one developmental reviews for all employees, with the emphasis on development, attitudes and behaviours.

And that was all that was needed to get them going over the first six to nine months of their journey towards employee engagement. Despite concerns over the behavioural and attitudinal challenges, essentially a fear of the unknown, the team agreed that the load was both readily doable and appealing.

The message here is simple. Kickstarting your cultural revolution need not be either time-consuming or daunting. You should see improvements in attitude quickly, followed closely by performance. If you are not experiencing either within a maximum of four to six months, there is a high probability that you're not doing it right. You could be over-delegating, sending out conflicting signals or simply not convincing the organisation of the seriousness of your intent. Keep going back over the quick wins until you feel confident of making progress.

Once you feel that the quick wins are indeed embedded, it's time to look more closely at your customers.

11
GOING FOR CUSTOMER DELIGHT

We have never yet encountered a company that claims to be *customer-unfriendly*. Nor have we ever met an employee who doesn't accept the vital importance of the *external* customer. They might moan and groan about the latter's unreasonableness, the late notice, 'feast and famine' and a total disregard for the supplier's position, but, in the end, everybody accepts that, without customers, there is no business.

However, over the years of scrutinising scores of companies on this very point, we can probably count the number of genuinely *customer-friendly* organisations on the fingers of no more than two hands. Whilst many of the companies claimed to be 'market-led' or 'customer-led', few actually exhibited any behaviour to support that boast. The truth is that many companies neither appreciate the concept nor know how to go about it.

Sometimes, this is extremely difficult. Take the example of a first-tier supplier to the automotive industry (**Figure 27**). If we define the customer as the assembler, then it becomes relatively straightforward. However, if the specifier is the end-user, then the situation becomes infinitely more complex.

Faced with such complexity, many first-tier suppliers simply give up and focus on their immediate contact. However, the specifier could be at any point further down the chain. So the definition of the external customer can be quite problematic.

Figure 27: Spot the Customer!

A similar logic could be applied *inside* organisations. Take a typical supply chain as shown in **Figure 28**.

Here, the only contacts between the customer and the organisation are the Sales function for the initial sales transaction, the Despatch department for delivery and the Customer Service function when things go wrong. However, when we examine what companies really mean by a 'customer focussed programme', we find that it only happens at the interface between the selling function and the end-customer. Given the usual friction between sales and non-sales functions, any attempt to create a pan-company approach usually evaporates very quickly. As a consequence, all bar those with this immediacy of contact lose sight of the real customer very quickly.

Figure 28: Internal Relationships

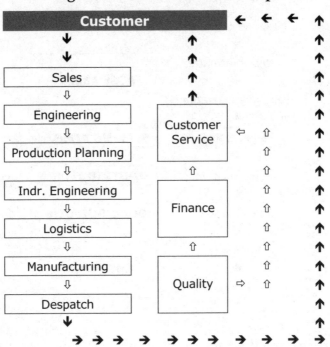

Given that this book is targeted at small to medium-sized enterprises, it would be nice to say that these problems are confined to their bigger colleagues. Sadly, this is rarely the case. Once your workforce gets into double figures and beyond, the same issues emerge. Only the severity varies.

Meeting customer requirements all the time is the minimum service standard for business nowadays. Competition is so fierce in all markets that the consequences of failure can be quite devastating. Upset your customers and they will:

♦ Go elsewhere.

♦ Tell everybody about you letting them down (customers do talk with each other).

♦ Tell your competitors, who will be delighted.

♦ Rarely come back.

It is probably *10 times* cheaper to retain a customer than to gain a new one. So many companies we encounter spend fortunes on marketing and promotional activity looking for new customers, yet don't seem to understand the concept of marketing to existing ones.

Take Lexus, for example, the Toyota offshoot designed to produce upmarket cars. It regularly comes out at the top of rankings on both vehicle reliability and on dealer support. This isn't accidental. The difference between its customer interfaces and dealerships elsewhere is quite remarkable. You are made to feel important at every stage of the Lexus experience, not just up to the point when you part with the money. Staff will call you to ensure that you are satisfied with the service you received, that everything is well. They are polite and seem to be interested and genuine. You might argue that this is just good training. That doesn't matter at all. My perception is that I have been treated professionally by people who are passionate about service. And in this case, my Perception is my Reality. What the Customer *perceives* is the most important part of the experience. If you provide excellent service and the customer doesn't realise it, then you have lost a major opportunity to realise highly valuable customer loyalty. And that is what customer focus is all about – winning and retaining customers.

So what, you might reasonably ask, has all this to do with employee engagement? After all, in the same way as the last chapter was hardly likely to do much justice to the huge subject of Management Style, then we are not going to convey a great deal on this equally complex and wide-ranging subject in one brief section.

There are three points to be made here:

First, understanding Customer Focus is a vital part of any organisation's strategy. The book we have found most valuable on the topic is *Once a Customer, Always a Customer* by Chris Daffy[4]. Not only has Chris made a complex subject relatively straightforward, each page is full of practical ideas on how to go about it. We heartily recommend it.

Second, to be successful, Customer Focus has to permeate every area of the organisation. In a traditional functional organisation, this is

---

[4]   Daffy, C. (2001). *Once a Customer, Always a Customer: How to Deliver Customer Service That Creates Customers for Life.* Cork: Oak Tree Press (ISBN 186076164X).

extremely difficult. In one based on employee engagement, the subject of customer care and attention is ideal for exploitation. Once the quick wins have embedded themselves successfully into the company, then people will be looking for ways to improve. Anything to do with the end-customer is instantly appealing. People see this as relevant, important and immediate.

And third, delivering exemplary Customer Service cannot be achieved by management action and intervention alone. Best practitioners in this field are characterised by an attention to detail and to service *throughout* the organisation. A participative organisation is the key here.

INTERNAL CUSTOMERS

One of the problems that companies encounter when developing customer focus strategies is that few employees actually ever come into contact with the end-customer. For most, the relationships are tangential and anecdotal. Others, a relatively small proportion of the workforce, act as the key filters of dialogue, information and instruction. As we will see later in this chapter, relationships between departments and functions in most enterprises are usually far from ideal anyway. Those between sales, service, customer support and the rest are more often than not characterised by fractiousness and resentment. Perhaps this should not surprise us:

- Sales departments are judged 99% of the time on sales volumes and, occasionally, margins. They see their jobs as being at the sharp end bringing in the business to keep the company going.

- Their colleagues don't quite see the matter so simplistically. They cite inadequate data, incorrect specifications, unrealistic due dates and a complete lack of understanding of the limitations of the supply side of the business. However, often the Sales Director will simply dismiss this as more evidence that the business isn't customer-led: *"People here expect customers to work around them!"*.

- Service departments see themselves as fire-fighters, salvaging the company's reputation in the face of general ineptitude. They are the conscience of the company, the real ambassadors of customer focus. Sadly, everyone else finds them arrogant, pompous, prone to exaggeration with a sadistic inclination to induce panic unnecessarily.

♦ Customer support areas see themselves in a similar light as their service colleagues. Their life is constantly dealing with immediate customer issues. They are usually the most stressed people in the entire company. Others in the company don't like them, simply because they perpetually bring bad news, they are harbingers of doom!

Against this background, it is fairly easy to see why customer dialogue in most companies is so vexatious. It is a subject of ongoing contention, rather than concord. It is associated with negativity, rather than positivity. And it is focused on complaints, rather than celebration. The ratio of compliments to brickbats from the sales department to the rest tells its own story!

To overcome this, we recommend that you undertake two 'campaigns':

♦ Introduce the concept of internal customers and suppliers.

♦ Make your standard 'customer delight' rather than 'customer satisfaction'.

We use the word 'campaign' deliberately here. Unlike much we have heralded before, this really will take a lot of management effort, attention and exhortation!

CAMPAIGN 1: INTERNAL CUSTOMERS & SUPPLIERS

It is difficult for people working at the same function or workstation every day to understand the impact that their work has on the overall satisfaction of the external customer. In the service sector, this is particularly evident. Most employees will be in the 'backroom', with little or no contact with the actual purchaser of their services. They probably receive very little information about customer reaction to the company's products, except when things go wrong. For that reason, if the organisation is going to be genuinely customer-focused, we have to broaden our definition of the 'customer'.

In reality, your business is just a series of transactions, starting with the customer, *order receipt*, and ending with the customer, *delivery of product or service.* Where individuals sit in that chain is only a matter of skill or specialisation, nothing to do with rank or capability. No-one has any claim to greatness by being at either end of the chain. What matters is the flow of transactions from order receipt to despatch. Customer service is dependent on the efficiency, accuracy and timeliness of each step along the chain. At the end of the day, the customer is not unduly concerned about *where* errors occur. S/he simply wants it right.

The approach here is relatively straightforward. We distinguish between those who have an end-customer and those who don't. And then for those who do not have a customer, we give them one! The philosophy is simple. We are all here to serve customers. If you are not directly involved in serving an end-customer, then serve somebody who is. We create the concept of an *internal* customer and then attach to it the same service standards as we do to our *bona fide* customers. Your internal customer is one who depends on you for the supply of products, services or information. Your task is to treat them (you'll have more than one usually) in exactly the same way as you would if you were sitting in the sales, despatch or customer service office dealing with end-customers. Your customers are dependent on you to provide a high-quality service. Otherwise, they can't provide the same to *their* customers and, ultimately, somebody will let the *real* customer down.

Interestingly, there is often a dual relationship here. Take Sales and Engineering back in **Figure 28**. Who is the internal customer and who is the internal supplier? The answer is that they are both. Whilst Sales might see itself as the 'customer' in demanding a product, it is also quite definitely an internal supplier in terms of the provision of data, specification, due dates and any other information needed to maximise the chances of meeting the end-customer requirements.

With this model, there is an immediate recognition that functions have to work together, rather than in spite of each other. This may seem fairly obvious but, as the next chapter will reveal, organisations have a habit of ignoring the logical.

Below, we list some useful approaches to be considered when 'campaigning' for internal customers and internal suppliers:

♦ Ensure that senior management messages and behaviours reflect this core philosophy. An example of NOT doing this was a very large company's mission statement:

> "We will put the customer at the heart of everything we do."

However, 95% of their workforce never encountered an end-customer and felt quite disenfranchised by this core value. They had no conception as to how to put the end-customer at the heart of anything. No information was received from, or about, the ultimate customer and they had little idea how their contributions impacted or otherwise on them. Perhaps the core value should have been restated as:

> "We will put the customer, internal and external, at the heart of everything we do."

The confusion then would disappear.

Equally importantly, management behaviour should reflect the balance needed across the organisation.

Charles was the Chief Executive of a consumer goods company. His background and forte was selling. He was infamous not just for spending most of his time with the sales force but also for taking their side in internal disputes. In fairness to him, perhaps he was too close to the Sales department and understood only too clearly the challenges and difficulties facing them. Unfortunately, he didn't share the same empathy for the 'support' functions, as he tellingly called them. The end result was not only internal hostility but occasional deliberate sabotage to catch his favoured sons out. Of course, the real victim here was the customer, but the internecine feuding conveniently ignored that.

♦ Create internal Supplier-Customer workshops, where small groups of informed employees are brought together to discuss issues between adjacent departments. The emphasis should be placed firmly on the positive, using independent facilitation to keep tempers and disputes under control. Both areas are asked to list the perceived problems with each other. The criticised party then carefully lists the challenges that they encounter in delivering the level of service demanded 100% of the time. The facilitator then gets both parties to constructively devise new ways of working together.

These multi-functional focus groups are ideal for the Action Planning phase of the Route Map as they promote:

◊   Real customer focus.

◊   The elimination of internal barriers.

◊   Process conformance.

♦ Establish formal Service Contracts between departments. We have always been a little wary of this approach as it can, in practice, turn out to be quite bureaucratic and reinforce prejudices rather than resolve them. However, used sparingly, in areas of complexity and sensitivity, they can be useful. It is vital that performance is measured across these boundaries and improvement is recognised as a shared victory.

♦ Communicate customer information. We talked extensively about communication systems in **Chapter 7**. People generally welcome information from customers, particularly where it refers to their contribution to the process. In most instances, however, communication will be related to macro rather than local issues. There is little advantage in bombarding the workforce with unnecessary facts and figures. Within the limits of commercial confidentiality, attempt to give each employee a focus on both the importance of end-customers and how effectively you are satisfying their needs.

♦ Ensure that your Quality Control processes reflect the needs of the end-customer not obscure internal diktats. Total Quality is a great idea if used properly, but at least 50% of all applications fail. Most of these failures arise because there is little or no ownership within the organisation, employees simply not being engaged. Frequently the terminology, the focus and the execution seem to develop a world of their own. TQM is then seen as just another piece of useless bureaucracy, instead of a genuine tool to improve processes, products and people to the customer's benefit.

♦ Ensure that all business activities are designed outside-in instead
   of inside-out. You start with the market and then develop your
   systems and strategies from these. This may seem to be yet
   another statement of the blindingly obvious, but sadly the
   majority of business processes are designed the other way
   round. The starting point too often is what the business would
   like to do, or what the business already has, rather than from the
   customer inwards. You end up selling what you want to sell,
   rather than selling what the customer needs. Customers need to
   be the focus of all activities. Make sure this is reflected in
   everything you do, from business planning to organisational
   design.

♦ You're not the first to underestimate the demands of Customer
   Focus and you won't be the last. The chances are that you are
   repeating the errors of others so test the things that go wrong
   commonly elsewhere before you go looking for original sins.
   Companies generally fail on:

   ◊ **Poor definition of requirements:** Many problems occur
      because the customer simply does not understand the
      product you are offering nor the processes needed to deliver
      it. Always discuss requirements in detail with customers and
      clarify ambiguity. Very frequently, your constraints and
      bottlenecks may prove to be totally avoidable.

   ◊ **Unrealistic expectations**: In their eagerness to 'clinch the
      deal', the sales force agrees to the undeliverable and then
      expects everybody to work miracles. Sadly, what then
      happens is that corners are cut and the supply areas fire-fight
      their way out of trouble. The hidden cost here is the
      disruption, waste, non-value added activity, overtime costs
      and the negative knock-on impact to other customers. Quite
      often, all this pain is either ignored or not understood.
      Planning goes out of the window and fire-fighting becomes
      the norm. Meanwhile, the sales force continues to operate in
      blissful ignorance of the sheer chaos and inefficiency they are
      inflicting on the organisation.

   ◊ **Ill-defined capacities and capabilities**: The supply chain
      here has not got down to defining its capabilities and hence

the danger of overload is ever present. In some areas, we
have seen a tendency to deliberately underestimate capacity
as a form of protectionism. This leads to a lack of credibility
in information and a subsequent second-guessing that will
ultimately be problematic.

◊ **Lack of consultation with internal suppliers and customers:**
Self-evident.

◊ **Lack of commitment to internal customers**: This arises when
internal suppliers become 'myopic', focusing on their own
problems rather than ensuring a smooth flow. This is often
evident with laissez faire management styles or companies
suffering from chronic 'siloitis' (see next chapter).

◊ **Requirements are not owned:** Often a consequence of
remote management or poor communication.

◊ **Remoteness of the Sales function**: Due to the geographical
dispersal of the sales force, often deliberately located away
from the main operation, communication can be sketchy.
Proper conduits for dialogue must be created. Better still, co-
locate!

CAMPAIGN 2: CUSTOMER DELIGHT

Until the authors came across Chris Daffy, Customer Satisfaction
seemed to be a fairly respectable goal. After all, to meet the
requirements of the customer regularly and routinely seems at first
sight to be a winning formula. But is it?

Unfortunately, nowadays, it isn't. Take quality for example. Just a
few years ago, quality in the automotive industry was a major
differentiator. You went to the maker who, in your view, could give
you the most reliable vehicle. However, nowadays, quality is a given.
Most cars, trucks and motorcycles simply don't break down anything
like they used to. And the same goes for many aspects of performance,
design and comfort. Customer satisfaction is a 'me-too' experience.
And a 'me-too' experience doesn't create customer loyalty.

Without customer loyalty, you cannot guarantee that your existing
customer will return automatically for their next purchase. More than

likely, they will shop around or go out to tender before making their final decision. As Tom Peters says, *"Customer satisfaction is no longer good enough to survive in today's market. What is needed is customer delight"*.

A delighted customer has many advantages. They will come back again and again. They will probably tell their friends about their experience. And they'll probably pay extra for the privilege of dealing with you. People recognise that good service generally costs more and are prepared to fork out more for it, as long as the delight continues.

The thing that attracted us to Daffy was his claim that delighting the customer need not be more expensive. In fact, cost is totally irrelevant. The only measure is perceived value. If you can create that extra perceived delight for little or no cost, then you are immediately at a major advantage over your competition.

Daffy's terminology for those extras that do so much to enhance the customer experience is the "WOW" factor. Here, the customer receives something over and above what is anticipated and instantly recognises and values the unexpected benefit.

Examples include:

♦ A travel agent including a foreign coin in your travel pack to pay for a trolley in your destination airport. Cost: insignificant. Value: out of proportion.

♦ Another travel agent sends you a postcard upon your return, hoping you've had a good holiday. Simple message, low cost, positive benefit.

♦ Staying at the Anse Chastanet in St. Lucia. Within 24 hours, half the staff address you by your name. How do they do that?

♦ You have a significant problem with a supplier. The Managing Director rings you up personally and promises to fix it. And then rings again to confirm everything is now on track.

On this last point, Daffy has an interesting theory. All organisations, from time to time, make mistakes. The difference between ordinary and excellent companies is in how they react to these problem areas.

The answer from a Customer Delight perspective is shown in **Figure 29**. The customer's satisfaction level with your organisation is somewhat damaged as you let them down with a quality or delivery problem. Your immediate challenge is to fix the issue, minimising the depth of dissatisfaction (d) and the time that dissatisfaction lasts (t). But beyond that you have to create a WOW event, where the pleasure at the unexpected outstrips the pain of the failure.

Figure 29: Killing the Pain

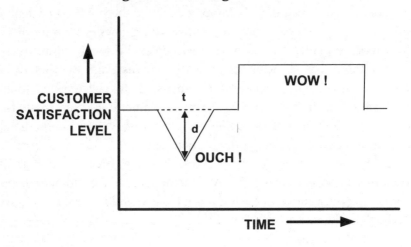

Case Study 21

An example: Alan runs a highly-regarded training consultancy. His customer base is very loyal, and repeat business is commonplace. One day, a key customer finds not one, but two, problems on an invoice. As luck would have it, both errors are in favour of Alan's company. The customer is not at all pleased. Alan immediately cancels the invoice and issues a new one. He then writes to the complainant and apologises, explaining how the mistake arose. He, truthfully, emphasises that this really is a one-off event and, as compensation, offers four free places on a forthcoming training course – a benefit of nearly £2,000 to the customer. The customer is staggered by the response and immediately sets aside any concerns about future dealings with Alan and his company. The WOW factor has completely submerged the original issue.

At face value, this is an extraordinarily generous gesture. But the course is running anyway, so Alan only incurs the minimal incremental cost for four extra places. Everybody ends up satisfied. A little imagination, a little thought may be all that's needed to create your WOW factors. For more ideas, read Chris Daffy's book.

SUMMARY

Employee engagement is all about getting your employees enthusiastic and motivated about company issues. The end-customer provides an ideal opportunity to create that buzz of excitement. People get a major kick out of seeing a customer satisfied or, better still, delighted. The more you can make employees feel a sense of ownership of the processes that ultimately fulfil customer requirements, the more you are likely to see improvement. If you can do that with both external and internal customers, you'll be well on the way to best practice.

12
WORKING TOGETHER

One of the great surprises arising from working with Perception Barrier Analysis over the past decade or so has been the number of companies that experience severe difficulties in the area of *internal customer focus*. Measured in terms of both severity and frequency, problems in this area seem to be second only to *management style*.

In organisations of any size, there seems to be a marked inability for functions to work together. The friction and antagonism shown in certain instances makes you wonder how these companies actually manage to do anything successfully. And yet, management, when challenged, usually admit that this is no surprise. With a shrug of the shoulders, they seem to accept the problem as a fact of life, *as if it doesn't really matter*! The odd eccentric is even inclined to view it as a matter of pride: *"Keeps them on their toes!"*.

Admittedly, it must be very difficult to quantify the dis-benefit to companies suffering from inter-departmental strife. To an outsider looking in for the first time, the damage is also too self-evident. It is huge. But those inside seem simply to get used to it. Perhaps they know no better!

Why is it important? If we were to take a fairly routine process, for example the processing of a customer order, we would expect to see something like **Figure 30**. The objective would be to complete each stage sequentially in a flow that would see a maximum added value, minimum waste and total process conformance.

Figure 30: A Simplified Process Flow

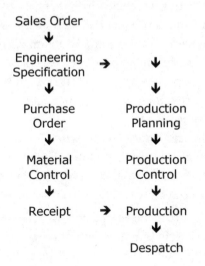

However, it is very unusual to see companies organised around flow – that is, organised horizontally. Much more commonly, companies structure themselves vertically or 'functionally'. So, our routine becomes more akin to **Figure 31**.

Figure 31: A Simplified Functional Flow

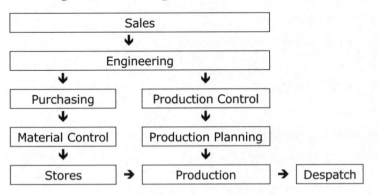

Now, instead of a flow through the organisation, we have a series of inter-departmental transactions. In itself, this is usually highly inefficient, because these transactions tend to *queue* at each stage. There is also the question of authority or *sign-off*, so the process may be diverted up the function or backwards if issues of clarification arise. All in all, elapsed times are extended and costs escalate, even in the unlikely event that the functions actually get on with each other.

But imagine the additional cost and confusion if these functions fall out, if they don't cooperate or worse. The waste has to be huge. The opportunity for improvement vast. Yet management's typical response is – a shrug of the shoulders!

Sadly, there are no quick fixes when it comes to this 'inter-departmental suboptimisation', where the interests of individual functions subvert those of the company at large. Unusually, this chapter contains not one new solution. This is down to:

♦ Many of the instruments advocated in earlier chapters – for
   example, those in External Customer Focus and in the adoption
   of multi-functional focus groups in Action Planning – will go
   some way to easing the severity of the problem.
   and

♦ There are so many potential causal factors here that we wouldn't
   know where to start!

Instead, we will discuss some of the most commonly-occurring reasons for departments not working well together and leave it to you to decide which, if any, apply to your company:

♦ System incapability.

♦ Senior management behaviour.

♦ Internal competition.

♦ Physical location.

♦ A blame culture.

♦ Poor organisational design.

SYSTEM INCAPABILITY

This is an area where the 'systems thinking' school would rightfully have a field day. **Figure 30** represented a process flow that ideally is designed from scratch as an integrated system. In reality, this rarely happens, even in the best of concerns. Individual functions are given tasks, and often ill-defined ones at that. They often design their own internal systems around that flawed understanding both of the task and of the real requirements of the next link in the chain. As a result, the interface between functions becomes less than ideal. This leads in turn to inefficiencies and frustrations. Each party sees the issue from their own perspective, not from the internal customer / internal supplier standpoint advocated in the last chapter. As a consequence, tensions arise, people fall out and dialogue is strained. Internal politics then intervenes and even mundane decisions become escalated upwards.

Getting the system 'right' theoretically would solve much of this dysfunction. However, this is a far from easy prospect that we will discuss in **Chapter 15**.

SENIOR MANAGEMENT BEHAVIOUR

In an ideal world, the average senior management team would be totally united, all pulling in the same direction. To a person, they would take decisions for the good of the company, even if the impact on their own function was occasionally adverse. They would exhibit 'cabinet responsibility' and generally set an example of cooperation, objectivity and humility.

Sadly, we're still waiting to meet a team like that.

In fairness, these utopian ideals are probably beyond the ambition of most organisations. Human nature, ambition and bonus schemes probably prevent the majority from actually reaching perfection. Nevertheless, this should be an aspiration.

There is only one person who can really pull this together and that's the Managing Director, Chief Executive, Proprietor or whatever title the organisation leader decides to adopt. If s/he demonstrates a lack of interest here, then there is no natural inclination to bond. This is not a natural state in the world of work. Even worse, many leaders operate a style that is politely described as *managing by creative tension*. Here, a certain deliberate aggravation is introduced as means of enhancing attention and motivation. However, very few are capable of playing this game with the necessary subtlety. There is a fine line between 'creative tension' and 'divide and rule', which most don't even appreciate, let along strive to avoid crossing.

There is little doubt that tensions within a senior management team can lead to even greater disharmony lower down the organisation. We often encounter a 'magnifying effect', where disagreement at the top becomes all-out warfare at the bottom. In one company, we felt the only way to describe their organisation structure was to construct a 3D model, based on parallel concrete silos each equipped with barbed-wire and machine guns. We hoped that this would embarrass the team but they just nodded in agreement! The problem is often obvious, but people just don't know where to start.

The answer is always with the man or woman at the top.

INTERNAL COMPETITION

A variant on Senior Management Behaviour, but we mention it separately because this is so often a deliberate policy. Key Performance Indicators (KPIs) are seen as measures of functional performance rather than corporate goals. However, in many instances, the objectives can be conflicting, or even mutually exclusive. Examples from manufacturing include Inventory Turns *vs* Build Flexibility. In some areas, the former is deemed the responsibility of the Logistics department, the latter that of Production. The Logistics head can readily improve his turns by shedding safety stocks. However, unless something else is done, production will suffer. Net result: a major argument and ongoing suspicion and mistrust.

Again, the responsibility comes back to the man or woman at the top. Be careful about setting individual targets unless you really understand the ramifications. And ask yourself – is your need to get your managers to compete with each other a reflection of your inability to manage? Be honest with yourself.

PHYSICAL LOCATION

When asked for the most obvious manifestation of inter-departmental dysfunction, employees inevitably cite poor communication across functions. For all the reasons noted here, departments seem incapable of talking to each other at the right time, to the right people and on the correct subject matter. Anecdotally, we would have to say that this very common problem seems to worsen with distance. The further the functions are apart physically, the bigger the problem seems to be.

Many dismiss this as irrelevant in the 21st Century. After all, we now have sophisticated communication systems: e-mail, intranet and all the paraphernalia of modern society. However, many of these issues are about *relationships* rather than mere information. E-mail is so impersonal that it is open to misinterpretation. People will read into it sentiments to which they have almost preconditioned themselves. On one occasion, we were shown an 'aggressive' e-mail. We couldn't find anything remotely aggressive about it, but the recipient insisted she had every right to feel insulted!

There is much to be said for co-locating personnel who manage adjacent links in the chain. If this can be done without walls, partitions and individual offices, many of these in-built tensions may simply evaporate.

A BLAME CULTURE

The concept of a 'blame culture' is a fascinating one. We often find in Perception Barrier analysis that people refer to a prevailing blame culture as a key problem in their company. But when we look for concrete evidence, we don't find any. It appears that the real issue is a 'fear of being blamed', which is quite a different thing altogether! Sometimes, this can be attributed to a past regime where autocracy figured highly and mistakes were punished severely. Occasionally, it's almost personally-inflicted, a fear of letting the side down. Perhaps more frequently, it's down to a fierce antagonism between 'competing' functions at junior levels.

In any event, the adoption of the employee engagement techniques advocated elsewhere in the book should help. In particular, the introduction of Recognition systems, alongside a greater tolerance of individual mistakes will improve matters enormously.

POOR ORGANISATIONAL DESIGN

A fairly obvious issue here that will be covered more extensively in the next chapter. We have seen some weird and wonderful attempts to construct organisations that must have made some sense to someone at some stage. But the end product in practice turns out to be confusing and ambiguous. A ready recipe for frustration.

SUMMARY

There are many, many reasons why internal departments don't get on. Often, it is very difficult to determine one clear, underlying causal factor. With most organisations where we encounter poor practice, our usual tendency is to ignore it for the purposes of Action Planning. This is not to say we underestimate the problem, far from it. However, experience tells us that the efforts in other areas, particularly those around the so-called quick wins discussed earlier, will have much greater organisational benefit in the short term – a better bang for your buck. There is also a fair chance that remedial action there will have a peripheral, but significant, benefit on Internal Customer Focus. The choice really is yours. If the solution to the problem screams out to you, then by all means tackle it head-on. But we do believe your efforts will be better served elsewhere in the majority of instances.

Figure 32: The Route Map updated 5

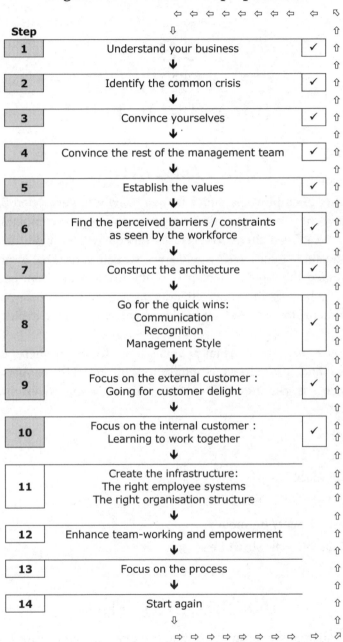

13
CREATING THE INFRASTRUCTURE

EMPLOYEE SYSTEMS

The subject of employee systems figures heavily in Perception Barrier Analysis for a very good reason – some of the biggest complaints are likely to be lodged there! Within this section will lie many of your more intractable issues, with rarely any easy solutions. That is why we have avoided the topic until step 11 of the Route Map. Your energies are initially best spent tackling the quick wins and then external and internal focus for greatest effect. However, we cannot avoid them forever.

Employee Systems is usually understood to mean those formal processes and procedures administered by the HR or personnel department, if you have one. Here, we are going to examine in sequence:

- ◆ Pay.
- ◆ Training.
- ◆ Appraisal.
- ◆ Demeaning systems.
- ◆ Recruitment / promotion.
- ◆ Organisational structures.

INFORMAL SYSTEMS

However, before we do that, we should ponder the benefits of *Informal Employee Systems*. We have looked at Recognition in some depth in an earlier chapter and have seen the enormous potential this tool has for improving motivation and, hence, performance very quickly.

Unfortunately, there are few other golden nuggets scattered around that can comfortably generate such short-term rewards. Nevertheless, other areas in the informal systems category are worthy of our attention.

Our end objective is to engage employees – that is, to improve their empathy with the organisation to such a degree that we establish a common objectivity. How we do that is of little consequence, as long as this empathy is based on a solid foundation and possesses the potential to be longlasting. The quicker we get to this understanding, the better.

Some commentators believe that informal employee systems can be quite powerful in building up this supportive culture. Others, like Ricardo Semler of *Maverick!* fame,[5] believe they are a waste of time and constitute at best a distraction.

We have decided to sit squarely on the fence here. You pays your money and you makes your choice! Both camps have a point. If you do go down this path, then you have to ensure that the social side of business life doesn't dominate at the expense of commercial reality. Should you be pushed for time and resources, we would advise you not to bother. If you intend to take a long term view, then, by all means, dip your toes in here. But always keep a sense of perspective and a clear understanding of their limitations. These are sideshows at best. The main attraction has to be the workplace.

Social Activities

The theory here is simple. We wish to encourage a spirit of team working both across, and within, departmental boundaries. By promoting and sponsoring extra-curricular events, we can accelerate this bonding process through employees getting to know each other better in a relaxed atmosphere.

If that is our objective, then we need to take steps to ensure that's exactly what we achieve. Much current effort and expenditure here is really about satisfying some sense of moral obligation felt by companies towards their local communities. Others do it simply from a paternalistic standpoint. For most of our readers in small to medium enterprises, neither tack is at all relevant. Therefore, you have to be

---

[5]   Semler, R. (2001). *Maverick!*. London: Random House Business Books (ISBN 0712678867).

very careful to ensure that every pound you spend really does improve that empathy.

The first problem area here is *management,* again. Unless you are an exceptionally mature organisation, the last thing any employee wants to do is to be ordered about outside work by his or her superiors. They get quite enough of that already, thank you, without volunteering for more. In addition, anything organised by management is likely to be viewed with suspicion. Often, this is well-founded. Tickets for the manager's favourite football team for example are hardly likely to be viewed as a gesture of pure altruism. We are looking for motivation, not handouts.

In our view, the best way of tackling this is first to decide a budget. This need not, and should not, be expensive. Initially, perhaps £25 to £35 per head per year. Second, you must draft brief terms of reference, defining the sort of events you would like to see funded or subsidised. Positive areas include:

- ◆ Sporting competitions.
- ◆ Family events.
- ◆ Quizzes.
- ◆ Keep fit.

No-go areas should include anything to do with drink, especially subsidised drink!

This is important as the final stage is to rope in a committee of responsible and interested employees and tell them to get on with it. Their job is to organise a series of events, funded and part-funded, with managers only in attendance as participants. Rank counts for nothing. The committee's objectives are the development of a social interaction amongst work colleagues and a consequent sense of affiliation to the company. Within the limits of the budget and the terms of reference, they have full delegated authority. In itself, this is a small example of employee engagement in action, but it is often very successful.

Experience tells us that such an approach can be hugely effective and enjoyable. The fact that events are being organised at a 'peer level' eliminates all the hassle, intrigue and resistance that usually ensues when management get involved. It is basically much friendlier and much less formal than an orthodox, top-down approach. Whilst you may get the odd problem (a subsidised visit to a transvestite bar springs to mind!), positive momentum will progressively build up. And it does have the significant benefit of not tying up management time.

Other Devices

There are many other devices for allegedly improving employee bonding. We would be extremely wary of the 'gifts for Christmas' type approaches, although the hamper salesmen will no doubt tell you otherwise. There are three potential drawbacks that frequently seem to undermine the goodwill behind the gesture:

1. Some people find the gift inappropriate. You can't please all the people, all the time.

2. Some people will have a greater expectation of value and be disappointed upon receipt.

    and

3. In bad times, companies always 'kill' the present to demonstrate the seriousness of the situation. This creates resentment rather than understanding.

Therefore, we are not inclined to support the idea but, then again, we've always had a soft spot for Ebenezer Scrooge.

Charity committees are often used to the same end. The company agrees to support an autonomous charity committee on a pound-for-pound basis, up to an agreed limit. For every pound the committee raises, the company matches it. Nearly everybody we encounter tells us that this is a great idea but, in our usual curmudgeonly way, we have to express reservations. For a start, we are not convinced that there is any correlation between the activity here and any real benefit to the company. These things tend to assume a life of their own. They can often be quite distracting during work-time and you will look an absolute killjoy if you intervene. However, on balance, the feel-good factor, especially when the cheques are being distributed to worthy causes, can make it worthwhile. Just keep a firm hand on the tiller!

Similar comments could be made for long-service events, although these again must never be subjected to budget cuts. Decide on a level that can be supported through thick and thin. Simple recognition of the anniversary, ideally in the presence of the employee's partner or family member, can be most effective.

Lifelong Learning

Many organisations are waking up to the fact that a significant proportion of the UK's working population has not yet recognised the importance of continual personal development, or 'lifelong learning' in the current jargon. Equally, there is an increasing recognition that an employee who decides to improve him/herself will be a more valuable asset to the company. Given this win : win opportunity, with scarcely any downside, perhaps any discretionary funding might be diverted to this area instead of the Christmas turkey or the annual dinner dance. With the latter, the benefits are elusive at best. With personal development, the payback could be immediate in terms of enhanced goodwill, with more to come through enhanced technical expertise. Elaborate schemes may be beyond the resources of many SMEs. Open learning centres, for example, allowing employees to access PC-based training programmes are said to be highly effective. Whilst it may be impossible for you to fund a dedicated facility, you may be able to negotiate access to a local link for a nominal outlay. Your local business support agency may advise here or even help broker an arrangement. Further Education Colleges are always eager to 'engage' with local employers. Occasionally, these agencies might also be able to access funds to help with expenses. The government, for example, is extremely keen to upgrade the nation's basic skills and computer proficiency. It is always worthwhile establishing contacts with such institutions so you become aware of opportunities, as and when they arise.

We have witnessed at first hand the transformational power that personal development programmes can have on employee motivation. Anything that has the potency of enhancing self-esteem and self-confidence has got to be good for both individual and organisation. We have seen good practice in training workforces in 'off-the-wall' practices such as positive thinking, stress management, personal objective setting and even meditation techniques. If approached on a 'train-the-trainer' basis, when one of your senior staff becomes the 'expert' and trains others, you might find this to be both exceptionally effective and economical. However, you have to ensure that the candidate selected to do the training is really suitable and that the values espoused correspond with the values adopted by the company. Any perceived 'clash' here will undermine, rather than reinforce, your efforts.

Informal employee systems can add as much value to an organisation as many of the more traditional approaches. Nevertheless, they are unlikely to have anything like the potency of the quick wins – Communication, Recognition and Management Style. If you do go down this route, make sure that you really have done sufficient to get the basics right – and you're not being led in this direction through fashion, fad or frivolity. The latter happens much more than companies would care to admit.

FORMAL SYSTEMS

Pay

Almost certainly, you will have been marked negatively in your Perception Barrier Analysis on any question to do with pay. The only exception to this appears to be questions that touch upon competitiveness. Here, you are likely to get a more realistic response. For the rest, you have to assume a 'norm' of about 35% to 40%, instead of the usual 50% to 60%. Above that, you're likely to be OK in the eyes of the workforce. Below that, you *might* have a problem, but we can't guarantee it!

The reason for the confusion is twofold. First, human nature intervenes. One client insisted that we had to be very straightforward about this issue and made us put the following statement into the questionnaire:

"I am satisfied with my pay level."

He then expressed acute dismay when agreements of only about 10% emerged. As we anticipated, most people interpreted this as:

"I would like more money!"

And only a fool would say anything other than "Yes, please!". Interpreting any question on pay and conditions, unsurprisingly then, is a bit of a minefield.

More importantly, this is an area that can attract the so-called 'protest vote'. People often feel dissatisfied about something or other that may have little to do with remuneration. But, emotionally, they have to express that dissatisfaction by striking out. This tends to manifest itself, in particular, on Management Style where the behaviour of senior management is often criticised, especially on trust, and on anything to do remotely with money. The cry really is *"We deserve more to be putting up with this nonsense"*, but the truth is that paying more will do little to solve the root cause of their complaint.

Last year, we had a conversation with the Human Resources Director of a high-profile national corporation. He was bemoaning the attitudes of his workforce. *"We've given them an above going-rate increase, the best pension scheme in the industry, family-friendly flexibilities, improved the working environment, etc, etc ... and they're still whingeing and moaning."* The thought that their concerns may have nothing to do with pay and conditions seemed to be completely missing from his radar.

In another organisation we dealt with, the preliminary findings from Perception Barrier Analysis indicated a deep dissatisfaction with pay. This came as a shock to us, as we knew the company paid 30% to 70% more than the local going rate. However, the more we talked to employees during the validation phase, the more it became obvious that they had really discounted any benchmarking with industry or local standards as irrelevant. Money seemed to be the only incentive at work and, simply, they wanted more of it.

Time and time again, this same phenomenon occurs. One of our colleagues was moved to observe, *"It seems the more you pay people, the more pissed-off they become!"*. Anecdotally, we'd have to say that this crude rule is right more often than it's wrong. We're not arguing against high pay, but we do object to pay being the only management tool in motivating a workforce. As we saw earlier, when we looked at Herzberg, money is not a good *motivator* but can be a devastatingly effective *demotivator*. Those who choose to manage by what seems at times to be little less than bribery will never engage a workforce.

In today's modern organisations, management needs to avoid the 'something for something' mentality that has bedevilled British business since the 1960s. Traditional approaches to pay negotiations reflect this flawed thinking. The time of the annual agreement approaches. Representatives get themselves ready by thinking of excuses to justify the maximum increase they can demand. Management meanwhile busies itself by working out the minimum it can get away with, plus a whole host of changes in working practices needed for next year and beyond. It is this latter element that clouds the picture. Given the intensity of the current competitive climate, you shouldn't have to wait for the next negotiating round to implement new working practices. What if the date of the annual review is 1 January and the problem isn't identified until 1 February. Do you have to wait for 11 months before you respond to the competitive threat? Will you still be in business? Why do changes, imposed by business threats and dislocations, have to be *paid for*? Surely the only real beneficiary here is the competition. In the short term, your company will suffer and, in the medium to longer term, your employees also, as their livelihoods are threatened by under-performance and excessive cost.

'Something for something' is a pernicious philosophy created by short-sighted, unimaginative and indolent management. In some companies, unfortunately, it has become habitual, a traditional creed resistant to change. If you already have the disease, then today is the time to start tackling it. The cure could take longer than you might care to think. Change should be permanent in every aspect of business life if you are to survive. There is no earthly reason why Pay should be exempt from the laws of commercial reality. Use your communication channels to get that message firmly across to all, especially management.

There is a temptation for a successful SME in its first or second flush of growth to reward employees through the pay packet. This is ostensibly quite laudable and will, for a short time, be motivational. People will feel recognised and bask in the glory of success. It will enhance, temporarily, self-esteem and self-confidence. Exactly what we're trying to achieve in this book, isn't it? Well, perhaps not, there are risks.

Recruitment will be easier. People will give up jobs to come to your company – albeit for money. Your employees will enjoy the benefits of higher pay and adjust their living standards to suit. Everybody wins all round. But then life becomes tougher. Growth means moving into more competitive markets where margins are smaller. Overhead costs increase. In time, these enhanced wage costs become unsustainable. Then what do you do?

We have seen this happen repeatedly with disastrous long-term implications for worker / management relationships. Trust has been destroyed. Your arguments for salary reductions may be plausible, but the consequences for employees can be devastating. Mortgage and hire purchase agreements will have been geared to anticipated income levels. Holidays may be booked, home extensions planned. In these situations, logic seems to fly out of the window. The damage to organisations going through this upheaval is invariably long-term. And all rooted in a well-intentioned, benevolent attempt to share the rewards of success.

That is not to say that you should never link reward with business viability, but you must consider both the long-term and the consequences of a change in the business's circumstances. If there is a risk that high pay rates are unsustainable in certain scenarios, then think twice before you adopt them.

For a small to medium business operator, the last thing you need is to be bedevilled by the complexities and traumas of complicated pay systems. If we agree with Herzberg's analysis that money is not necessarily motivational, and we understand that 'normal' fluctuations in business fortunes are rarely anything to do with effort, logic tells you that you should adopt the simplest of pay systems you can find. Obviously, this is not going to be one flat pay rate for everybody but use that as a starting point and work from there. We would advise you to avoid grade bandings unless you accept that, progressively, all will migrate from bottom to top with an inevitability that will have nothing to do with capability or skill acquisition. And make sure you also budget for the wage drift that such payment systems automatically incur. Otherwise you may find that your 'cost of living' projections could be badly underestimated.

Likewise, care must be taken with bonus schemes linked to one element of performance. You have to deliver on a whole host of parameters if you are to achieve the business viability and the 'customer delight' we spoke of earlier. Incentivising employees to deliver but one of these elements is a classic recipe for the 'suboptimisation' we encounter repeatedly. Margins are sacrificed for volumes, quality suffers in the cause of maximising production, the long-term is forgotten on the altar of short term gains. Business has enough challenges of its own. Don't add to them unnecessarily. Keep your pay systems simple, fair and transparent.

Training

The role of training, development and education is one of the most important aspects needed to implement a culture of employee engagement. We in management are often guilty of thinking our enthusiasm for this brave new world of engagement will be automatically shared by others. Unfortunately, this is rarely the case. The usual reaction is a combination of uncertainty, hostility and suspicion, even from the most enlightened of workforces. Many will perceive employee engagement as a threat. For some, this may be real. Those whose power base is rooted in status or tradition will inevitably find the going difficult. And they may well convey that uncertainty to others. Improvements in Communication, Recognition and Management Style will certainly help but, for many, the crux will be exposure to new practices – through training.

However, we have to accept that the role of training is not always valued by every company, especially those in the small to medium category. They often find it difficult to relate actual training programmes to beneficial outcomes. Too many owner-managers, for example, see training as a luxury that may be appropriate for their larger counterparts but is irrelevant to their size, cost and management structures. This is so dangerous.

If your major concern about training is a difficulty in seeing a tangible benefit to the bottom line, make sure that clear commitments on outcomes are given by the training provider before commencement. Alternatively, find ways of minimising costs, up front. This should not be too difficult. If one assesses the key training needs for most organisations going down this road, the following are likely to emerge as priorities:

- Immediate priority:
    - ◊ Senior management awareness and conviction.
    - ◊ Senior management architecture and involvement.
- Second priority:
    - ◊ Management style and leadership (top tier).

◊   Understanding perceptions.

♦ Third priority:

◊   Communication, Recognition and Management Style.

◊   Supervisory skills.

◊   Team facilitation and problem-solving.

♦ Fourth priority:

◊   Continuous Improvement techniques.

◊   Process 'management'.

There are many benefits in doing much of the above in-house. After all, employee engagement is for life. Management consultants or trainers are too expensive to be anything other than initial catalysts. An effective home-grown training resource is likely to be better informed, more accountable and more acceptable than any external provider. If this training is also carried out by senior decision-makers, then people will understand from the outset that this is more than the usual flavour of the month. In addition, the programme can be carried out in bite-size chunks to suit operational resources. Care should be also taken to synchronise the training to the point and time of need. Much valuable resource is wasted here by training the wrong people or training too early.

The selection of your internal 'champions' understandably becomes all important. The first quality you need to look for is enthusiasm. You want people who are likely to become evangelistic about this new approach. Second, they need to have a certain doggedness. Resistance to culture change can be fairly fierce at times from all quarters. Traditionalists will feel threatened as they see their natural power base eroded. Middle management may fear for their jobs. And the fire-fighting fraternity will see it as an unwanted distraction. Your champions have to be resilient enough to overcome the consequent cynicism, criticism and occasional outright hostility. Obviously, therefore, the higher the status of the champion, the more likely they are going to be able to rise above all this negativity. You do not want people who are too easily discouraged.

Third, and this is a key point, you want champions to be able to empathise with the workforce and to possess the necessary attributes of persuasion and presentation to get the message across. Much of the latter will come with practice, but, again, the candidates have to possess the resilience to go through this learning curve without losing self-confidence. We have seen some very unlikely characters absolutely blossom here, given time and training. However, they were all natural enthusiasts and strong-minded.

These champions will have to be trained, but, again, this can be done reasonably. There are plenty of 'best value' organisations about who are more than willing to open their doors to interested parties. Your local business support office can probably point you in the right direction. Visiting and reading about good practice is probably the best way of acquiring the necessary knowledge and skills needed to drive such a radical change as employee engagement. Fortunately, nowadays, there is no shortage of places to visit, nor books to read on the subject. Training in-house is a real, and ultimately more satisfying, alternative to relying on third parties. In any event, never regard training as a luxury, a discretionary option. The cost of *not* training is always much higher than training correctly.

Appraisals

Our interest here in formal employee systems is not to recreate the copious body of knowledge found elsewhere on each of these topics. Instead, we are merely trying to assess how best they can be used in support of employee engagement. The Appraisal process is a classic example of an essentially good idea that more often than not goes terribly wrong.

Fortunately, it is not our task to enumerate everything that can, and usually does, go awry in the application of Appraisal systems. However, we need to draw attention to three key irritations:

+ Performance Appraisal.
+ Pay.
+ One–way dialogue.

If your single objective in appraising your employees is to pass judgement on their performance, usually by assigning a specific grading, then read no further. However, most employers recognise that the real power of meeting employees once or twice a year in a formal setting for anything up to an hour is in allowing the *subordinates* to raise their concerns. The world of work can be both an impersonal and complex place for all of us. Over the course of a year, individuals may be subject to stresses, strains and irritations that may cloud their views of the organisation and hamper their performance and attitude. To the casual observer, the complaints may seem to be very minor, if noticed at all. To the *injured* party, their importance may become increasingly irritating as time goes on. It is, therefore, vitally important that a forum exists for employees to share and discuss these concerns with their supervisor privately.

However, it is equally important that the employee holding the sense of injury or grievance approaches the session in the right mind-set. The ambience needs to be friendly and unchallenging if they are going to be sufficiently motivated to offload their frustrations. Nobody ever got incentivised by outright, insensitive criticism, except perhaps occasionally on the sports field!

Contrast this with the average Appraisal meeting. The subordinate goes along with one objective: to get out of the session as quickly as possible with a rating compatible with their ambitions. Their mind-set is hardly going to be open and relaxed. On the contrary, it is much more likely to be apprehensive and introverted. This is hardly conducive to an effective two-way dialogue, especially if you create the perception of one person sitting in judgement and the other waiting for the verdict.

Does that mean you should never numerically rate the performance of your employees? We have no real view on this subject, as we understand the current fashion to do so but are yet to be convinced of its real effectiveness. The only way you are going to motivate employees is to get everyone on to the top rating ultimately. We suspect that this artificial ranking is meaningless, unless you want to use the information as part of a planned redundancy programme. And that's hardly motivational!

In our view, these one-to-one sessions should be rechristened 'Training Needs Analyses' or 'Developmental Reviews', to emphasise that this is all about moving forward, not retrospective judgement. If you insist on quantitative performance appraisals, then we suggest you reserve those for a separate session. However, properly handled, a useful qualitative assessment of performance almost inevitably will emerge anyway. The healthier characteristic here is that this review will be triggered by a self-assessment, where the employee starts the discussion by giving his/her summary of prior performance, strengths and weaknesses. By starting the session with the manager in listening mode, the chances of a meaningful dialogue are far greater. The whole theme of the hour should be along the lines of: *"How can the organisation help you improve your performance and your satisfaction with the world of work"*. This contrasts with the usual: *"Let me list all your weaknesses and then you tell me what you're going to do about them!"*. The same objective but one framed positively, the other negatively.

We remain astonished at the number of organisations that link pay increases into these sessions. Performance assessment is a flawed routine at the best of times. To have your annual increment hanging over the outcome of your appraisal is bound to influence your approach to it. You are going to be on edge, over-eager to please and averse to disagreement or anything that could be construed as complaint. The end product is inevitably stilted and ritualistic. Not at all conducive to employee engagement. Most managers, incidentally, hate these sessions as much as their subordinates.

To promote effective self-assessment, we encourage you to use something like a 'Citizenship Wheel', an example of which is shown in **Figure 33**. Ideally, each segment on the wheel should correspond with one of your 'Company Values'. Prior to the interview, employees self-assess themselves on each area on an arbitrary 1 – 10 scale. Your job is not to sit in judgement on the validity of that score but to use the rating as a guide to discussion. *"Why have you rated yourself lower / higher on that element? Give me some examples to support your assessment."* The skilled interviewer can gently draw out strengths and weaknesses in a responsive, rather than aggressive, manner. When dealing with managers and supervisors, the Management Style Questionnaire of **Chapter 9** may also be a useful discussion point.

Figure 33: The Citizenship Wheel

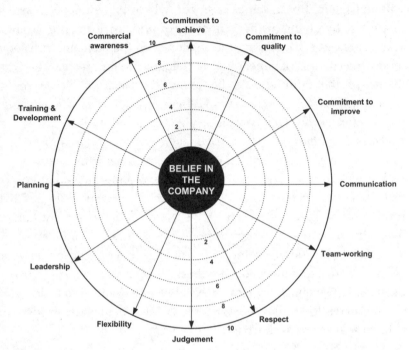

In summary, a few pointers for guidance to ensure you achieve healthy 'appraisals', or whatever you're now going to call them:

- **The primary objective is to assist the employee improve their work performance.** This is, therefore, an exercise first and foremost in motivation. Filling out the form in advance isn't a terribly good idea!

- **Pay should be barred from discussion – both ways.** It only distracts from the primary objective. This is a developmental review.

- **The interview should be between an employee and their immediate boss.** The habit of Personnel or HR Officers conducting the interviews in a search for 'third party objectivity' misses the point.

- **Promotion or future prospects can be discussed in general, but rarely specifically.** The objective is to raise and encourage aspirations, but it is desperately important not to generate false hopes or give rash promises. Interviewers tend to ascribe far less gravity to this process than the subordinate who may easily misread signals.

♦ **Discussion of performance should start with self-assessment.** There should be no surprises in the interview. If you have criticisms, these should have been made at the time of the perceived failure or weakness. Any such criticism, implied or direct, should be based on objective standards. The focus here is on development and support.

♦ **Both parties need time to prepare for the interview and, hence, adequate notice needs to be given.**

♦ **Responsibility for the outcome is shared equally.** An employee is personally responsible for his/her development. However, a manager is also charged with maximising the contribution of their subordinates and, hence, any failure implies joint culpability.

♦ **The outcome is not a comfortable chat, but a plan.** Both parties must agree on a plan to go forward. The manager must ensure that this is monitored throughout the year, not just left for review next time around.

Demeaning Systems

A very brief word on some of the unconscious consequences of many employee systems. Most of the latter are designed by human resource specialists who might be assumed to have an interest in people. Sadly, in many instances, this is very much a misplaced assumption! Personnel professionals, it is said, tend generally to be turned on by systems rather than people. They are not automatically the most empathic profession. Care needs to be taken to ensure that any new system does not create barriers between one group of workers and another or worsen existing ones. Canteens we debated earlier. We also touched upon companies that insist that blue-collar must clock, whilst white-collar don't. Some organisations have one group hourly-paid, with others paid a salary. Car parks can be another demeaning differentiator.

You might argue that, in your organisation, such arrangements have been around for years and don't seem to have caused any real problems. There are two responses: first, *"Do you really know?"*. Second, if you are going to create a culture based on *radical* levels of employee engagement, is this good enough?

We would strongly advise you to review progressively all your employee systems, existing and proposed, to ensure that you don't unintentionally create a class of winners and a class of losers. If you do, you could fail entirely to convince your workforce that your approach is different and serious. The cynics, barrack-room lawyers and the sceptics will have a field day.

Recruitment, Promotion & Induction

Managing people is a good deal easier if you can make sure you get the right people in the first place. When you pick a new member to join your team, you are exposing yourself to two levels of risk: first, will the new recruit be capable technically of doing the job and, second, will s/he gel with the rest of the workforce. In traditional organisations, the latter is rarely considered. For those intending to develop a culture based on employee engagement, this *social* element is paramount.

Your first challenge is to ensure that the people doing the recruitment for you not only understand that latter point but that they themselves also fully comprehend the underlying philosophy. Owner-managers / managing directors should take a keen interest in recruitment activity to ensure that the message gets home and stays home. Any bad decisions should be the subject of a post-mortem to ensure the same mistakes aren't repeated.

This should not be terribly onerous. Presumably, part of the initial recruitment process includes both a job specification and a person specification. The latter must be extended to reflect your new company values, particularly in terms of team-working, respect for others and in ideas generation. Questions within the interview and follow-up on references need to reflect these 'softer' demands of working life.

Similar principles apply to your promotional practices. The next generation of management must be capable of both maintaining and improving the people practices we have explored in this book. Your momentum could easily be arrested by promoting the wrong person. Not only could the successful candidate be personally disruptive, but their selection may send out a signal to the organisation that you were not as serious about culture change as you might have maintained. A couple of case studies illustrate the potential damage here.

Case Study 21

Jim worked for an offshoot of an American company. He inherited his medium-sized operation in rather a poor state. Attitudes were poor, with confrontation much more common than rational dialogue. Systems were highly traditional, based upon a longstanding autocratic management style.

Jim approached the problem in a very aggressive and radical fashion. He flattened organisational structures, introduced a very open management style and challenged employees to accept accountability and responsibility for their own workstations. The place was scrupulously cleaned, updated and employees entrusted with maintaining these new standards. The response was enthusiastic and performance progressively improved. Within three years, Jim had established himself as the vibrant head of a highly competitive facility. His reputation spread, as visitors flocked to see the visible signs of such a dramatic transition. The place was friendly, sleek, efficient and impressive. Young Jim was a star and, eventually, was promoted to bigger and more challenging pastures.

Unfortunately, the US-based recruitment team seemed ignorant of the plant's new and radical characteristics. They merely took the next name off the succession plan and parachuted him into the operation. Alex was a middle-aged traditionalist, a Scottish firebrand whose forte was fire-fighting. He was renowned as an old fashioned autocrat, a street-fighter of a manager.

Within 18 months of Jim's departure, the plant had reverted back to its old ways. Efficiency sank in line with attitudes. And all because the central personnel department didn't do its homework and balance the needs of the operation against the personal profile of the applicant. Ironically, every weakness that Alex displayed was well-known inside the company. Nobody bothered to put the two together.

Case Study 22

Rochesters was a medium-sized operation that had been through *Team Enterprise*, their version of employee engagement. The process had been relatively successful, with the financial returns more than justifying the approach. All areas embraced the philosophy enthusiastically, with some recording quantum improvements. Assembly, however, had been more difficult than was expected. This labour-intensive area probably handled more complexity and more disruption than the rest of the operation put together. One of the major obstacles was in finding appropriate candidates for the key position of Assembly Manager. External recruits fell by the wayside at an alarming rate, with average tenure less than eight months. Understandably, attempts to change culture advanced in fits and starts. Progress had been made but not to the level experienced elsewhere nor to the undoubted potential of the unit.

Management decided that radical action was needed. Looking outside seemed fraught with risk, so they decided to have a fresh look at internal possibilities. One candidate, Alan, stood out as having the relevant technical experience and a strong, determined character. However, he was very junior and seemed to lack subtlety. Nevertheless, the risk was taken and Alan was promoted.

Within six months of his appointment, virtually all the goodwill generated by *Team Enterprise* had evaporated. Attitudes hardened, morale plummeted and performance suffered. Alan's abrasive, and often crude, autocracy completely jarred against the philosophy previously espoused. The company is very much back to square one.

The latter case is a sad one. Perhaps the area is unmanageable by one individual and that might be the next step. But it does illustrate that the goodwill and benefits of employee engagement are somewhat fragile in the early years of change. And the quickest way to unlock them is to appoint the wrong people. Succession policy should be the responsibility of the key decision-makers in the company. Big or small, organisations should be preparing for the unexpected, whether that be positive in the form of business expansion or negative in the form of unplanned departures. When you do have to recruit from outside, at whatever level, you must ensure that your induction process includes an intensive exposure to the cultural demands of the business. Most people will react positively to this. However, one rotten apple can really upset the barrel.

Organisation Structures

There are two great ills in modern organisations. The first is managerial ineptitude. The second is the inability of these inept managers to resist the temptation to be tinkering constantly with new organisational structures.

A new man or woman comes into a position of authority. What do they do? They reorganise.

The company hits a sticky patch. What does it do? It reorganises.

The company has a good run and expands. What does it do? It reorganises. We could go on but you've got the point.

Two facts about organisational change:

◆ It rarely works.

◆ It distracts everybody for perhaps months, depending on the extent of change.

Every manager we have ever talked to on this subject emphatically agrees – but then goes and does it anyway! In other words, everybody's incompetent except me. We were tempted to restrict this section to one word:

◆ **DON'T**

but perhaps that might be misconstrued. Instead, we limit our advice to:

◆ Remember, changing your organisation can damage your health, and a lot more besides!

In other words, when it comes to changing your organisation, sup with an enormously long spoon.

Fortunately, most our SME readership should not have experienced the severity of the problems encountered by their bigger counterparts. But experience tells us that once companies get beyond 50 to 60 employees, they tend to pursue orthodox structures. And that's when problems emerge.

A few pointers for companies likely to grow in the short to medium term:

◆ **Always keep your management hierarchy as flat as possible.**
The enemy of employee engagement is a 'deep' management structure. The effectiveness of employee engagement is said to be inversely proportional to the number of management levels in the organisation. A traditional management pyramid is a self-generating structure: it feeds upon itself. It becomes the rationale for its own existence. Some managers spend all their time in the

pyramid in meaningless meetings and transactions, fetching and carrying information as well as discussing and debating decisions endlessly. Keeping your hierarchy flat will maintain a high value added in your most expensive resource – management.

♦ **Try to make sure your organisation follows processes, not functions.** In our discussion earlier on Internal Customer Focus, we saw how easy it was for functional interest to disrupt the process 'flow' through the organisation. As you move into the final steps of the Route Map, you will learn how important this 'flow' or 'heartbeat' is. Your objective will be to expedite this series of transactions through the organisation with a minimum of waste, maximum added value and total process conformance. And 'maximum added value' also means that processes are continuously tested for relevance. For example, should you be warehousing intermediate stock? Could you not get direct delivery to point of use? In a flat organisation based on flow, these questions are immediate. In a traditional functional organisation, they can be lost, hidden by sectional interest.

♦ **Avoid baking 'mistrust' into your organisational model**. One of the key sources of non-added value in most organisations is in inspection or checking routines. Often driven by auditors and accountants, they arise through a need for high-level accountability. Things must be checked, approved or sanctioned before action. This, in turn, creates delays, inactivity, queues, unnecessary inventories, inefficiencies and, ironically, worst of all, inaccuracies. Build into your systems local accountability, supported if necessary by Audit or exception reporting. In the end, it is far more effective than the alternative.

♦ **Ensure that dialogue takes place across functional boundaries, not up and down them.** In many respects, functions are necessary evils in organisational design. They are there essentially for bread, rations and 'professional' integrity. Over the years, we have seen many attempts to replace functionality by matrix organisations, project organisations and some weird and wonderful constructions. None of them actually, in the end, appeared to offer extra benefits in clarity and in operation. Our advice is to recognise the advantages that functional structures bring, but also to ensure that they don't interfere with process flow. If every functional manager is charged annually with ensuring that this happens on their adjoining patches, life would be much easier. One way of spotting inefficiencies here is to track dialogue across functional boundaries. In the same way as you seek to eliminate extraneous activity in process flow, you do likewise with dialogue. You do not want unnecessary delay whilst an individual seeks approval, authority or advice. Try to avoid this as much as possible and you reap the twin benefits of improved efficiency and less frustration.

Autonomous Work Groups

If one takes the 'flattened organisation' to its natural consequence, the concept of self-managing teams or 'autonomous work groups' comes into consideration. Theoretically, this brings a number of benefits:

♦ The elimination of one layer of management.

♦ A greater involvement / engagement for the workforce.

♦ Greater efficiency and quality arising out of real 'ownership of the problem' and 'ownership of the solution'.

♦ Higher morale and job satisfaction.

♦ More logical process flow.

However, sadly, that's just the theory. Practice is a lot more difficult. You cannot start out by simply launching self-managing teams, unless you have the unusual opportunity of a 'greenfield' start-up operation. This area is fraught with risk, and any weakness in the supporting infrastructure will eventually undermine all the good intentions. As many companies will witness, there is but a fine line between delegation and abdication. To be successful with autonomous work-groups, you have to be sure that you have the basics of a robust supportive culture in place. Effective delegation is a *consequence* of good practice, not a creator of it.

Assuming, however, that you have been through the steps of the Route Map and have evidence that the organisation has embraced the philosophy, then this is certainly the way to go. Take your time and move progressively to your ultimate model. There are no real rules here and no 'one size fits all' solutions. In fact, it would be highly unusual if one model suited your entire organisation. You could, readily, see the potential in a warehouse, factory or in a retail outlet. However, we have never yet encountered much formal self-management in Finance departments, for example. Here, you can have a lot of the practice, but within an orthodox structure. This doesn't make it any inferior, it simply reflects the nature of the operation.

For those areas that are suitable for autonomous management, we suggest you consider the following:

♦ Split the function into logical, discrete teams. Maximum size will be probably 12 to 16 people.

♦ Carefully define areas of responsibility and accountability. Develop meaningful measures so you can track progress. Establish limits of delegation clearly and communicate where higher authority lies. Spell out consequences of failure.

♦ Select 'Key Operators' to 'run' the teams. Their duties will be very similar to traditional supervisors but without any responsibility for discipline.

♦ Appoint local 'champions' within the teams, to handle specific responsibilities such as housekeeping, quality, health and safety, consumables and so on.

♦ Define and execute training needs for all personnel.

We strongly advise that, at least initially, the Key Operator is not paid any increment over his/her colleagues. They do the job for self-esteem, interest, job satisfaction or promotional prospects. This is not intended as a cost-saving initiative. The most important dynamic in the whole equation is the relationship between the Key Operators and their colleagues. You want, for example, the Key Operators to stand in for the 'Champions' in the group whilst the latter, from time to time, attend to their new duties. This may become quite difficult if there is a pay differential between them. Remunerating the Key Operator increases the ever-present risk of he/she being psychologically separated from the group and assuming a quasi-supervisory role. This will undermine the team spirit and the group harmony you are trying so hard to achieve.

SUMMARY

There are many exciting opportunities within employee engagement to improve organisational flow. As well as autonomous work groups, business unit type structures, for example, seem to work exceedingly well in the right context. Here, functional representatives are gathered under an operational umbrella. The benefits are cited to be faster problem-solving, reduced bureaucracy and lower overhead costs.

However, all of these good ideas share the burden of being disruptive in the short-term and returning the investment only on the longer horizon. Until you reach the maturity level when you are both robust and healthy enough to guarantee success, we strongly recommend that you restrict your organisational efforts to planning and reviewing.

You will be sorely tempted to disregard this advice. The intellectual attractions of organisation upheaval seem to be irresistible to most managers, particularly those new in the job. However, before you leap in here, remember what we said earlier about organisational change. It rarely works; in fact, it distracts and disrupts like crazy for much longer than its originators would care to admit!

Figure 34: The Route Map updated 6

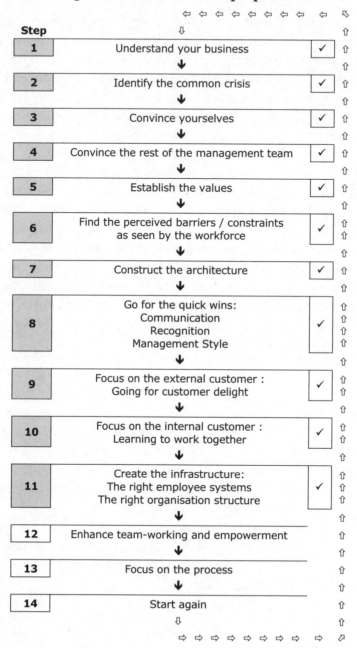

14
TEAM–WORKING & EMPOWERMENT

Ask any manager involved in a culture change programme to describe *employee engagement* and the chances are that the words *team-working* and *empowerment* will figure strongly in the reply. They are seen as clear manifestations of the ultimate culture, conveying both a sense of harmony and effective personal accountability. As such, they are both to be pursued vigorously.

However, in many ways, these are *consequential* outcomes of developments implemented elsewhere rather than crusades in their own right. When we undertake Action Planning (**Chapter 6**), for example, we will discover major improvements in both team-working and empowerment without any obvious efforts being seen to tackle the issues head-on. If you followed the recommendations in that section, you will have attempted to solve issues emerging from Perception Analysis through 'multi-functional focus groups'. This unfortunate piece of jargon simply means putting a team of suitably qualified people from a number of different departments together to help solve a longstanding problem. Despite the limited time this focus group is in existence, the individuals will experience real and powerful team-working, perhaps for the first time in their working lives. As the frequency and opticality of these focus groups increases, more and more people get to experience or witness the sheer potency and enjoyment of effective team-working. In time, they will transfer the lessons learnt into their daily routines.

Similar outcomes and consequences will be seen with empowerment. In traditional organisations, this approach may be very new to employees. Getting involved in a small team gives them a taste of personal empowerment in a much wider context than their usual job description. They find the experience enjoyable and stimulating. They want more of it, so they volunteer for other focus groups, come up with their own ideas or even simply contribute more in their new team meetings. The whole thing becomes a virtuous spiral towards employee engagement.

There is, therefore, no urgent need to leap immediately into formal structures of improved team-working or empowerment. As you strive to embed communication, recognition and management style into the organisation's psyche, you will be making huge progress in both areas anyway. So there is no need to rush. Organisations differ in both starting points and responses. You have the flexibility of finding your own best fit.

A few examples illustrate the point.

Case Study 23

We had been warned about Fred. Fred was a fork-lift driver in a retail warehouse where we were conducting a Perception Barrier Analysis. The general manager gave us a quiet warning that Fred was seen as a 'complainer'. He did his job OK, but generally made everybody else's life a misery by his constant bickering. Nothing was ever right, nobody did anything good enough for Fred. He was, as his boss said, "to be avoided for the sake of your ears, if not for your sanity".

As the process developed, Fred was indeed talkative, especially during validation where he managed to wheedle himself into one of the sessions. The interviewer, however, was less damning than management. Although Fred did complain a lot, unusually, the targets of his venom were the inefficiencies surrounding his own job. He seemed very frustrated.

Unsurprisingly, when the Action Planning conclusions were announced, Fred wanted to jump the gun. He bombarded his immediate supervisor with pleas for a local group, despite Fred's issues not being on the initial priority list. Fred eventually got his way, as his boss caved in under the onslaught.

As the group got into debate, it transpired that Fred's real beef concerned the unavailability and unreliability of the fork-lift fleet. Things had got much worse over the previous 18 months with the addition of a second shift in the warehouse. Time that had been available for routine maintenance was now absorbed by the night shift. Major maintenance had to be done largely at weekends, which meant that equipment could be out of action for days. The solution had been decreed to be additional trucks, but the request was still lodged in the Finance department.

Fred had lots of ideas, some radical. He had already dismantled the planned maintenance schedules and identified some of the more time-consuming elements that could be undertaken by the drivers themselves. This left the maintenance department with a much more manageable load twixt shifts.

All the group's recommendations were accepted. Within weeks, the problem of fork-lift availability had 'gone away' to such an extent that the request for additional trucks was withdrawn. Fred had a new conduit for his energies that reduced his propensity for negativity. In short, he now felt 'empowered'.

Case Study 24

Ewan was always known as a conscientious and highly-competent worker. He was quite unassuming, if occasionally frustrated by what he saw as the same things going wrong over and over again around him. In the past, various approaches had been made to him to become a supervisor but he had declined. As well as simply not fancying the hassle, he did not feel he possessed the necessary interpersonal skills to do the job properly.

His first reaction to the company's culture change programme was one of polite cynicism. His long experience had taught him that, once a year, some big new idea would emerge from on high, all well-intentioned and ably-presented. But they all had a habit of disappearing as fast as they emerged – 'flavours of the month', if indeed they lasted the month. However, he was intrigued by the concept of getting people involved to solve their own problems, especially continuous improvement. He volunteered, not just to go on the continuous improvement course but also to teach a simple version of it to his colleagues. He argued that it would carry a lot more weight coming from him rather than 'just another training initiative from some faceless office-bound oik'.

With some concern, his boss gave him the OK to run a trial programme. To everybody's surprise, except perhaps Ewan's, the outcome was more than satisfactory. Ratings and comprehension were a good percentage above the normal course.

Since then, Ewan has become a leading light in continuous improvement, responsible both for much original thought and, more importantly, for great enthusiasm from his colleagues.

Ewan and Fred are two of the many 'heroes' we have seen emerge through this process. Individuals with real individual talents and expertise that may have been hidden over decades, due to the prevailing culture. By providing modest opportunities for empowerment, against a background of even limited team-working, both were able to prosper for the first time.

It is interesting to note that, in both examples above, and in many more we could cite, the transformation of attitude came very early in the process. Structures, systems and even thinking hadn't really crystallised and yet huge progress ensued. This is a real learning point. The key driver of successful implementation is not the sophistication and technical excellence of your structures but the spirit and intent behind them. The workforce has to perceive that:

♦ The approach is genuine.

♦ The new ethos offers *real* opportunity for involvement.

♦ The approach offers *real* opportunities to make a difference.

♦ The contribution will be valued.

One might conclude that the real determinants of success are management sincerity and enthusiasm rather than intellectual completeness! This concept of 'making a difference' is also important.

Over the years, we have interviewed scores of people in the world of education, particularly further education. When asked why they had chosen to enter and, more importantly stay in, the profession, this phrase came up over and over again. 'Making a difference' is a key aspiration for all our potential heroes. Management must create an ambience where this is seen to be possible. Structures are mere embellishment, the real power coming from the spirit and intent in which they are developed.

We are great enthusiasts for Investors in People and for the European Foundation for Quality Management (EFQM). Both have their critics, but the abiding virtue for us is that they really do focus on the people side of the business in a way that many SMEs may not automatically find natural. Unfortunately, there is no guarantee that excellence in either qualification will result in genuine excellence in employee engagement. We have encountered many award-winners who have every structural element firmly 'ticked in the box'. However, they fail to reap the real benefits because they haven't convinced the workforce of their enthusiasm and beliefs. The key has been located, but they have yet to find the lock. This is the real power of Perception

Barrier Analysis (**Chapter 4**). Managers have a fine propensity for deluding themselves. Workforce perceptions will always give a much more realistic picture.

In summary, challenge yourselves very rigorously before embarking on some of the techniques to be discussed in the rest of this chapter. Are you adopting them because they are the natural development of your employee engagement programme? Or are you looking at them because you've not yet succeeded in your first steps? If it's the latter, go back to Step 1 and start again. Without that attitudinal foundation, there will be little added value in mere structure.

THE NATURE OF TEAMS

One of the big growth areas in management training nowadays is in 'team-building'. Groups of people are taken on 'Outward Bound' activities, where they cross rivers, climb mountains and generally enjoy chronic discomfort in the hope that they'll eventually work together more effectively. Alternatively, they retreat to a classroom and do strange things with packing cases and planks. All good fun, but highly questionable in terms of value for money.

One might be able to justify the energy expended here if the activities were geared to a specific team and a specific task. Unfortunately, the way of the world of work isn't quite as simple as that. Teams are not usually groups of people who happen to be located together in the same department. Interaction here is more often on a tangential level, with individuals carrying out separate and distinct activities. Real team-working takes place, either across departmental boundaries in pursuit of the 'process' or in temporary affiliations dedicated to a specific task.

Those teams that operate effectively are collections of personalities, skills and experience, where the total outstrips the sum of the parts. By working together over an extended period, they get to know each other's strengths and weaknesses and strive to achieve an optimal 'balance'. Whilst individually, they might be very different, they share both common objectives and a desire to succeed. However, it is precisely these individual differences that, in finality, make it all work.

Team-building training programmes often attempt to reduce teams to a sameness. However, in our experience, by promoting shared values, culture and even jargon, there is a danger of creating cliques and clans. Sure, the harmony within the team *may well emerge* to be extremely powerful, but this may create tensions across team boundaries. And as we've seen elsewhere in this book, the inability of departments, sections and functions to work together is a major generator of waste.

If you really want to develop a robust approach to team-working within your organisation, we suggest you ignore formulaic teambuilding approaches and ensure instead:

+ That you develop a clear set of organisational Values, indicating how individuals are expected to work and relate to each other.

+ That team development is dedicated to the task of the team – that is, that training is geared to the best way of achieving the specific business need, not 'how to be a good team member' or whatever.

+ That you also introduce powerful recognition systems to demonstrate that the achievement of business objectives by teams is really valued by management.

Tackling team development this way means that you will add value immediately to the business process. In addition, you will also have an approach that handles changes in personnel and task.

WHY TEAMS & EMPOWERMENT?

Back in 1989, when Leyland Trucks was trying to think through the requirements of a new culture, it came up with the following *Principles for Effective Employee Engagement*:

+ Decisions must be delegated to the lowest practical level of the organisation.

+ Communication must be natural and ongoing at the supervisor / subordinate level.

+ Demarcation lines should only be drawn on capability.

- Consultation is not enough, we must educate and train to exploit and develop the individual talents and expertise of the workforce.

- No-one should feel more or less an employee than any other.

Today, many years on, if you were to ask this now-renowned exponent of employee engagement about the validity of these initial thoughts, it probably would not deviate from them. True, Leyland might want to change some of the terminology, but the spirit and intent remains intact. These principles will be at the heart of any engagement programme.

Interestingly, if you crawl through these statements and attempt to distil further, you will come up with lots of references to 'empowerment', but little that points to 'team-working'. Does that mean the latter is less important or even not needed?

We think not. Teams are not just the product of social engineering, nice things to have. Experience tells us that they are vital instruments in achieving your business's necessary competitiveness. The key word here is synergy, a term that has come to mean much more than its dictionary definition of a 'combined or coordinated action'. It is now recognised that, properly managed, a collection of disparate personalities, experiences and knowledge can achieve far more than the mere sum of individual contributions. To most of us, this is fairly obvious, it's nothing new. And yet, the vast majority of teambuilding workshops tend to strive for a bland sameness that could undermine the real dynamics of a 'synergetic team'. Differences need to be celebrated as well as managed.

In essence, therefore, the whole rationale behind organisations having teams is to improve business performance. This includes:

- Productivity, quality and efficiency improvements.

- Involvement, participation and ideas generation.

- Lead time, cycle time and inventory improvements.

- Flexibility, added value and process reliability.

- Design advances, innovation and creativity.

- Motivation, satisfaction and empowerment.

The energy or vitality of a team characterised by differences, linked to a common desire, will take you much further than down these paths than any robotic groupings. Ensure, therefore, that your establishment and management teams seek and sponsor that spark.

TYPES OF TEAMS

It is important to recognise that not every team needs the same level of nurturing and support. Their requirements vary considerably. For convenience, we often distinguish between four specific types:

- ◆ Directed teams.
- ◆ Lean teams.
- ◆ Self-managing teams.
- ◆ Project teams.

Directed Teams

These are traditional teams, such as departmental or functional groupings, that operate under a rigid hierarchy and are characterised by largely-centralised decision-making. Some limited latitude is allowed, but generally the term 'team' is probably a misnomer. Examples would be a Finance function or Information Systems department. These are convenient affiliations of people operating under a functional, or even professional, banner. Interaction within the group is probably fairly limited. The motivational force here, aside from the usual top-down direction, is the camaraderie and comradeship obtained from being part of a designated group.

Training requirements depend on how much interaction and interdependence is required from the group. In many instances, the use of the communication, recognition and management style recommendations noted earlier will suffice. We have already observed how the introduction of 'early morning huddles' can have a profound effect on bonding. Where there is only a limited need for individuals to *work* closely together, we would see little benefit in formal teambuilding training.

Lean Teams

Lean teams are usually found in high-volume, short-cycle manufacturing or parallel areas that replicate the 'high-task, low discretion' characteristic of the work. A team of check-out operators in a supermarket perhaps would fall into this category. They are a natural development of Tayloristic thinking, as usually their use is encouraged by their greater efficiency over other models of workplace organisation. A degree of empowerment is encouraged, but only at the margins of their activity, as generally they are far too busy to do anything other than address the direct needs of the process.

Training requirements here are very specific, therefore. First, employees in Lean Teams need to be encouraged to think much more holistically about their role. Faced with a moving conveyor, a fast-moving machine or a telephone that must be answered in a rigorous and repetitive routine, it is easy for an operator to think solely of the task in hand. It is also just as easy for them to become bored or even resentful. This encouragement and attention becomes absolutely vital in avoiding the negative consequences of the role.

Second, they have to be trained in very specific disciplines to maximise the benefit of whatever discretionary time they have at their disposal or time earmarked specifically for continuous improvement. One of the dangers of 'Quality Time', for example, where the process is stopped to allow workers to contribute to process improvement, is poor direction. If this valuable time is not controlled and earmarked specifically for effective problem-solving, the workforce may come to regard it as a legitimate relaxation period or an opportunity to 'skive'. Once this thought becomes embedded, then it becomes very difficult to shift.

Finally again, the quick wins of communication, recognition and management style are needed to reinforce the seriousness and worthwhileness of intent. There is little point in resorting to the more elaborate teambuilding training activities here, as most of it would never be used.

Self-managing Teams

Also known 'Self-directed Work Teams' or 'Autonomous Work Groups', these can be found in any area of business, commerce or industry. The key differentiator here is the extent to which they are responsible for much of the detailed decision-making undertaken on a daily basis. They feature an absence of hierarchy and high levels of interaction within the group. Commonly, the perception of hierarchy may be masked by the appointment of Team Leaders, where hopefully the view of the latter is that of a 'principal peer' within the group. This is absolutely vital, as care must be taken to avoid the alienation of the 'leader' from his/her colleagues. Otherwise, they will not perceive themselves to be self-managing.

Self-directed teams can be found anywhere where the task offers the opportunity for high individual, or collective, discretion. Their training and maintenance needs are high. First, the surrounding culture needs to be supportive. Second, individuals need to be armed with skills to help them perform as effective team members. Within this category, you could include listening skills, problem-solving techniques, facilitation, working with others, etc. Many of these can be addressed by short bite-sized sessions run by local managers.

There is also a key requirement for those responsible for the teams, or those administering routine support, to understand the dynamics here. Self-managing teams are notoriously difficult to get going in traditional organisations. Mistrust, suspicion and a fear of a blame culture can undermine the best of intentions. Self-managing teams are, in summary, the most difficult to establish and maintain, but the rewards of successful implementation are considerable.

Project Teams

Project teams can be found anywhere and are usually constructed for a specific purpose. The team will be created around a task that, when complete, will result in the group disbanding. In Action Planning, 'multi-functional focus groups' are, in essence, short-term project teams designed to promote involvement and empowerment by expediting problem resolution.

Training needs will vary according to the size, nature and intended longevity of the group. At the smaller end, good facilitation may suffice. At the other extreme, the group may need help in working together and in understanding each other's strengths and weaknesses.

In some respects, the project team is the most important type of team for an empowered organisation. Self-directed teams are enormously powerful, but are risky and take time and effort to create. Project teams need less maintenance and also offer lots of additional benefits, including:

♦ An effective way of solving problems.

♦ An effective way of countering interdepartmental disharmony.

♦ An effective way of developing and retaining organisational high fliers.

The last should not be dismissed. In both small organisations and those that have seen fit to flatten management hierarchy, the opportunities for traditional vertical promotion are limited. Project teams offer the prospect of 'diagonal' progression, where individuals can be developed by greater responsibilities on a short- to medium-term basis. As they advance, they can be given projects of greater complexity and importance.

The use of project teams in promoting cross-departmental interaction is also to be recommended. In fact, many companies view the classic T-chart organisation structures as just a frame for 'bread and rations'. The real work takes place at the project group level. Whilst it is difficult to draw this as a two-dimensional model, there are few difficulties with implementation. In essence, what you are trying to create is a 'dynamic matrix' structure, something that sounds extremely complicated. In layman's terms, what you want is a traditional functional organisation alongside lots and lots of project teams! Simple enough?

DEPLOYMENT

Some might think the description above is a little too *ad hoc*. Students of organisational design may be much more vociferous in their opinions. However, again, the key determinant of success is not in the actual structure, but in how you manage it. For example, it is absolutely vital that project activity mirrors organisational priority – in other words, that project teams work on the things that are important to the company. Whilst this may seem to be self-evident, in our experience, most companies fail miserably here. They neglect to inform sufficiently on either task or targets. Teams end up working on secondary, or even tertiary, issues, without any knowledge of priority or aspiration. This is not just wasteful, it will also turn out to be demotivating and demoralising.

Case Study 25

In the early 80s, Quality Circles were all the rage. Philip ran a satellite operation of a large company. He learned that the Central Quality Group had ordained the early introduction of the concept. Philip's area, a foundry, was the first of the pilots.

Philip was a bit perplexed about the logic here. He was told that neither he nor any other manager could have any say in the selection of the project. Likewise, implementation had to be the exclusive province of the selected teams and their new friends, the consultants sent in by Central Quality.

A product was duly selected for the first quality circle, much to Philip's protestations. However, protocol dictated that he wasn't allowed even to articulate his concerns. On paper, the outcome eight weeks later seemed a roaring success. Floor-to-floor times were reduced by 60%, likely defects by 30% and overall costs by 25%. The proud team duly reported to Philip what they'd done and how they'd done it. He didn't have the heart to tell them the product was being discontinued in six months.

Sadly, when news broke out, the damage to Quality Circles was terminal and not at all very helpful to future engagement proposals. The company quickly learned that 'top down' quite definitely has its place.

Figure 35 shows the Employee Engagement Deployment Model used at several companies we have encountered. We strongly recommend that you follow this discipline, especially in smaller concerns where distractions can so often make you lose sight of the real end game. You can make this as complicated as you see fit. At its simplest level, you could complete the entire process in a few hours and, at the end, have a list of priorities for the entire organisation cascaded down to team, or even individual, level.

Figure 35: The Employee Engagement Deployment Model

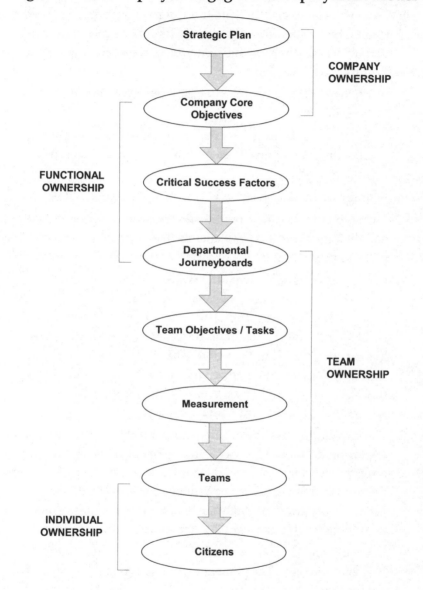

Follow these simple steps:

1. From your Strategic Plan, either written down or in your head (preferably written-down!), identify four to six core objectives that reflect the direction and ambition of the company. Examples could include:

    ◊ Making a 15% return on sales, 20% return on capital investment.

    ◊ Eliminating the overdraft after 12 months and, thereafter, operating with a positive cash flow over each 12-month rolling period.

    ◊ Improve market share by 12% within two years.

    The emphasis should be on the most relevant business targets and their quantification. Statements like 'to grow the business' or 'to be profitable' are not allowed, as they have no numbers.

2. Each function reviews what they have to do to help the company meet the Core Objectives. By discussion, you arrive at a set of Critical Success Factors (CSFs), the achievement of which will support the attainment of the Core Objectives. There are likely to be more CSFs than Core Objectives but don't go daft! You want to retain focus. In addition, most CSFs will be cross-functional targets rather than merely functional ones. Here's where your project teams come in handy.

3. The Critical Success Factors are further broken down into departmental aims. Each department accepts the CSFs appropriate to them and analyses further. Note that a department here could mean a function or a major project group. A departmental 'journey board' is created, listing and describing its objectives and how it intends to achieve them.

4. This targeting is further cascaded, to give individual teams objectives or tasks. The great benefit here is that the team now knows that their efforts are going to be expended in an exact fit of company requirements.

5. Each Stage from 1 to 4 has quantified targets attached to it. You have to ensure that progress is monitored routinely and non-compliances investigated.

The appropriateness and relevance of team efforts in continuous improvement are vital. By carrying out the above, the team first will see the bigger picture. Second, the team will know that it is using its energies optimally in pursuit of objectives that tie in directly with those of the company. Done correctly, teams will see that the deployment of challenges and responsibilities reflect real needs and priorities. This, in turn, generates real ownership, the holy grail of engagement.

We recommend that, within the limits of commercial confidentiality, you promote this through visual displays. Your offices, shops or plant should be adorned with posters, pictures and billboards prioritising in plain English your principal aspirations. Whilst care needs to be taken not to lapse into spin or propaganda, we can learn a lot here from the advertising industry.

CONTRACTING WITH TEAMS

It is often very productive to allow teams a little time for quiet reflection facilitated by a particularly empathetic manager or specialist. One highly effective routine is to get the group to consider what it wanted from management and what they thought the company wanted from them. This is then distilled into a 'team contract' that reflects the behaviour they expect from each other. A sample is shown in **Figure 36**.

Team contracts can be highly useful for the group in a number of ways. First, it can help address tensions in the team as the voice of the majority is heard. Second, it helps develop, for them, a unique code of behaviour that reinforces its distinct identity. But, most importantly of all, it gives all the team members a chance, perhaps for the first time, to think through the whole rationale behind team-working and its role in the common good. We in management take such things for granted, as it is part and parcel of daily life and debate. For others, however, this is new and challenging. Allowing them the opportunity to cogitate and challenge can be enormously beneficial.

Figure 36: A Sample Team Contract

Contract - Team B

We, the undersigned, agree that during the 'Development
of the Empowered Team Process', we will act and behave
with the following considerations:

♦ We will trust in each other, by showing honesty and
   openness, to develop belief in one another and in what we
   are trying to achieve.

♦ We will adopt a flexible attitude,

♦ We will show full support of each other, allowing input from
   all.

♦ Advice will be offered, not dictated,

♦ We will operate in an environment that allows occasional
   foul-ups and in which constructive criticism is valued.

♦ We will commit to the team and the development process
   with enthusiasm.

Signed: ... ...

Problem Areas

As you dig deeper into the world of employee engagement, you will
see lots that can go wrong with team-working. The answer is total
vigilance, especially in the early phases of introduction. The key
indicator, as we have said repeatedly, is employee perception. If they
feel there is a problem, then there probably is!

A few case studies:

Case Study 26

Jimmy was a manager in a manufacturing outfit that was
undergoing a transition from hierarchical management to an
essentially team-based one. Jimmy ran one half of the operation,
a colleague the other. The latter had been selected to pilot the
philosophy and structures. Considerable progress had been made
by reinforcing local identity, new communications and recognition
systems and by increasing subordinate-to-supervisor ratios.
Accordingly, Jimmy was given the green light to go ahead as well.

Jimmy was a huge enthusiast and an embracer of the new. It was
not surprising that he tackled his new challenge with energy and
gusto. Within days, the whole area was rechristened 'The A
Team', locker and rest areas painted in distinctive team colours
and a local mission / value statement published. As time passed,
he could proudly cite significant improvements in performance,

quality and morale. Everything seemed to be going in the right direction ... but ... !

Before too long, senior management's attention and focus was drawn to the consequences of excessive competitiveness between the 'A Team' and its counterpart. Due in no small part to the desire of Jimmy and his colleague each to be seen to be doing the best, both teams ended up at each other's throats with frequent arguments about service levels, capability and even alleged sabotage.

In short, in their haste to get local team-working underway, senior management had allowed the big picture to slip by. Instead of improved harmony all round, they found themselves dealing with two conflicting tribes and a battleground readily delineated by separate colour schemes. The selection of a neutral and calming shade of beige was only the first step in rebuilding!

Case Study 27

Bill was very enthusiastic about moving to self-managing work groups in his organisation. His business was not terribly suited to top-down management, due to its volatility and uncertainty. Decisions had to be taken as close to the customer interface as possible and local autonomy seemed to be the right way forward. Accordingly, Bill set about restructuring his team. Supervisors were redeployed to support functions. Key Operators were selected after rigorous interpersonal skill and capability testing. Despite no differential being offered for this new position, there was no shortage of applicants. However, the intensive training programme may have appealed to some.

Transitional arrangements complete, Bill launched his self-managing work groups to universal acclaim. To his surprise, nobody had a problem with them. Over the first two months, Bill marvelled at the smooth introduction. Productivity, cost and quality targets were comfortably exceeded.

However, cracks began to appear in month three. Key Operators complained of stress and alienation from their teams. Team members complained of inadequate support and many urged the restoration of orthodox supervision.

After much investigation, and reference to others who had been down the same journey, Bill discovered the root of the problem. He hadn't got rid of supervision, he'd merely replaced it with someone far less trained, probably less capable and without the real or natural authority to carry it off. In short, the Key Operator had been so overloaded that a pseudo-hierarchy had been created, replicating in the eyes of the workforce the model that had been deleted.

The solution was to create within the group several 'champions', specialists who could look after specific activities. The Key Operator would merely coordinate their roles or fill in if necessary, where time off the job was needed. Ultimately, the Key Operator became less the focus of attention of the group and more a peer with additional responsibilities. Peace resumed.

Case Study 28

Chris worked as a plant manager for a chemical company undergoing a culture change inspired by a change of ownership. He followed all the rules assiduously and ensured that all management received sufficient training and that they moved in line with a carefully-constructed plan. In his support areas, Chris saw an immediate payback, as employees reacted really positively. However, his production units did not seem to respond at all and much of his communication and training activity seemed to sail straight over their heads. Chris was completely bemused. He had carried out exactly the same process with the two groups under his control. On one, it worked like a dream. On the other, it worked like a drain. He could not understand it at all.

Detailed investigation identified the problem, but not the solution. Production, in common with most chemical plants, took place on continental shift systems. Each shift would be staffed by a small number of process operators and a supervisor, the plant being very capital-intensive. As these were permanent arrangements, these groupings were longstanding, with people working with the same colleagues for many years.

The company had experienced a troubled history, both competitively and internally. Relationships had traditionally been very poor all round, with particular weaknesses between the shift teams and dayshift management, as well as between one group and another on adjoining shifts.

The net consequence of all this was the emergence of a micro-culture that was infinitely stronger than the corporate culture. So Chris's well-intentioned, but limited, interjections were futile. A solution is still sought.

SUMMARY

Team-working and empowerment are much used expressions in the vocabulary of anyone entering the world of employee engagement. Much has been written about both areas, and a whole army of consultants and trainers are ready to help with an array of persuasive tools.

We strongly advise any organisation going down this road to move with caution. Your biggest challenge is in understanding the dynamics of what is going on rather than seeking 'one size fits all' solutions. Improvement will be happening anyway, as your work on communications, recognition and management style begins to bite. This will be augmented by the outputs of multi-functional focus groups on external customer focus, internal customer focus and, to come, continuous improvement.

So, unless you see an immediate need to leap into autonomous work groups, we advise you to leave such embellishments to the second or third iteration. Then you'll have far fewer problems when you come to introduce them.

Figure 37: The Route Map updated 7

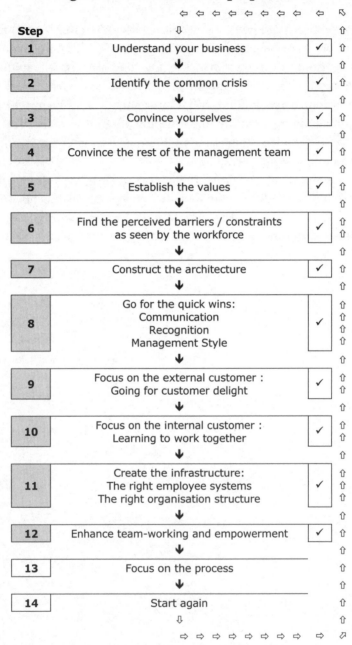

15
CASHING IN I: BACKGROUND

There has been a temptation to start every chapter so far with the words: *"This is the most important section of the book"*. We will continue to resist doing it again but, believe us, from here on in lie the critical stages in reaping the rewards of all the hard work vested in your cultural foundation.

Many organisations, perhaps most organisations, do not actually get to this point. Some fail because they have simply been unable to win the 'hearts and minds' *of the workforce*. As you will have discovered already, this is always down to managerial weakness rather than any insurmountable resistance from the ranks. Others are so chuffed at the attitudinal benefits of employee engagement that they lose the ambition to push the organisational development further. This is a pity, as the pace of change quite easily can be quickened and, almost certainly, will result in an even more motivated workforce. Sitting on your laurels is not the wisest thing to do in this highly competitive world, either.

THE DRIVING FORCE

There is perhaps a natural concern that employees may not empathise innately with all the cultural stuff we have banged on about so far. Inevitably, goes the theory, all this latent goodwill and enthusiasm will rapidly evaporate when you start on the real challenge of improving business processes.

However, we might accept some validity in this statement in more traditional, hierarchical organisations. Employees here see processes as instruments of control or bureaucracy. Their natural tendency, therefore, is to be cautious, if not downright sceptical. On the contrary, in an engaged workforce, processes and procedures will become 'owned' by employees, who, in turn, become far less tolerant of weaknesses and waste. It is questionable which is the most frustrating for the average worker: management inadequacy or poor process performance? Irrespective of relative merit, we can all agree that the latter is a major contributor to the stresses and strains of daily life. Once employees are empowered to do something about fallibilities in the ways that work is conducted, the chances are that they are going to be more than keen to get involved.

Within Perception Barrier Analysis, it is usual to include a number of questions on this very subject, for example:

> *"I feel I could make a greater contribution to the organisation."*

> *"I can see ways of operating more efficiently."*

> *"My job could be made more interesting and challenging."*

In well over a decade of surveying even the most resistant of organisations, we have yet to encounter anything less than a positive response to all three. Once people get involved and see themselves making a difference, their desire and energy to do more increases dramatically. This is a real win : win situation. The employee benefits through:

- Less frustration.
- Less hassle.
- A feeling of accomplishment.
- Improved self-esteem.
- Improved interaction with colleagues.
- Ultimately, improved job security.

Likewise, the organisation will see:

- Better quality.
- Better process conformance.
- Better flow.
- Better customer satisfaction.
- Better performance.
- Fewer 'industrial relations' issues (less 'us and them').

If you have successfully executed steps 1 to 12 in the Route Map, you will almost certainly be ready for this next exciting push. It is unlikely that you will have fine-tuned every cultural idiosyncrasy, but that is not a concern. Over the years, you will constantly revisit, reiterate and enhance your cultural foundation, as it flexes and responds to new challenges and circumstances. The key determinant is whether a critical mass of the workforce is ready for this big step forward. Once you're happy that they are, then it is time to press on!

THE FIRST STEPS

Business process excellence starts with senior management, the men or women at the top. Experience tells us that organisations that flourish in this area do so because senior management drive the approach 'top-down'. They show interest, enthusiasm and determination. They build structures. They set priorities. They scrupulously measure, audit and review.

To some readers, this may seem to reflect the 'command and control' style this book is trying so hard to undermine. However, the new management paradigm, *inspiring people to manage themselves*, demands that management efforts are shifted from micro-management, or 'control freakery', into a carefully-constructed architecture for effective delegation. Otherwise, the prevailing culture will lapse into abdication and apathy. The trick is to combine strong management with self-generating, bottom-up ownership and involvement.

In the earlier chapter on Team-working (**Chapter 14**), we introduced you to the Employee Engagement Deployment model. In essence, this is simply a means of constructing a business plan that becomes relevant to all employees. By identifying and cascading top level goals, you can ensure that all departments, teams and individuals work on priorities that are meaningful to the company and which do not simply emerge as a product of departmental self-interest.

We stress very strongly here that, whilst it is sensible to identify goals covering the entire remit of management responsibility, it is impossible for the organisation to work on everything. Business Links, we noted earlier, for example, are expected to respond to upwards of 140 KPIs. This is grounded in the false notion that the more you measure, the more you get done. Government itself is often a classic example of creating numerous priorities, often in an attempt to avoid making the crucial, but essential, choices. The danger in such a notion is that management efforts will be so dispersed as to become an impotent, bureaucratic paper-chase. To be successful, your senior management team must limit the priority targets to a few important variables, the 'critical few'. And then chase them like hell!

Recent research by Stephen Covey and Bain & Company point to sustained profitable growth being a function of:

♦ **Focusing on the core:** Carefully determining those few critical variables which will impact on the organisation's immediate future, and

♦ **Executing with precision:** Ensuring the organisation keeps a clear, determined emphasis on the delivery of these targets and does not allow distractions to get in the way.

Some might now be throwing their hands up and saying that this is yet another statement of the obvious. We agree, but, sadly, the difference between knowing and doing in some British institutions is enormous. If you remain sceptical upon this point, we simply encourage you to take a short, informal survey of attitudes to 'change and improvement' in your organisation. There is an 80% chance that one or all of the following comments will appear repeatedly:

> *"We're starters, not finishers."*

> *"We suffer from initiativitis."*

> *"We dread it when the boss goes on a course. Back comes the latest flavour of the month."*

> *"Paralysis by analysis."*

> *"We never, ever, see anything through."*

> *"We've no idea where this company is going. We change from day to day."*

Sadly, in larger organisations, many of these comments will come from your middle management team! If they don't know where they're going, how can they possibly direct others to the eventual destination?

Our starting point, therefore, is **Figure 38**. From your overall Vision, you will set a discrete number of core objectives as discussed in **Chapter 14**. You need to prioritise if this number exceeds four or five. For each of these priorities, you first set budgetary-type targets to satisfy your investors and bankers. Each department then decides how best it is going to contribute to these core objectives, by determining its own Critical Success Factors. Remember, it will not be possible to 'departmentalise' everything. Many objectives will be achievable only by departments working together.

Figure 38: Building the Platform for Business Process Excellence

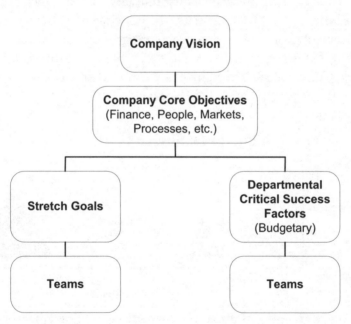

However careful and sensible you are about conducting this phase, you will inevitably stick in the 'land of the readily achievable'. Budgets, especially those for external consumption, tend to reflect only modest, incremental change. Managers, as a consequence, tend to reside in their comfort zones and are not tempted to 'think outside of the box'. Unsurprisingly, that's where they'll stay, until overtaken by crisis.

Increasingly, many companies are adopting 'stretch goals' in key business performance areas. Say, for example, we want to enhance cash flow by improving the number of times we turn our inventory over in a year. The budgetary approach would probably limit improvement to, perhaps, 5%, as the management team feel that sort of level is deliverable. They would work diligently towards the 5%, but are highly unlikely to exceed it as, frankly, there is no compunction or incentive to do so. But if, as well as the budgetary target, we give them a stretch goal of a 30% improvement, a different mentality emerges. Here, they have to look afresh at all the variables that influence inventory turns and *think again*, often challenging the fundamental assumptions and processes that underpin their conventional approaches. In these situations, quantum leaps in efficiency can often be attained. **Figure 39** demonstrates the principle here. By going for an improvement goal of Snowdon, we might get there or thereabouts. By targeting Everest, we may not get there, but could finish up at an intermediate point such as Kilimanjaro. And, when we went to school, Kilimanjaro was a lot higher than Skiddaw!

Figure 39: Stretch Goals

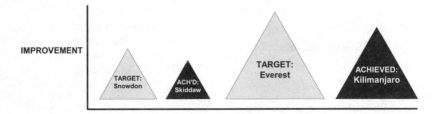

Naturally, the setting of Stretch Goals demands a different supporting methodology to simple budgetary targets. We have to encourage people to be creative, to take controlled risks and to question conventional wisdom. It is therefore best pursued in a spirit of adventure, with senior management acting both as cheerleaders and consciences! Properly managed, the concept of stretch goals can be both tremendously motivating and enormously productive. In your competitive world, it is an opportunity that cannot be neglected.

TIME – THE ENEMY!

The lack of focus on process integrity can be quite alarming in many companies. Business processes seem to 'work' (we use that expression loosely) through a combination of good luck and permanent fire-fighting. In other words, processes are usually controlled by attention to 'outputs'. And, inevitably, that's inefficient and often too late.

When asked why management doesn't spend more effort in first ensuring that business processes run the way they are designed and, second, in optimising their effectiveness, the answer is invariably: *"Time"*. It is not difficult to feel sympathetic here. Business nowadays is so much more complex and difficult than as recently as 15 to 20 years ago. Then, it was fairly common for companies to succeed by being 'niche', good at a few variables but moderate in the rest. Today, it seems you have to be good at everything, otherwise you will be picked off by a competitor who is exactly that. As a consequence the typical load of your average manager is much greater than yesteryear. And they know it.

How then does one break out of this increasingly vicious circle? We heartily recommend that you do this by first *understanding your load*. Here is a little exercise that should take no more than a few minutes over a month:

♦ Keep a sheet of paper with you during your working day. Every time you do a different activity, write it down. Continue to do so over a 'representative' period, usually two to four weeks.

♦ Once you feel you have covered every aspect of your working life, go back to your list. For each activity, come up with a quick estimate of how much time each week you really need to devote to it *to carry it out routinely and effectively*.

♦ Add up these time elements.

And the result? A major mismatch. Typically, in small to medium-sized enterprises, managers are loaded with 50 to 70 hours per week against a standard 35 to 40 hour envelope. Something has to give.

We respond in a number of ways:

1. **We put the HOURS in.** Despite so many UK managers nowadays doing exactly this, it is not guaranteed to be effective. So much of our daily grind has to be carried out in the 'normal' working week that simply adding excessive overtime doesn't work. But lots of us do it anyway, because it makes us feel better.

2. **We run FASTER.** This is the second favourite option, beloved especially of operations managers. A quick glance at the typical nicknames bestowed by knowing workforces gives us a clue to effectiveness here. 'Crazy Horse', 'Geronimo' and 'The Roadrunner', for example, probably tell us all we need to know about this approach!

3. **We take SHORTCUTS.** We don't have the time to do everything properly so we look for quick answers, leading to errors and misjudgements.

4. **We take RISKS.** Working life for all managers becomes a matter of continuous risk-taking in any situation, particularly in the private sector. However, as time gets compressed, we tend to become bolder, with the inevitable consequences. Alternatively, we may do the same thing out of sheer desperation.

   or finally, quite simply,

5. **We plan to FAIL.** Very few of us in management actually own up to this. We may even delude ourselves by simply not considering the possibility. But the truth is that many in authority handle the constraints of time by focussing on a few priorities and wishing / hoping the rest will manage itself. Unsurprisingly, it doesn't, but we comfort ourselves with expressions like *"We did our best"*.

None of the options above are acceptable either to the efficient running of the business or the quality of life of the manager. We need to appreciate that the complexities of modern life created by technological, competitive and social shifts have made traditional management styles redundant. In particular, it is clear that 'command and control' is nowadays only appropriate to a minority of situations. If we truly want to achieve both effectiveness and life balance, we must give up on attempting to 'manage' people. The real added value comes from encouraging, educating and training people to manage themselves. By doing this, we can transfer responsibility and accountability for the execution of operational detail and minutiae to individuals and leave management to concentrate on broader strategic issues.

Moving to radical levels of employee engagement does not increase managerial workload, as many fear. Ironically, the reality is the opposite. All those who successfully exploit this philosophy find that they have much more time to plan and organise than ever before. The shift from a preoccupation with operational detail to a clear focus on operational strategy is not only intellectually more attractive, but it's even better for your blood pressure!

However, achieving this heady state is going to take some time, as everybody becomes accustomed to the new management paradigm and the necessary trust and respect builds up. In the meanwhile, we have to do something about our time constraints, otherwise we will continue to put in excessive hours, run faster, take shortcuts, take risks and plan to fail. It is time to examine our own Personal Effectivity.

This is again a simple, but highly beneficial, exercise if carried out diligently and intelligently. The objective of Personal Effectivity is to create an awareness of how you spend your time. In particular, it examines how much of your daily life you spend positively 'adding value' to the organisation and how much on waste or 'non-added value', where you are preoccupied with the consequences of your own, others' or system failures.

Step-by-step:

1. Over a set period (one to two weeks, say) keep a detailed diary of your day, listing all activities and the amount of time you spend on them. Ensure that your full working day is accounted for, from the time you arrive until the time you leave.

2. When complete, carefully analyse each activity. Was the activity genuinely 'adding value', in other words doing work essential to the ideal flow of processes and procedures across the company? Or are you in 'non-value added' mode, where you are preoccupied addressing the consequences of failure elsewhere.

3. Quantify the percentage of your time spent on waste or non-value added. In many management positions, this can be

surprisingly high. Often the major part of a working week can be devoted to the consequences of not getting things done 'right first time'.

4. Prioritise the areas you will gain most from by eliminating the causes of waste. Set about resolving the issues by working with your internal customers and suppliers as often the source of the problem lies across interfunctional boundaries.

Merely undertaking this exercise can be a real eye-opener. Typically, managers find themselves spending a goodly proportion of their time in unproductive and distracting meetings. Is it really necessary for you to attend that meeting if your contribution is limited? Is it necessary for the meeting to be held at all? If we have to have meetings, are they being conducted properly? Do they have terms of reference and followed-up action points? Are they kept to the point or do participants meander and cross-talk?

Similarly, we all complain about being submerged in paperwork. However, do we tell the originators of the multitudinous reports, correspondence and spurious e-mails that litter our companies that we don't need to know everything? So often, we find people sending out acres of print on the basis that others want and need to understand when the reality is the reverse.

When done across the entire management team rather than individually, Personal Effectivity can be both illuminating and high beneficial. At the very least, it will increase individual awareness of how much time they continually spend 'rectifying'. It will also encourage a more constructive dialogue across departmental boundaries, breaking down the 'silos' we encounter so frequently in companies. However, care must be taken not to *compare* individual added-values. It is relatively meaningless. Someone working in quality or logistics department is likely to have a higher percentage of non-added value than a colleague in sales or engineering. These levels should be datums, starting points for self-improvement.

Second, do not become over prescriptive about the definition of non-value added. As this is not an absolute science, we can alter the definition as we progress. Some people start with an extremely rigorous interpretation, others with a more liberal version. There is little benefit in engaging in long intellectual debate. The objective is to get individuals and teams first to recognise the waste around them and then to start to eliminate it. The more they work on it, the more they'll appreciate the subject. Like elsewhere in this book, Personal Effectivity is as much about motivation as it is about prescription.

SUMMARY

The real benefits of radical employee engagement start to flow when these new levels of interest, enthusiasm and commitment are used to tackle processes. Using the expertise and talent of a much greater proportion of the workforce, we can start to unlock business process excellence.

However, before we launch into it, we need to ensure that our cultural foundation is best placed to drive forward. Management, therefore, needs a top-down framework of understanding and priorities to ensure employees are steered towards the important areas. Stretch goals, alongside normal budgetary targets, can help enormously here. This should cause us to break the mould that is best expressed by the maxim 'doing what we have always done, gets us what we have always got.'

Covey's advice on focussing on a few key variables and 'executing with precision' is invaluable in helping to avoid the distraction and dilution of effort so often seen here. And, finally, the journey has to start with managers looking at their own effectiveness, particularly in relation to their own time management. Done successfully, this will both set an example and inspire others to go further.

16
CASHING IN II: TECHNIQUES

There are thousands of books written on the subject of Continuous Improvement. There are a similar number of different techniques and tools that can be deployed to smooth your path towards business process excellence. The dilemmas are often: which technique, which approach and which guru?

Because of the industry that surrounds this subject, there has been an increasingly unhealthy emphasis on *instantly* applying some of the more familiar tools. Given what we learned earlier, it should therefore be no surprise to us that failure rates are often high. With sizeable financial outlays, long payback periods and frequent failure, it is little wonder that badly-burnt management back away from venturing twice into the world of continuous improvement. This is a real tragedy, as many of the more common approaches can be instrumental in transforming business results.

With this in mind, it is self-evident that a book of this nature must be very cautious about steering its readership towards specific tools and techniques. From the huge catalogue of well-intentioned management initiatives devoted to continuous improvement, how do we decide which is best for the typical small- to medium-sized operation?

At first sight, our choice of application may seem surprising to our average reader. However, the work of Jim Sumner (Operations Director) and Allister Butler (Materials Manager) of Leyland Trucks is felt to be entirely appropriate here, despite the physical size of this complex operation in comparison to that of our average SME reader. What Jim, in particular, has done is to take the best of the many alternative strategies available to companies and to distil them into a simple, resilient and workable philosophy. As a consequence, the business has graduated to genuinely world-class status in all its products, processes and procedures. There are few exemplars of that level anywhere in UK business today and even fewer in the manufacturing sector. By carefully analysing Jim's approach, we can construct a platform suitable for any of our SME readership.

Typically, the routine adopted by most organisations in going down the continuous improvement path is, in sequence:

♦ Identification and acceptance of the need for change.

♦ Selection of appropriate tools and methodologies – for example, TQM, Six Sigma or Kaizen.

♦ Creation of an internal organisational structure to support it.

♦ Management commitment, belief and enthusiasm to drive it home.

Sadly, experience tells us that each stage becomes successively less effective, the further down the list you go. In the end, more often than not, the 'change initiative' fails.

Jim and his team recognised the deep cynicism characteristic of many organisations when it came to top-down-inspired, new initiatives. 'Flavour of the month', unfortunately, has become the stamp of organisational disapproval, leading to resistance, subversion and, ultimately, rejection by the workforce at large. With this background common to the majority of enterprises, we can readily see that simply inflicting some complex, and often alien, initiative on the resistant masses is not ideally positioned to succeed.

A better approach is:

♦ As before, identification and acceptance of the need for change.

♦ Build up the organisational structures and infrastructures to tackle the situation. In essence, this involves the Business Planning and Employee Engagement Deployment models described in **Chapters 14** and **15**. Here, we seek to ensure that the bigger picture is understood and that direction and priorities are clearly set by management. 'Top-down'-created, but 'bottom-up' awareness and involvement.

♦ Constant attention to maximising management commitment, belief and enthusiasm to ensure the process becomes embedded into the organisation psyche.

♦ Involvement, engagement and empowerment of the workforce.

♦ Selection of appropriate tools and methodologies.

The key difference here is that the priority is given to developing both the organisational infrastructure and collective attitudes towards continuous improvement BEFORE the actual approach is selected. The company, therefore, is driven by its overall vision, not the artificial, externally-inspired tool or methodology. TQM, Six Sigma, Kaizen, etc become viewed as mere artefacts in the process, not the process itself. This greatly enhances the overall sense of ownership, responsibility and accountability.

Figure 40 describes the overall approach here, where business processes are inextricably linked to both Leadership and Culture. To be competitive, a company has to have all three work synchronously and smoothly with no gaps, barriers or disjoints.

Figure 40: Your Improvement Model

Each area is co-dependent on each other, creating at its core a culture of *Team Enterprise*.

With this background firmly in our minds, we can start now to examine Jim's approach to continuous improvement. He starts by defining his 'ESO' methodology below:

- Sumner's ESO Methodology:
  - ◊ Process **E**limination
  - ◊ Process **S**treamlining
  - ◊ Process **O**ptimisation.

STEP 1: PROCESS ELIMINATION

Interestingly, Jim always starts with the 'E' in 'ESO', which stands for 'elimination'. The rationale behind this is very straightforward.

Very rarely do we have the opportunity to construct organisational processes from scratch. Even more rarely do we get the time to examine how systems and processes *really* work in action, as distinct from the theoretic plan. Looking at **Figure 41**, the routine commences with someone constructing the 'macro-process'. This is then interpreted and reinterpreted at least twice in supportive micro-processes, activities and tasks.

Figure 41: Process Hierarchy

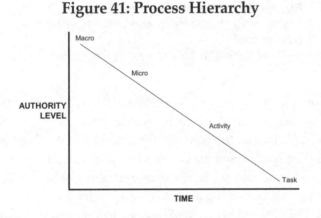

What tends to happen is that great care is expended on addressing the needs of the macro process at the top. However, due to all sorts of reasons, including lack of information, time and understanding, others develop subsidiary processes that are less than ideal. As a consequence, additional unnecessary steps become accepted as standard practice. Your organisation will be riddled by such waste or, to use the expression used in **Chapter 15**, 'non-value added activities'.

Look at the example in **Figure 42**, which describes a simple assembly operation. Within this six-minute cycle, analysis identifies 14 separate and distinct activities. However, only three, the ones in bold, actually add value. In other words, these are the steps that arguably the customer only wants to pay for. By focussing our efforts on eliminating the other unnecessary elements, we can both improve the effectiveness of the process and the competitiveness of the business.

Figure 42: Value Added Analysis

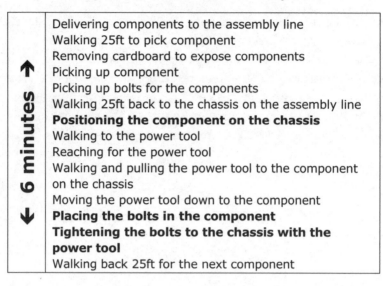

This is a manufacturing example. Traditionally, this is where the efforts on process elimination have been focused over the years. However, experience tells us that the potential for improvement is even greater in service and administration functions. Managers rarely look at efficiency here, due to the 'siloitis' we have mentioned so many times already. It is too easy to blame system malfunctions on internal customers or internal suppliers. Challenging such weaknesses can often lead, in traditional establishments, to an even greater aggravation between departments, so many simply opt for a quiet life. As a consequence, the inefficiency and waste continues unnoticed and unseen.

Tackled multifunctionally, great benefits can be realised immediately. Again, the approach is simple but highly visible.:

Brown Paper Planning

We suggest that you select a complex and troublesome process. You commandeer a sizeable conference room and cover the walls in brown paper. Upon the paper, you get people to build up optically the actual process flow, using the physical paperwork or computer-generated equivalents. We emphasis the fact that the picture has to reflect reality, not theory. One of our clients saw its order receipt process starting as shown in **Figure 44**.

Figure 43: Order Receipt Processing

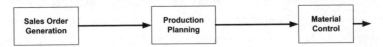

Three simple steps. However the reality was as shown in **Figure 44**.

Figure 44: Order Receipt Processing – The Reality

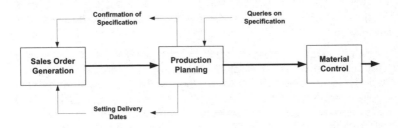

These additional routines, created by a combination of unknowing errors on the part of the internal suppliers and a total lack of understanding of process capability, actually absorbed twice as much time as the 'official process'! By highlighting and quantifying these unofficial diversions, we can improve both the efficiency and quality of the process. In another example, a process with five nominal stages turned out to have 18! It was little wonder that the company had so much difficulty with it.

Having carefully constructed the reality of the system flow, you then invite members of the various departments to come along, scrutinise and sign-off the integrity of the brown paper exercise. Unofficial diversions as these noted above should be quantified. So if 30% of invoice requests have to be returned to Sales for clarification or correction, the numbers should be clearly stated for everyone to see. This may cause some surprises!

This exercise is not just confined to Process Elimination, of course. It also becomes a useful starting point to Process Streamlining and Optimisation (which we will talk about later). However, the first approach should always be to tackle why the actual process flow differs from the ideal, theoretical model and to migrate to the latter. Persistence and clarity are two of the qualities needed here. Very frequently, these process diversions are nothing more than crutches used by employees to keep them in their comfort zones. Resistance can be quite vigorous and hostile!

An example from Jim's experience tells a story.

Case Study 29

For many years, Leyland held a dedicated and sophisticated high bay warehouse at the start of its production process. Here, the thousands of individual components were taken from suppliers' vehicles, loaded into customised containers and stored in a huge computerised warehouse, to be 'called off' as build requirements dictated.

The justification for the building of the warehouse was, at the time, commonsense and logical. Thousands of part numbers were needed to support uncertain logistical systems, unreliable suppliers and erratic customer demands. However, in turn each of these barriers was progressively improved until the cost of intermediate warehousing far exceeded its benefits. Nevertheless, the decision was not an easy one, particularly for those who relied on the 'belt and braces' approach to cover a less than totally disciplined approach to working life. Jim and his team needed to be brave in the face of opposition from the traditionalists.

The result? Material previously handled up to eight times now just needed one transaction. Inventory costs plummeted, alongside the sizeable write-offs each year for redundant or excessive stocks. In total, the company saved over £1m in annual operating costs. Not bad for a bit of lateral thinking and a lot of courage!

In short, process elimination should be the first step along any journey towards process excellence. The two examples above may not be relevant to your situation, but the principles most certainly are. We strongly recommend you select two or three complex, priority business processes that cross departmental boundaries and subject them to the same treatment. There is no real cost, aside from the brown paper! You don't need consultants, trainers or any external expert help. But by harnessing the interest and support of all involved in the system, you can unleash a great deal of motivation, enthusiasm and local knowledge. The very fact that they have contributed to the improved process will stimulate a desire for further and greater involvement. By then, your newly acquired managerial task of 'inspiring them to manage themselves' will become so much easier.

STEP 2: PROCESS STREAMLINING

Having tackled the 'E' in ESO, we now move to the 'S', which stands for 'Streamlining'. This is a generic title for a host of approaches, including:

- Cycle Time Reduction.
- Defect Elimination.
- Mistake Proofing.
- Simplification.
- Standardisation.
- Preventative Maintenance.
- Quick Changeovers.
- Reduced Waiting / Walking.

As a starting point, your brown paper system plotting will be more than useful here. If you are dealing with a physical system – for example, manufacturing, warehousing, retail etc, a physical model can also help tremendously. Jim advocates a process called 'Visioneering', where the occupiers of a particular activity participate in producing a physical model of their process. This is a simple 'Blue Peter' paper and glue exercise, where operators can visualise exactly how things are going to operate. By playing with movements and operations visually, staff can more clearly understand what's expected of them and where problems are likely to occur.

Of course, you do not have to resort to such detailed, pictorial representations. Often a two-dimensional process map will be more than adequate. Again, however, we re-emphasis the need to track reality. Paperwork flows, whether orders, invoices, receipts or whatever, can be particularly illuminating if delays, queries and returns are tracked and quantified. Quite often the majority of the life of a document supposedly flowing in the organisation is spent in a queue. By carefully building up a picture of these delays and establishing causality, solutions often follow readily. Jim is particularly taken by the experience of Edward Bear, and uses it to illustrate the point to his questioning workforce.

"Here is Edward Bear, coming downstairs now, bump, bump, bump, on the back of his head, behind Christopher Robin. It is, as far as he knows, the only way of coming downstairs, but sometimes he feels that there really is another way, **if only he could stop bumping for a moment and think of it.**"

How many of your people have been banging their heads for years without thinking of either the consequence or the solution?

There are many simple tools to aid you in your efforts to undertake the necessary streamlining of inefficient and ineffective systems. The 'basic tools' could be described as:

♦ Process Mapping (the brown paper exercise).

♦ Pareto Analysis.

♦ Five Whys.

♦ Eight Wastes.

♦ Cause and Effect Fishbone Diagrams.

♦ Process Walk Through.

♦ Spaghetti diagram.

♦ Kaizen Blitz.

There is no need for you, or indeed anybody else, to know everything about each of these tools. You, as the key decision-maker, simply have to have an overview on when they should be used. Individuals within the organisation can be trained up to become the experts in individual techniques and used to facilitate or train others when the need arises. However, the key learning point is to appreciate that this is a continuous approach, challenging all systems constantly and aggressively.

The last point is often difficult for owners and managers in SMEs to absorb. *"If it ain't broke, why fix it?"* is a common response here, which underlines an unhealthy affection for the *status quo*. For people like Jim and his team, the *status quo* is the enemy. If we continue to do tomorrow the same things as we are doing today, then any hope of competitor differentiation will evaporate. Your key source of competitiveness may well be slipping as you read, gradually but perniciously.

Second, we have to accept that there is no such thing as a static, balanced system. All systems are destined to deteriorate once they have been established. One of the famous Parkinson's Laws is that an organisation begins to decline as soon as its edifice is built. Without scrutiny, decline is inevitable. A culture of continuous improvement throughout the company is essential, even to stand still.

There are many good books on these simple approaches – for example, *Kaizen*, and its follow up, *Gemba Kaizen*, by Masaaki Imai.[6] We will not repeat all their detailed explanations here. However, it may be useful to explore a couple to emphasise the general principles involved.

Five Whys

In writing this book, we have tried to steer away from complexity and to focus on simple, effective routines. We are seeking quick wins to demonstrate the power of employee engagement. This is definitely not in any way to demean the audience. We believe passionately that most managerial issues are rooted in not 'doing the routine things routinely'. By introducing these simple checks and disciplines, we can learn quickly and together. The purists may decry management style questionnaires, perception barrier analysis, personal effectivity and so on for their simplicity, but they cannot deny their potency.

This is what attracts me to the Japanese practice of asking *"Why?"* five times. Nothing could be simpler, but each stage of questioning gets you nearer to the root cause. An example:

Q: "Why are you throwing sawdust on the floor?"

A: "Because the floor is slippery and unsafe."

Q- "Why is it slippery and unsafe?"

A: "Because there is oil on it."

---

6   Imai, M. (1986). *Kaizen: The Key to Japan's Competitive Success*. Maidenhead: McGraw-Hill Education (ISBN 007554332X). Imai, M. (1997). *Gemba Kaizen: A Commonsense Low Cost Approach to Management*. Maidenhead: McGraw-Hill Education (ISBN 0070314462).

Q: "Why is there oil on it?"

A: "Because the machine is dripping."

Q: "Why is the machine dripping?"

A: "Because oil is leaking from the oil coupling."

Q: "Why is it leaking?"

A: "Because the rubber lining inside the coupling is worn out."

Now there is a skill to carrying out this technique, believe it or not. It is vital that the questioner asks the question *empathetically*. There is nothing worse than some smart-arse repeatedly and smugly asking *"Why?"*, *"Why?"*, *"Why?"*, *"Why?"* and, by the way, *"Why?"*. Done incorrectly, the best outcome will be resentment. The worst could be a fat lip!

This is a powerful, yet simple, device where subtlety and tact become all important.

Kaizen Blitz

Kaizen is a Japanese term meaning gradual, unending improvements – doing little things better and progressing through evolution to higher and higher standards. It is viewed as an umbrella term for a host of practices developed in the United States but refined and polished in Japan. It is characterised by:

♦ Being long term and creating long lasting impacts.

♦ 'A journey of a thousand steps' – rather than one big one

♦ Being continuous and incremental, not stepchange.

♦ Involving everybody, not just an elite few.

♦ Tackled usually on a team basis, not individual.

♦ Focusing on refinement and maintenance of processes, not upheaval.

♦ Using simple, conventional techniques.

♦ Emphasising the process rather than outputs.

In short, it is ideal for employee engagement and SMEs starting down the road of continuous improvement. It is a beautifully simple concept, often made too complicated by its practitioners. Imai's books, quoted earlier, are wonderfully clear guides for anyone interested in improving their business.

Jim has rarefied the technique at Leyland Trucks with the introduction of the '*Kaizen* Blitz'. Here members of support functions go into an operational area and 'live the process' alongside the operators for three days. Armed by a battery of standard basic tools described earlier, they produce a list of 'concerns'. On day three, they consolidate this list, gain agreement from the operators on the validity and importance of their findings and allocate a responsibility to resolve each issue. Each recommendation is tracked intensely over the next two weeks to a point of closure.

The immediate benefits are obvious:

♦ Greater access and understanding of key processes by internal suppliers and customers.

♦ Enhanced sense of teamwork between the 'operational' team and its support functions.

These alone are worth the price of the entry ticket. However, the greater power of the *Kaizen* Blitz is its ability to uncover a multitude of process weaknesses. Early in the development of this process, a phenomenon referred to as the 'iceberg theory' was discovered (**Figure 45**).

Figure 45: The Iceberg Theory

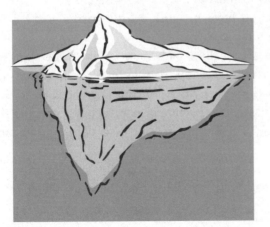

Above the water issues
Not Accepted by the organisation
Below the water or hidden issues
Accepted/Tolerated by the organisation

Before the blitz, everyone was broadly aware of those issues that were simply not acceptable to all. However, progressively, they also uncovered a multitude of non-compliances below the water level that were routinely taken 'as a fact of life' by the operational staff. Their tolerance level, based no doubt on years of system malfunction, was inordinately high by process excellence standards. The *Kaizen* Blitz was able to uncover and, ultimately, rectify and eliminate them.

A version of the *Kaizen* Blitz could easily be tailored for your area, whether that be a call centre, a retail establishment, a service provider, a building society or whatever. Just imagine the power this technique would have in the Health Service – in hospitals or doctors' surgeries! Don't worry if your colleagues are not yet fully conversant with all the potential that *Kaizen* can provide. After all, you can always go back and do it again. But done properly in a spirit of employee engagement, you could see very swift returns.

STEP 3: PROCESS OPTIMISATION

Thus far, we have managed to keep things relatively simple. This last section however, the 'O' in Jim's ESO, can be somewhat complicated to the uninitiated. Rather than omitting it, we have decided to retain a potted version of process optimisation. Once you have explored and exploited process elimination and process streamlining, the opportunities to go even further are tremendous. One way of looking at it is to see the first two as harvesting the 'low hanging fruit'. If you want to clear the tree, you have to work a little harder! And that's where process optimisation comes in.

In essence, what we are dealing with here is first understanding and then maximising *process capability*. People tend to think that this only applies to manufacturing activities, but nothing could be further from the truth. All processes, irrespective of nature, have a propensity to fail. To make progress, it will ultimately be essential to understand the nature of that failure.

To demonstrate this, we will look at an example far away from the manufacturing arena. Inspired by John Seddon's excellent work

Freedom from Command & Control,[7] which looks at the application of the Toyota production system to service industries, we here gaze into the world of call centres.

Case Study 30

Geraldine has been appointed manager in a sales and service department. Her principal task is to take calls from clients regarding sales promotions, service enquiries and general complaints. She must satisfy them through a reasonably predictable, formulaic routine. She has 12 call-centre operators under her control.

She finds the department in disarray. Morale is rock-bottom, with constant staff complaints, arguments and general bickering. Absenteeism is rife, especially the casual variety, with labour turnover an increasing problem.

She talks to Dave, her immediate predecessor who 'couldn't wait to get out'. He launches into a tirade about the lack of work ethic in this largely unskilled workforce who, in his eyes, were more suited to 'burger-flipping' than dealing with customers. He described how each operator was expected to close 60 calls per day. If they failed to do so, they lost bonus but he still needed to 'jump up and down'. If you kept on top of them, they could do the 60 but take your eyes off them for a minute, and they'd start slacking! He'd proudly averaged 91% of the target over the previous year – 55 calls per day per operator. But it was bloody hard work!

Geraldine, having read John Seddon's book, wants to adopt a different approach. She asks each operator to log just how many calls they can do unfettered in an average day. She has a nice management style that her subordinates find immediately refreshing after Dave's ranting and raving. They agree to cooperate.

The results over a couple of weeks are quite surprising. Geraldine logs them on a process control chart, which she displays to all.

7   Seddon, J. (2003). *Freedom from Command & Control: A Better Way to Make the Work Work.* Buckingham: Vanguard Education Ltd. (ISBN 0954618300).

Figure 46: Process Control Chart

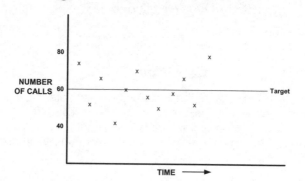

After discussion with the staff, she concludes:

♦ The average number of calls handled over the period was around the 60 targeted.

♦ However, the number handled each day by each operator varied enormously. Some days, the number could easily exceed the target 60, although this rarely happened under Dave's tutelage as there was little incentive to do so. Other days, despite the apparent goodwill of the staff, the number could be as low as 40.

♦ The process appears therefore to be incapable of achieving the management demand of 60 calls per day, each and every day, from each operator.

Geraldine then splits her staff up into small groups and asks them to identify why there is such a large daily variation. The voluminous report includes:

♦ The sales force have a large discretion on how deals are structured, with varying discounts. They also regularly offer sales promotions. Neither is communicated routinely to the call centre office so they have to put customers on hold, whilst they check. This is particularly bad 'at the end of the month'.

♦ Service calls are often delayed, due to the quality of the on-line service records. Again, the service department has to be contacted before the specific equipment details can be identified and the appropriate service engineer summoned.

♦ Given the large staff turnover in the department alongside the increasingly complex product range, some operators find it difficult to respond to customer complaints. They frequently requested training from Dave but 'there was enough time to carry it out'.

Armed with this understanding of the causality of the problem, Geraldine does two things. First, she gets permission to change the payment system away from individual contribution to a scheme related to the performance of the department as a whole. Second, she initiates corrective action to ensure the most important of the problems identified are addressed. In future, for example, complaints are to be handled by two trained staff on a dedicated phone line.

Eight weeks later, she repeats the exercise.

The outcome?

♦ The variation, day by day, has dropped by 50%.

♦ The average number or calls handled per day increases from 54 to 71.

♦ The staff are much happier, committed and motivated. Absence and turnover are significantly reduced.

Figure 47: Process Control Chart 2

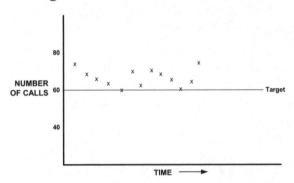

This is a simple tale, but the same story is being repeated daily right across British business. The traditional 'carrot and stick' approach is being used incessantly by managers to drive employees who *do not really have any control over the process they're using*. The net effect is employee alienation and a lack of productivity. We constantly encounter situations where uplifts in complexity are invariably followed by requests by management for increased resource. The end result is often higher overheads and greater inefficiency instead of the desired control. The routine in such situations should be:

♦ Are we sure the process is capable?

♦ If we're not, what are the variables?

♦ Once we know them, the key variables should be measured and compared against specification.

If the process is shown then to be lacking, remedial action can be put in place to eliminate excessive variation. This is far easier, far more effective and far less stressful than simply shouting even louder at the poor unfortunates who just happen to operate the system. It also provides a wonderful opportunity for real employee engagement, as employees tend to react very favourably to approaches where they can influence the outcome.

Commonsense it may be, but such simple logic is far rarer than we imagine!

Six Sigma

Increasingly, companies across the world are implementing a system of process optimisation called Six Sigma. Originating from Motorola in the United States but made fashionable by Jack Welch at General Electric, Six Sigma is a sophisticated approach to understanding process capability and ensuring minimum process variability.

For students of statistics, the theory goes back to the 19th century Gaussian distribution of the 'normal distribution curve'. Variation in a process taken over sufficient readings will probably represent the bell curve of **Figure 48**.

Figure 48: Defining the Process

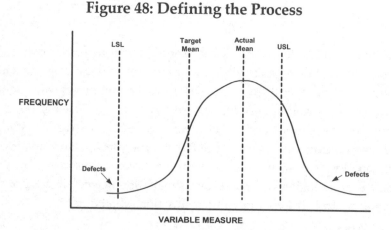

Six Sigma sets out to reduce defects or non-conformances by reducing the variation in the process. We start by "centring" the process, ensuring that the actual mean meets the target. This is the first step in reducing defects (**Figure 49**), the whole curve shifting rightwards so that the upper and lower specification limits (USL and LSL) are balanced across the mean.

Figure 49: Defining the Process 2

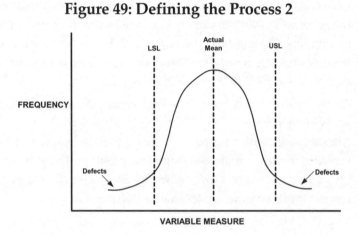

The second part of Six Sigma is to reduce variation in the process. As variation is reduced, defects are eliminated (**Figure 50**).

Figure 50: Defining the Process 3

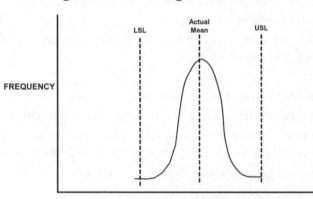

The objective with Six Sigma is to reduce defects to less than three parts per million. In essence, it is simply the application of statistical methods to eliminate or reduce variation. It has five phases:

- **Define:** Start by clearly defining both the problem and what constitutes a 'defect'.

- **Measure:** Using your definition above, describe the internal processes that will influence the parameters you seek to control. Collect data to identify inherent variation so that the reality of the process is clearly understood, as well as its theoretic, targeted parameters. (It sounds a bit complicated, but the simple exercise we described earlier in the chapter on Geraldine's call centre dilemma is a good example of this stage.)

- **Analyse:** The objective of Stage 3 is to understand why defects are being generated. This is where you can really get complicated, using a range of statistical tools to isolate and measure the key variables creating the problem. The general idea is to pick out the most influential parameters that have the biggest impact on the process and tackle them first.

- **Improve:** Having raised the possibility that certain variables may be much more influential than others, your task here is first to confirm that and to quantify the impact. Once sure that your measurement systems are actually capable of locating the variability, you set about modifying by reducing or eliminating variation.

- **Control:** The hard work has been done in gaining a clear understanding of the problem. Your challenge is now to keep it under *control*. You will do this with simple process control charts or characteristic check lists.

Nothing in the above is particularly new. The great attraction of Six Sigma is in its discipline. Those successful in Six Sigma have adopted it as a wholesale organisational philosophy, ensuring a standard, consistent approach across the company. Jim's approach to Six Sigma also has the twin aspirations advocated so frequently in this book for effective employee engagement:

- Top-down direction, energy, commitment and consistency.
- Bottom-up involvement, ownership and self-direction.

Once internalised successfully, the opportunity is then presented to expand to great effect with external suppliers and even customers. So whilst we wouldn't necessarily encourage our readers in SMEs to immediately leap into the complex world of Six Sigma, we would certainly recommend that they keep it as an aspiration. By progressively adopting the techniques of continuous improvement advocated here, we feel sure that Six Sigma will emerge as the natural end product of your radical employee engagement strategy.

Making Choices

Before we leave the area of process excellence, let us turn to a very common weakness in business today, *making choices*. Managers have to make selection decisions daily on a whole host of topics, ranging from recruitment, promotion, new capital equipment and all the way through to new software. Faced with a pick from two options, the decision may be obvious. However, when the alternatives become numerous, then finding the optimal solution becomes problematic. Sadly, too many managers still rely on gut instinct, experiential judgment or some other largely unscientific approach. How often do you find managers using highly sophisticated decision-making techniques to purchase a key piece of capital equipment and then being almost cavalier in their approach to staff recruitment and training?

We do not wish to overcomplicate matters but the adoption of a simple Selection Matrix can aid clarity of thinking. There are only four basic steps:

1. Identify all the important factors that will shape your decision. Separate those we term 'constraints', qualifications that are mandatory and need only be classified as 'go' or 'no-go'.

2. List all the non-constraining factors and ascribe a relative priority, usually out of 10. So, for example, if you are buying a car, having more than four seats may be relatively unimportant and rated 3, whereas reliability may well be vital and judged to be 10.

3. Construct a matrix and rate each alternative on a scale of 0 to 10 against each factor.

4. Multiply the 'weighting' of (2) with the rating of (3).

Adding up the totals gives us a balanced, numerical view of a *potential* decision.

An example to illustrate the point.

Case Study 31

Archie has built up his software business from scratch and now wants to recruit a deputy to facilitate a stepchange expansion. He has operated thus far very much as a one-man band, in terms of managing the company. Bringing another strong personality on the scene is a huge step for him and he can't afford to make a mistake. He knows that one of his weaknesses is impulsiveness, so he has to ensure that his selection process is objective.

He starts by identifying the important characteristics of the likely successful candidate.

- A good team-worker.
- Compatible with Archie's personality.
- Customer-friendly.
- Entrepreneurial in outlook.
- Financially-literate.
- Good experience of the software industry.(Mandatory)
- Graduate-level education.
- High energy levels.
- Successful track record. (Mandatory)

He decides that both a successful track record and good experience of the software industry are mandatory requirements or constraints. He rates the rest in relative importance:

- Compatibility   6
- Customer-friendly   9
- Financially-literate   8
- Graduate-level   4
- High energy levels   6
- Team-working   5

Upon reflection, he realises that an entrepreneurial flair is unnecessary and this does not figure in his selection decision.

He then calls in the four candidates shortlisted by the headhunter and rates each against his predetermined factors.

His matrix looks like this:

Quality	Weighting	Candidate 1		Candidate 2		Candidate 3		Candidate 4	
		Rating	Out-come	Rating	Out-come	Rating	Out-come	Rating	Out-come
Team-working	5	7	35	4	20	6	30	4	20
Customer Friendly	9	8	72	4	36	8	72	7	63
Compatibility	6	10	60	7	42	9	54	4	24
Financial Literate	8	8	64	7	56	8	64	9	72
High Energy	6	5	30	6	36	7	42	6	36
Graduate Level	4	6	24	10	40	7	28	8	32
Totals:			285		230		290		247
Constraints:									
Track record			Go		Go		Go		No Go
Experience of s/w industry			No Go		Go		Go		Go

Archie gets a shock when he does his final evaluation. Instinctively, he warmed to Candidate 2 who had a track record, experience of the software industry and an intellect off the scale. However, overall, he came out worst of the four. Archie agonises for 10 minutes, but then realises that, not being a graduate himself, he probably places a disproportionate emphasis psychologically on educational achievement. Without the pre-planning and the matrix, he would have probably been so impressed and overawed by the academic standing of Candidate 2 that he would have selected him. The evident downsides on team-working and customer friendliness, probably related to an intrusive arrogance and haughtiness, would have been forgotten.

Likewise the gap between candidates 1 and 3 is imperceptible and could have caused a dilemma. However, by thinking out in advance the desired attributes, Archie's stated 'constraint' of experience in the industry becomes the deciding factor. Had he not spent time in preparation, he would probably be agonising for a lot longer.

Making the wrong decision can be both expensive and disabling. Time spent on a little forethought and preparation is rarely wasted.

SOME FINAL THOUGHTS

The great quality of the ESO methodology that we so admire is less about the clarity with which it tackles specific techniques but more about the holistic philosophy that surrounds it. At all times, we must remember that the keystone to delivering benefits to the organisation is the individual worker, the 'hero' of this book's title. Your process excellence journey must recognise that success is likely to be much more about motivation than technique. Six Sigma, we can confidently predict, will fail miserably in most applications. It will be introduced as yet another top-down, brave new world, flavour of the month. The emphasis will be on the technique rather than the problem and the people. Hopefully, this book has given you a few clues on avoiding this oh-so-common pitfall.

A few general pointers, most of which have been covered before:

◆ **Resist the prescription of the traditional.** Putting in operations to 'check' on people is both demotivating and expensive. There is no need for inspection, individual quality control, intrusive supervision, rectifiers and so on, provided employees are encouraged, trained and persuaded to take ownership. You may have to take a few brave pills to disassemble these trappings of traditional command and control. However, done correctly, experience tells you quality goes up and costs go down. Period!

◆ **Resist the cocoons of functionality.** British businesses of all types and descriptions seem to be bedevilled by inter-functional strife. We often see managers take the easy route and focus on functional improvement, in splendid isolation from the rest of the organisation. Unfortunately, business processes and procedures have little time for organisational boundaries. Departments are for 'bread and rations', processes demand unfettered progress across boundaries as in **Figure 51** below. Therefore, always tackle improvement through cross-functional teams.

Figure 51: The Importance of Cross-Functional Teams

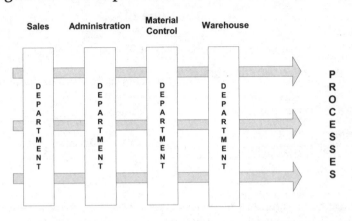

◆ **Resist the negative 'East-Enders' approach to language!** Process excellence is all about 'can-do'. The organisation sets unrealistic, stretch targets and then works together to achieve the previously thought impossible. We in management can actually subvert this process by unconsciously using negative language. We talk about *problems* rather than *challenges*. We allow qualifications to lessen expectations – *"I'll try to do that!" "Hopefully we'll achieve the target!" "My best guess is we'll do it!"* 'Probably' replaces 'will'. We must ensure at all times that our language, tone and demeanour reflects the positive approach we apparently so desire.

◆ **Resist the temptation to delegate process excellence.** The kiss of death for any key initiative is for senior management to distance itself from the activity. The leaders of the organisation have to not just set an example but also to play a key role in seeing through to completion each strand of development.

According to Jim, each of his key managers and leaders must exhibit the following 'additions list' (**Figure 52**). To this list could be added 'adopting an evangelistic fervour' for the key decision makers. Only then will the organisation realise that THIS IS SERIOUS!

Figure 52: Leadership Qualities in Process Excellence: The 'Additions List'

◆ Champion process excellence.	◆ Remove road blocks.
◆ Be dissatisfied with the *status quo.*	◆ Stimulate creative thought.
◆ Balance team and task.	◆ Take time out to reflect.
◆ Demonstrate involvement, not just commitment.	◆ Balance detail and strategy.

The correct management of process is vital to the future health of the organisation. Hopefully, by following the prescriptions of the ESO methodology, you will be equipped to best use the efforts of your new found 'heroes'. You can be patient here and do things progressively. But always ensure that the ultimate vision is in sight and understood. This really is the key if you wish to be truly world-class.

Figure 53: The Route Map updated 8

Step		
1	Understand your business	✓
2	Identify the common crisis	✓
3	Convince yourselves	✓
4	Convince the rest of the management team	✓
5	Establish the values	✓
6	Find the perceived barriers / constraints as seen by the workforce	✓
7	Construct the architecture	✓
8	Go for the quick wins: Communication Recognition Management Style	✓
9	Focus on the external customer : Going for customer delight	✓
10	Focus on the internal customer : Learning to work together	✓
11	Create the infrastructure: The right employee systems The right organisation structure	✓
12	Enhance team-working and empowerment	✓
13	Focus on the process	✓
14	Start again	

17
CASE STUDY: UNIWORLD COMMUNICATIONS LTD

We have long argued that the principles of employee engagement expounded in this book are simple, straightforward and commonsensical. Difficulties only emerge when you try to implement them! To demonstrate this, we would like to devote an entire chapter to just one case study – Uniworld Communications Ltd.

Colin Potter, the inspirational brain behind Uniworld, had never heard of *Team Enterprise*, employee engagement or whatever when he started his company. However, he does have the enviable talent of approaching any problem from a 'clean sheet of paper' standpoint. In other words, he takes nothing for granted. As we will see, he adopted many of the steps recommended in the Route Map naturally, simply because they were logical and made sense at the time.

His story makes a fascinating counterpoint to the perhaps academic approach we have developed in *Growing Your Own Heroes*.

Colin left school in North London in 1966, armed with a handful of 'O' levels. His failure to perform properly at school, despite being an able pupil, meant that he had to eschew the traditional route into employment *via* academia, and chance his hand immediately in the world of work. After a few years in modest roles in accounting in a couple of commercial outfits, he managed to gain a foothold into the mighty world of IBM. Despite starting as a relatively lowly invoicing clerk in 1970, he forged his way up the corporate ladder to the heady heights of Divisional Financial Controllership in 1979. IBM gave him the opportunity to do this, based on his work performance and abilities rather than accounting qualifications. Realising that further progression in financial disciplines was unlikely without these qualifications, he moved across to a new Business Development unit in the computer service division, where he applied his invention and ingenuity to developing marketing strategies for a business that had never previously sold itself to its clients.

However, the world of big business became increasingly frustrating for Colin. He found the bureaucracy and the prescription more than a little claustrophobic. Being possessed of a lively mind, and being also somewhat entrepreneurial in spirit, the natural risk-aversion and change-resistance of his working environment increasingly demoralised and constrained him. He had a choice. Grow comfortably old, grey and frustrated in corporate Britain, or throw it all up in pursuit of intellectual and emotional enlightenment. In 1984, he elected for the latter and left the comfort zone that was IBM.

At this point, the usual case histories tell of opportunities uncovered and successes achieved at a stroke. Unfortunately for Colin, this was not to be. Prior to leaving IBM, he had set up a small business at home, which he worked on in evenings and weekends. This was cutting and wrapping clear polyester window film into DIY kits and selling by mail order to parents who wished to reinforce glass doors in the home. This venture, though modest, was enough to solicit an invitation from his supplier to join him in his established business. Colin took a 50% share and, between 1984 and 1988, he worked in a partnership that grew very substantially and profitably. However, like many business partnerships, there was no real understanding or common goal, and they fell out.

So, in 1988, he took an even bigger step and launched himself into the business world, solo. Colin remained in the same industry effectively competing with the successful business he had developed. The majority of his business came from protecting the glass in buildings against terrorist attack. After more downs than ups, this foundered and finally went into liquidation in 1992. Frustrated and absolutely broke, Colin took himself off to Africa and earned a living of sorts there in the same field until late 1995. Having found himself going deeper and deeper into Africa, and with no prospect of sustainable income or real future, he returned to the UK.

In late 1995, he stumbled over the fledgling industry providing businesses with an alternative telecoms service to BT, as the telecoms industry became de-regulated. In reality, his wife Barbara found the idea, when she started to use an alternative when calling Colin in Africa to discuss their latest financial plight. A newsletter from the supplier advertised for agents and Colin seized upon this opportunity to carve a new life for himself and his family. The main benefit was that he needed no cash for stock, debtors, offices, etc. All he needed was enough money to see him through until the new business started earning enough income to put his family onto a sound footing again.

He started out as a commissioned agent and graduated, four years later, as a reseller buying from carriers (including BT!) and providing the complete service to business. This included invoicing the customer and meant ownership of his customer base.

The concept of providing an alternative telecom service to business was seized on by many and Colin talks of vast competition. Yet he fought through to real success. Colin's USP here, his 'unique selling proposition', was not particularly unique in concept, but unique in that he delivered on it, knew the product and industry in depth (surprising how few do bother), empathised with the client and his needs, and delivered to the standards that he would want to receive.

He describes the approach thus:

> "It's my belief that people like to be treated as individuals. They like to be served well. People in business get frustrated with what they perceive to be bureaucracy and indifference. They rarely trust and always dislike machines. They want to be dealt with by someone who knows what they are talking about and in whom they can place their confidence. They want to know that action is going to take place. They object to pressing 1 for this or 2 for that. They feel disempowered when leaving voicemails. *'Will anyone ever hear the message or, if they do, will they actually take any action?'* ... Whatever the system the company has, it must be triggered by a human being with a face or voice to the client".

Taking the elements of the Route Map one by one and matching them, with the obvious benefit of hindsight, to Colin's approach, we see:

Step 1: Understand the Business

Colin spotted that Uniworld could create a niche here, addressing some of the basic frustrations of the business user. By understanding and tackling their fundamental needs with a service geared to exemplary and friendly interaction, he felt his could create a real differentiation between Uniworld and the competition.

Step 2: Identify the Common Crisis

Identifying the crisis is never a problem for the budding entrepreneur! The first critical element was financial. Colin and his small band all had families to support, mouths to feed. That's more than enough drive for most. However, in addition, Colin had a burning ambition to succeed. He wanted to prove to himself that there was life outside Corporate UK and that business could be conducted more efficiently, more effectively and more acceptably to the key person in the equation – the customer.

Steps 3 and 4: Convince Yourselves (and the Management Team)

Again, not a problem for Colin. His experience in big companies had taught him that the traditional way that organisations dealt with employees and customers was both stultifying and mind-bogglingly inefficient. He was a man on a mission, a passionate advocate of a philosophy neither he nor many others had at that point articulated.

Step 5: Establish the Values

Interestingly, from the outset, Uniworld was a values-driven business. Experience and reflection had taught Colin that an organisation imbued with a much more 'personal' set of values had a far greater chance of success with both customers and employees than the traditional model. The essence of these values will emerge as we track through the remaining steps. However a quote from Colin will illustrate his fundamental philosophy:

> "Good service is only ever provided by people who care. People only care if they are given a reason to care. Usually that stems from a sense of **belonging** and **understanding**. They feel that they belong because they have a clear, autonomous role. They understand because they share in the **goals** of the company. If the company is successful, they will share in that success both emotionally and financially. They feel valued because they are valued.

These people deliver good service because they genuinely feel good about themselves and the company they represent.

Great customer service can only come from people. It is not possible to do it without them".

Stage 6: Find out what the buggers think!

In a start up situation, the challenge is different but the problem is still the same. You have to find out continually what people think. In medium- to large-sized operations, techniques like Perception Barrier Analysis are needed to get through the distortion, the posturing, the reticence and the resentment. With micro-organisations, the solution is open and frank communication.

Colin, again:

"Starting off is difficult. Staff just don't believe aspirational owners. In the beginning, you can only paint a picture. You don't have the money to deliver any financial incentives. You can't even reassure staff that the business has a future.

But what you can do is demonstrate your integrity and commitment by sharing everything you know with them. Honesty in your dealings is absolutely vital. If, even just once, you are dishonest or inconsistent, you lose trust for years. Most people are distrustful, they've heard it all before.

It becomes a step-by-step process, patiently building the bond between owner and staff. Fifty per cent talking (communication) and 50% listening – with both ears!"

Step 7: Construct the Architecture

In a start-up situation, the architecture is hardly complicated but still vital. Colin routinely embedded routines, which will be described later, to ensure that there was a structure behind his philosophy. Employees have to see evidence of management seriousness. Without being embedded into routine, the sceptics and the cynics prevail.

Step 8: Go for the Quick Wins

Quick Win 1 – Communication

"First, I would stand up in front of the company once a week and tell them exactly what was happening. No punches were pulled. I was totally honest with them and they knew as much as me as to what was going on, the plans I had, what I was thinking about and what might be troubling me.

This had a dynamic effect. People could see that the company would grow and that there was a place for them in the future. This particularly appealed to the ambitious.

Ultimately, others would take over part or all of the meeting with me as a guest. People were encouraged to ask questions about anything and everything.

After a couple of years, I didn't consider the weekly meeting to be enough. So I brought in the *Wednesday Breakfast Club*. My Operations Director and myself would invite two senior staff and two junior staff to breakfast at a local hotel. People on average attend three times a year. The idea was to create an informal opportunity for free-flowing conversation on problems, challenges or simply suggestions. The outcome was sensational. They were fun, dynamic, and very, very effective, especially in generating 'off-the-wall' ideas". Most importantly, when either ideas or problems surfaced, we took action – immediately. On many occasions, as soon as we arrived back at the office. First, it made sense and, second, people could see that it was worthwhile voicing their views and participating, because the management took them seriously."

Quick Win 2 – Recognition

Colin's whole philosophy revolves around his customers and employees maintaining a high sense of self-esteem, a feeling of being valued. With employees, he devised a number of instruments to ensure that the pervading sense of individual value was sustained. However, the one thing you can't manufacture is sensitivity. Colin's approach was genuine, heartfelt and perceived to be precisely that.

"The pat on the back is worth tens of 'kicks up the backside!'. We would recognise frequently, often with informal awards. The latter might range from a bottle of champagne, to a dinner for two where an outstanding contribution had been made. Only the deserving were rewarded. 'Buggins turn' never entered our vocabulary. To be recognised, you had to have made a positive or significant contribution.

However, we also did other things. Everyone's birthday was remembered and celebrated. I would deliver flowers or champagne, with a birthday card, to the celebrant's desk – in person.

It doesn't take much to say 'thank you' but it really works!"

Quick Win 3 – Management Style

Colin's great problem with corporate UK really centred upon the unnatural 'command and control' style that most managers adopt in these organisations. When fettered with artificial symbols of status, real barriers can be created between the managers and the managed. From the outset, Colin was determined to avoid this.

"All management had the same desks as everyone else and we all sat in the open-plan office, side-by-side with staff. There were no distinguishing features or different facilities enjoyed by management.

The role of management was to support staff. We firmly believed in the concept of the inverse organisation (**Figure 54**). Management support the staff who serve the customer. The end objective is exemplary customer service, not inflated management ego."

For example, we operated a system of escalation. If a member of staff was having a problem getting a result from a supplier, then they escalated the issue to their manager and so on. There was no stigma, no sense of failure or blame culture. The 'natural' process was management simply responding to support, guide or coach staff. This was vital if we were to achieve our shared goal of delivering great service to the customer. Our philosophy was simply to accept responsibility when there was a problem and help resolve it.

The test comes when customers complain. Management never, ever, ducked a call. We had to take ownership and get involved in the resolution."

Figure 54: The Uniworld Inverse Organisation

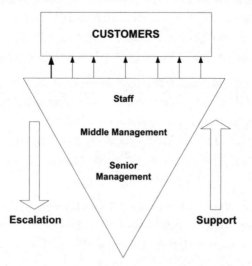

Colin believes in leading by example. He worked alongside his colleagues, using the same furniture and with none of the trappings of management:

"I ate in the same cafeteria, and made my tea in the same kitchen. This brings you really close to your team and they genuinely liked this sense of 'oneness'. No-one ever lost sight of my role, I was Managing Director. I was just more accessible than most! No-one ever confused me as 'one of the lads', although friendliness to everyone comes naturally to me. By taking the leadership role at our staff meetings and exercising control at key moments, no-one was ever confused about my role."

Steps 9 and 10: Focus on the Customers – Internal & External

As will be absolutely clear from the foregoing, the whole *raison d'être* of Uniworld was its obsession with customer delight. Each team member looked after their own clients in totality:

> "Employees were involved from the start. They would set the client up initially with the requisite services from Uniworld. Then the same person would handle every need. Our buzzword was 'proactive' care, with the individual employee taking responsibility to achieve exceptional satisfaction.
>
> Customers, therefore, became known as 'my customer', as strong and healthy relationships were built up between the two. Progressively, all customers received fantastic attention by staff who showed they really cared. Individual reputations and personal pride were always on the line as standards rose and rose.
>
> A little example. It was a matter of importance that customer calls were always, without fail, answered in person. Our golden rule was never to pass the customer to another colleague. If consultation was needed, we did it, not the client.
>
> The outcome? First, staff really identified with this ownership, both front line and back office. Second, we delivered really brilliant service levels. Customer after customer would comment along the lines of "You are by far the most outstanding of our suppliers!". Anything like this was always read out at company meetings, often triggering the recognition we noted earlier.
>
> Internal Customer Focus? Well, I understand it is a problem elsewhere but we rarely encountered it. Our client obsession alongside our real esprit-de-corps meant that the greater sense of team prevailed. And we always work through processes not functions. The latter was relatively meaningless to us!"

Step 11: Creating the Infrastructure – Employee Systems

Interestingly here, Colin takes a sharp departure from the book. He believes that individual financial incentives in small organisations (less than 50 employees) do have a powerful role to play:

> "You have to win hearts and minds. Money usually oils the wheels, especially in the early days. A fair bonus scheme, no matter how small, which rewards people for performance and recognises company objectives, is vital. It builds trust in those early stages, particularly when you do what you say you are going to do.
>
> As time goes on, you can move to profit bonuses based on team or corporate goals. The latter is particularly effective in getting people to work as one team.
>
> However, it took about four years to build up sufficient trust in the business and in me. I think there are two forces at work here. First, people come along with the baggage of traditional organisations. They are naturally suspicious and mistrustful. It takes at least two to three years of consistent management behaviour day in, day out, before these barriers are sufficiently eliminated. After all, they've probably been exposed to many other false starts in the past.
>
> Second, the issue of trust is more difficult when dealing with an entrepreneurial owner. We are probably more self-centred than the norm, excessively optimistic and certainly more driven. They have to get to know you, and it takes time.
>
> Nevertheless, you have to get there. Only when you get to the point of absolute trust will employees take personal ownership. Once they believed in me and the business, this 'collectivism' really took off.
>
> Although small, we tried to be imaginative with our employee systems. Two examples:
>
> First, after a number of debates, we decided to become involved in a chosen charity. Committees were appointed and authorised to run events. One group, for example,

organised a cycle ride across the USA for a team of four policemen. The benefits to us were:

a) The feel-good factor of raising money for a good cause.

b) Practicing the organisational and managerial principles embraced by, and learned from, the company.

c) Building up team skills.

Interestingly, some individuals prospered so well in their charitable work that they became candidates for internal promotion. Some were simply grateful for a free trip to the USA but, all in all, the charity projects were a great way of uniting the company.

Secondly, during the *Breakfast Club* meetings, people frequently raised an issue that they were so busy on the telephone throughout the day that they never had time to do basic administration. I pondered this over the summer holiday and came back with a proposal. The suggestion was to start one hour earlier every day. In return, employees could have every other Friday off. 50% one week, the rest the second. No-one really noticed the extra hour but the benefit of a long weekend every second week was really appreciated. That was just lateral thinking that created wins all round, for customers, the company and, very importantly, the employees."

Step 12: Enhancing Team-working & Empowerment

"Our staff worked in teams, each with a team leader. The team became a kind of business entity. However, we stated unambiguously from the outset that the most important team was the company itself. No individual or team could win if Uniworld couldn't win. This became a mantra, repeated incessantly, until it became engrained in everybody's unconscious. There was no room or tolerance for politics, points scoring, brownie points, petty jealousies or bitching within or between teams. Only one thing really mattered – great customer service that the client recognised and valued.

It was this single objective that improved pay and conditions. We all knew it and believed it.

We didn't take on employees who just wanted a job. We wanted people who desperately wanted to be responsible for something they could identify with. That's why we allocated individual customers to individual staff members. Armed with the knowledge of turnover, margin etc, in essence they created their own mini-business. That promotes both ownership and interdependence.

Everyone who joined us loved the concept of empowerment, of ownership of their customers and the freedom to get on and do their job without all the barriers and frustrations that they had experienced in previous employments."

Step 13: Focus on the Process

Due to the very nature of Uniworld's product, process excellence became a mandatory requirement rather than an option. In the early days, however, this proved quite a problem.

"Aside from trust, one of the key constraints preventing employees warming to the job was the basic inadequacy of our administrative processes. Management should never underestimate the frustration and demotivation created by inadequate or poorly performing systems. They tend to be just as disabling as weak organisational cultures.

It was so bad in the early days that employees found it difficult to respond to customer calls. They had to wade their way through a number of tedious stages to find the relevant information or to make a decision. The worse it got, the more morale would plummet. This is a common feature in small companies. Because, almost inevitably, the optimal systems take some time to get in place, employees get frustrated. Asking for their involvement often provokes a feeling of helplessness. 'We'd love to help you – but the systems are crap.'

The solution is precisely that described in **Chapter 14**. Those at the top have to work determinedly to right the situation.

They have to be as interested in process excellence as they are on business outputs. Cash, profitability, quality and customer delight are all vitally important, but they are simply consequences of downstream processes functioning effectively. The entrepreneurial owner-manager has to set an example, dragging his/her staff with them until all is well. Ironically, you need the 'cultural' support to help you address administrative malfunction, but you only optimise the culture, creating your own team enterprise, when you achieve process excellence. The entire approach is iterative".

Stage 14: Do it Again

Colin's not too sure of our approach here:

"I do believe that you must constantly revisit what you've done. However, I'm not sure it's such a discrete step at the end of the process. In small businesses, you have to constantly revisit, refine, learn and move on. I'd prefer to see it as lots of concentric circles rather than one big loop. Nevertheless, taking time to re-configure your overall strategy and challenge your fundamental assumptions is definitely beneficial. Stage 14 is valid – but perhaps there's more to it than that."

So there we have it, one man's experience in developing a business. Each of the steps advocated in the Route Map falls neatly into Colin's journey with Uniworld. This is no coincidence, for Colin was armed with the same tools as others who have ploughed this path. In his corporate life, in his partnership, and in his adventures as a sole entrepreneur, Colin experienced the good and bad. His greatest asset was his ability to learn from mistakes, his own and others. Eventually, the benefits of the Route Map became obvious, even commonsensical.

Now there would be little point in relaying Colin Potter's story if it all ended in failure. Fortunately for us, the reverse was the case. Uniworld was a fantastic success and eventually made the national press for reasons typical of Colin. In March 2004, Uniworld was sold for a considerable sum to a bigger player enamoured by the quality and performance of the operation. Colin deservedly made a lot of money. But, in keeping with his overall philosophy, Colin voluntarily donated a large chunk of the proceedings to his colleagues. Each employee was given £5,000 for each year of service. Some walked away with £35,000. In the world of the ubiquitous fat cat, this story was so different that it even hit the tabloids!

We believe the story of Colin Potter and Uniworld to be the benchmarks for all small businesses to follow. They key messages are:

♦ Integrity and commitment.

♦ Enthusiasm and hard work.

♦ Inspiring, not managing, people.

♦ Putting customer delight at the heart of everything.

♦ Recognising the twin foundations of cultural and process excellence.

We call the last item *Team Enterprise*, the fusion of the optimal culture with effective and efficient systems. Neglect one and you'll be permanently walking with a crutch! Achieve both and you'll be walking on air.

FOOTNOTE

No doubt, Colin could have taken his money and retired into the sunset. After all, he'd worked very hard for it. But the easy life is not for restless Mr Potter. He has established a small team in a small company in a new market, but this time armed with the lessons of Uniworld.

Document Genie is a software house that specialises in automated document creation, particularly sales proposals. However, it is much more than that. It possesses marketing flair, good design and an exceptional customer fixation. John took the opportunity to visit the offices in Portsmouth in 2005. Although still a small team and no doubt on their best behaviour, he reported that he had rarely experienced such energy, focus and teamwork. He prophesised a healthy future, especially if they stick to the Route Map!

18
BACK TO SQUARE ONE

By now, we hope we have convinced you that employee engagement is less of an initiative than a prevailing philosophy. It is way beyond expectation that anyone will get everything right first time here. In fact, we can guarantee that nobody will get anyway near exhausting the potential that employee engagement can offer in probably 20 years! You just keep on refining and refining. The benefits will continue to flow.

However, its implementation can often be exceedingly complex as you attempt to draw together the threads of motivation, involvement and process integrity. Therefore, it is vital that, from time to time, you take stock of where you are and revisit each stage in the process with a more experienced and, hopefully, more enthusiastic eye. Stage 14 is therefore START AGAIN, go back to Stage 1 and commence afresh.

In the case study discussed in the last chapter, Colin Potter argues that there should be a constant process of examination and re-examination. We couldn't agree more. It is essential that we take time out to question ourselves, our direction and our philosophy. Nevertheless, we need a disciplined approach to do that within our routine and we believe there should be a regular staging post in our Route Map where we formally commence another iteration. We 'start again'.

By the time you have been through the Route Map twice, you should start to see some of your initial aspirations becoming firmly embedded in practice. The rudiments will be:

- ◆ A sense of vision
- ◆ Knowing where you are going
- ◆ Taking everyone with you
- ◆ Re-visiting your values and understanding your culture
- ◆ Checking that your Continuous Improvement architecture is effective and all-inclusive

♦ Checking whether you have significantly improved since the start of the journey.

A SENSE OF VISION

Everybody should now understand what the organisation is about and where it's going. In your early days, this will probably constitute an appreciation of the *crises* faced by the company, portrayed constructively. Eventually, this will transform into an aspirational goal rather than a reactive response.

However, there is little point in having a vision statement unless it inspires people. Reminding employees that they are swimming in a sea full of sharks is simply a threat. It must represent an intention, an ambition. It must be clear, a visualisation of a different, and a better, future. It must both be enthusiastic and inspire enthusiasm. And it must convey a sense of leadership characteristic of the organisation.

You need to ask yourselves the questions:

♦ Does your Vision meet these requirements?

♦ Is it much more than a bunch of words written on a wall?

♦ Do the majority of employees understand, empathise and feel inspired by it?

If the answer is 'No' to any one of these questions, start again.

KNOWING WHERE YOU ARE GOING

By now, you should have used your vision to quantify your *objectives* for the future. Some of these objectives will be budgetary, but a select few will have stretch goals. You will also have carefully segregated a small number of priority objectives that your and your team will seek to 'execute with precision'.

Are you happy you have achieved sufficient clarity here?

TAKING EVERYBODY WITH YOU

The budgetary targets, the stretch goals and the 'critical few' will be supported by departmental and cross-functional critical success factors to ensure that we have a commonality of approach across the company. They, in turn, will be subdivided into team and individual goals, which ensure that everybody not only works to the same hymn sheet, but that they also sing in tune!

RE-VISITING YOUR VALUES & UNDERSTANDING YOUR CULTURE

Although many of us in business will wisely devote much time to discussing and debating shared values with our employees, we should always remind ourselves that, in finality, *only the leaders of the organisation can establish cultural values*. It is the conscious and unconscious behaviour of the key decision-making group that sets the culture of a company. We should constantly test ourselves, therefore, to ensure that the values we loudly espouse are genuinely held by the senior group and that management behaviour constantly and consistently supports them. Otherwise, they are wallpaper at best, or acute organisation irritations at worst.

Thornbury's model (**Figure 55**) can help you understand here. Your entire culture is dependent on the way you construct and apply those vital core values at the centre. People must see the image of these values, their underlying philosophies and the way they are applied to be entirely consistent. At the extremity of the model are the artefacts, the consequences of culture. These are the visible signs that we use to gain our own impression of the prevailing culture, irrespective of what the core values may proclaim. Sadly, too many companies in our experience tend to think that articulation and advertising of a few 'motherhood and apple pie' statements is sufficient. Bigger companies seem to fare worst here. Faced with an undoubted logistical challenge to disseminate and embed the message, they resort to trinkets. Credit card value statements are all the rage but soon become meaningless if not pursued by reality. Our advice: save your money and put your resource into auditing and reviewing behaviours.

Figure 55: Thornbury's Framework for Understanding Culture[8]

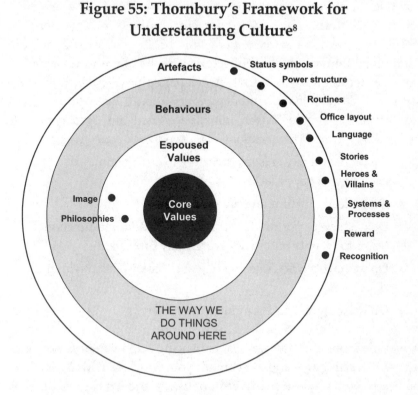

Don't underestimate the 'war stories' that surround your company. Nor the grapevine, 'heroes and villains' and local legends. You may not accept that they represent the reality of life at work but, if they are sufficiently commonplace, they probably do reflect accurately the perceptions of many of your employees. And as we said before, their perception is their reality.

IS YOUR CONTINUOUS IMPROVEMENT ARCHITECTURE EFFECTIVE & ALL-INCLUSIVE?

Many people go down the employee engagement route simply in search of greater harmony in their world of work. That is a laudable

8   Thornbury, J. (2000): *Living Culture: A Values-driven Approach to Revitalising Your Company Culture*. London: Random House Business Books (ISBN: 0712669590).

intention if, in our view, somewhat short-sighted. The majority, however, will want to achieve fundamental business improvement.

The barometer of success here will be the robustness of your Continuous Improvement architecture. This has little to do with the tools and techniques you adopt. An elaborate Six Sigma programme superimposed on a malfunctioning organisation is likely to be far less healthy than a simple Kaizen initiative carried out by a genuinely engaged workforce. The questions you need to ask yourselves are:

♦ Do we have a recognisable structure to our Continuous Improvement approach?

♦ Do we lead, monitor and review top-down?

♦ Do we have opportunities for functional and multi-functional teams to identify and to resolve priority problems?

♦ Do we have a wholesale and ongoing dissatisfaction with the *status quo*?

♦ Do we recognise and communicate success?

One of the more effective ways of enhancing self-awareness here is to visit best practitioners and benchmark your progress with them. Over the years, we have seen many visitors to Leyland Trucks, and indeed Runshaw College, leave with their eyes wide-opened to the art of the possible.

HAVE WE SIGNIFICANTLY IMPROVED SINCE THE START OF THE JOURNEY?

This is again a question where you have to be ruthlessly honest with yourself. Unless there is something horribly wrong with one or more of the fundamentals of your business, your employee engagement endeavours should be paying off in spades, even over the short-term.

If you have truly got it right, then these paybacks should be significant, stepchanges not mere incremental improvements. If the answer is negative, then in all probability, you have neither raised the philosophy above the usual 'management flavour of the month' nor progressed into channelling energies into organisational improvement.

Do not despair if this is the case with you. Many organisations get fired up in the early stages and then become distracted, often unavoidably. Go back to the fundamentals and embed the disciplines into management routine. Recognise that you have probably let the workforce down with failed promises and denied expectations. It will require a good deal more effort second time around, therefore, to persuade them that, this time, you really mean business. Behaviours now count for so much more than words, so rather than getting your managers talking about change, ensure they lead this time. They need to set the example and become *permanent* exemplars themselves.

Go back for your Perception Barrier analysis, extract a few 'litmus test' questions and canvas opinion:

- Has trust in management improved?
- Has 'mutual' trust developed?
- Are relationships between departments healthier?
- Do people enjoy working in your company?
- Would they leave if offered a similar job elsewhere at similar rates?
- Do they believe that colleagues are more prepared to go the extra mile for customers?
- Do they believe that the quality of products and services is increasing?
- Do they believe your company is a better place to work since your last survey?

Try also to quantify the benefits in the following areas / terms:

- Absenteeism.
- Labour turnover.
- Operating costs.
- Total overhead costs per £ of output.
- Quality costs.
- Quality improvements.

THE REAL TEST

Life in business is now generally accepted to be much harder, more complex, more competitive and more volatile than it has ever been. Companies that standstill die. Companies that become excessively inward-looking and conservative, ultimately, fade away too. The debacle that was British Leyland / Rover clearly illustrates the point but, in the same industry, similar signs seem to be emerging from General Motors, Fiat and, surprisingly, Mitsubishi in Japan.

The message is clear. Maximise your competitive edge permanently or recognise that the long decline is not that far away. Increasingly, the gurus of our profession are coming to the same conclusion: only by changing the traditional role of employees in the world of work will we find the key to survival. Organisations have to become self-learning organisations. Each individual has to take on board responsibility and accountability both for self-development and for task development. The enemy is outside the gates. There is simply no room for energy to be spilt negatively inside the organisation.

Is your company using employee engagement to constantly question the *status quo*? To continually improve, adapt, challenge and overcome? If you hesitate, even fractionally, you probably have your answer. More needs to be done, so let's do it again. And do it better this time.

And the best of luck.

Figure 56: The Route Map updated 9

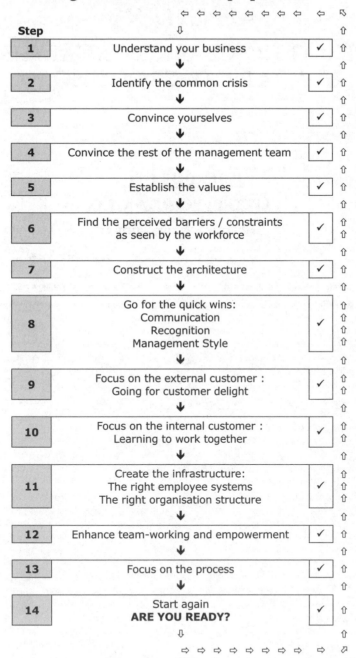

Step		
1	Understand your business	✓
2	Identify the common crisis	✓
3	Convince yourselves	✓
4	Convince the rest of the management team	✓
5	Establish the values	✓
6	Find the perceived barriers / constraints as seen by the workforce	✓
7	Construct the architecture	✓
8	Go for the quick wins: Communication Recognition Management Style	✓
9	Focus on the external customer : Going for customer delight	✓
10	Focus on the internal customer : Learning to work together	✓
11	Create the infrastructure: The right employee systems The right organisation structure	✓
12	Enhance team-working and empowerment	✓
13	Focus on the process	✓
14	Start again **ARE YOU READY?**	✓

APPENDIX 1

PERCEPTION BARRIER ANALYSIS: A TYPICAL GROUPING

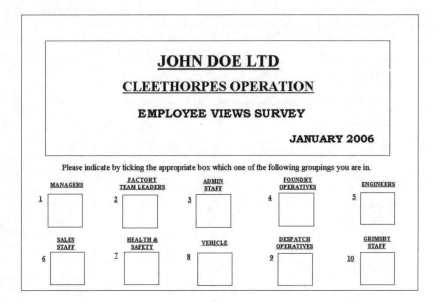

APPENDIX 2
PERCEPTION BARRIER ANALYSIS: QUESTIONS

Communication

1. I am told on a regular basis how the company is doing.
2. I am given sufficient information to do my job properly.
3. I would find it really useful to know more about the company.
4. The information I am given is easily understood and useful.
5. My manager only communicates when there is a problem.
6. My manager communicates change clearly before it happens.

Employee Systems

1. Training and development is treated as an important issue in the company.
2. I get the training I need to do my job effectively.
3. My manager lets me know how I'm doing.
4. I know what my performance targets are.
5. There are opportunities for me to progress within the company.
6. Pay levels are generally in line with other comparable companies.
7. Health and Safety is treated as an important issue in the company.

Continuous Improvement

1. The company is constantly improving its product and services.
2. My manager does **not** want to change the way we do things.
3. Time is set aside to review and improve the way we do things.
4. Everyone is encouraged to find better ways of doing things.
5. I have the opportunity to get involved with problem-solving.
6. I can see things in the company that could be improved.
7. I have the skills and capability to solve problems.
8. I would like to be more involved in problem-solving.

External Customer Focus

1. People here show a good attitude towards customers.

2. I receive feedback on how satisfied the customer is with our product and service.

3. People are prepared to go out of their way to keep the customers satisfied.

4. The quality of our product is excellent.

Internal Customer Focus

1. Communications between departments are good.

2. Departments in the company support each other well.

3. People in other departments are happy to help me.

4. I get good support from people in my department.

Organisation Structures

1. The way we are organised is clear and easily understood.

2. I can see that, if we were organised differently, we would be more efficient.

3. The organisation structure does not create problems of bureaucracy.

4. The number of levels in the organisation structure is appropriate to what we need.

Management Style

1. I am happy with the way I am managed.

2. My manager says 'Thanks' for good work and effort.

3. My manager shows me respect and consideration.

4. The employees get on well with management.

5. Managers listen to my views and suggestions.

6. Mutual trust exists between managers and employees.

7. The company understands when people make mistakes

Team-working

1. I feel part of a team.

2. We are organised on a team basis.

3. We are encouraged to work in teams.

4. We need more team-working.

5. My department works well as a team.

Empowerment

1. The company uses all my skills and experience.

2. People make decisions for me that I could easily make for myself.

3. I am encouraged to take more decisions about the work that I do.

4. I am able to act on my own initiative.

5. My job could be made more interesting and challenging.

6. I feel I could make a greater contribution to the company.

Working for the Company

1. I think that my employment is reasonably secure.

2. If I was offered a similar job in another company at the same pay, I would take it.

3. I enjoy my job.

4. The company is good to work for.

APPENDIX 3
BUSINESS LINK CASE STUDY

We talked earlier in the book about the challenges facing both private and public sector organisations. We think this is often overplayed and that it is often better to focus on the different approaches required when dealing with large and small organisations. No matter how much we hear about the need to inject 'small business thinking' into the big company heart. we still see endless big corporate solutions being offered up to small business.

Some organisations exist in the twilight zone between the private and public sectors – organisations that win various public sector contracts and mix that with European and other funds along with commercial income. Business Link Lancashire is one of these organisations.

When the idea of Business Links was introduced in 1992. the Parliamentary Select Committee on Trade & Industry commented *"the establishment of Business Links is likely to be seen in the future as one of the most important reforms of the 1990s"*. They came into being, from 1993 onwards, with the admirable brief of putting in place a world-beating system of business support, with a clear goal to help businesses to compete successfully and win in world markets. In a nutshell, the ideal was to be the 'one stop shop' for small and medium-sized businesses – a single point of access to the widest possible range of support services required by a business. In many parts of the country, there was in existence already a range of support from Chambers of Commerce, the now extinct Training & Enterprise Councils, Local Authorities, Enterprise Agencies, DTI … and the list went on and on. The role of the Business Link was to pull together this mass of diverse support and make it more coherent and effective.

The story since 1993 is mixed and, like most large networks, quality and impact was variable. One of the main problems was the sheer size of the network – back in 1999, there were 24 Business Link organisations alone in the NW – today there are five. Another major problem was that they were subject to the vagaries of, and constant changes in, government policy and, like many organisations in receipt of public sector monies, they are measured to death. The pig doesn't grow any bigger if we keep measuring it, and we're afraid that this is a lesson that government fails to grasp. No-one objects to a sensible set of key measures that are both demanding and relevant to what is really important. However, at one point, Business Link Lancashire was subject to about 150 individual targets. There was always plenty of talk about rationalising this number, and really prioritising the key objectives, but this never happened because the various fund-holders wanted everything and refused to give up any of their own targets for the collective greater good.

The genius of management is to make complex issues easy and understandable and it is therefore somewhat disappointing that we therefore make the world so complicated with so very many different strategies and priorities. We've got: national, regional, sub-regional, local, sectoral, thematic – the list goes on. Business Link has to try and reconcile the irreconcilable and make sense of this and satisfy a diverse host of fund-holders and stakeholders, who often see partnership as no more than 'the suppression of mutual distrust in the pursuit of money' or put more succinctly 'partnershaft'.

Business Link Lancashire has built an enviable reputation over the last seven years for sound financial management, good operational performance and as a pivotal organisation in developing enterprise, business and skills support.

Perhaps the key to the success of the business is that it sees itself essentially as a private sector business whose immediate priorities are: cash, customer satisfaction and employee morale. If we get that bit right, the rest will follow. The management accepts that it is a relatively small, but highly complex, business and that their job is to deal with this complexity and make their operations as simple as possible. This has led to some outstanding results. When the company was formed in February 1999, there was an extraordinarily thin balance sheet and lack of available cash. From the outset, the business has always generated positive cash and has built a balance sheet that is required to enable that company to grow safely. The market penetration has doubled in four years and accounts for 30% of the businesses in Lancashire. Customer satisfaction levels are excellent throughout this period of sharp growth: 93% would recommend the company to others to use, 90% would use it again, 92% report a business benefit working with it, and over the last two years the percentage of very satisfied customers is a remarkable 59%. The Workforce Development service has a nationally-renowned reputation and has been amongst the top-performing deliverers of Investors in People in the country for a number of years.

In terms of the staff, the main indicators of staff morale are excellent – there is basically zero staff turnover and absence rates rarely rise above

1.2% to 1.5%. As the Chief Executive is one of the co-authors of the book, you would expect there to be in place the things this book encourages you all to undertake yourselves: regular management style surveys – with assiduous follow-up on the results of these surveys; meet the boss lunches every month for the last five years; staff surveys; sensible performance reviews of all staff, as opposed to non-productive appraisals; a highly-developed home-based working culture for advisers, etc, etc.

The most important thing that underpins all of this is the obsession with providing an environment where staff have the opportunity to use their abilities and are given the space to do this. Rule number one – use your best judgement at all times. Rule number two – there isn't one. Working like this involves calculated risk and there are implications. Some staff initially think this is an easy ride, but they soon realise that this company expects you to bring your brain to work with you and is very demanding on issues of performance and productivity. The return is that it is a fun and satisfying environment to work in. The staff of the company have coped with many changes in external policy and contract management that are too numerous and tedious to list – the testament to the staff is that they continue to drive up performance and productivity, despite all the well-meaning changes in direction thrown at them by the policy-makers. Change is tough but, if you manage it well and involve your people, it can be coped with and will not be an obstacle to success.

Last, but not least, the reputation of the business is excellent in terms of customers, fund-holders and stake-holders. It consistently delivers what it says it will and has a reputation for openness, transparency and integrity. It has proven that the private sector heart can still beat effectively in the public sector arena and that, if management is determined and provides the necessary leadership, it can shield both its employees and customers from the complexities and frustrations of delivering public sector services. Businesses are interested in what this company has to say and what it has to offer, and the success of Business Link Lancashire can also be measured by the fact that its influence is considerably greater than the size of the organisation merits.

INDEX

OAK TREE PRESS
develops and delivers
information, advice and resources
for entrepreneurs and managers –
and those who support and educate them.

Its print, software and web materials
are in use in the UK, Ireland, Finland,
Greece, Norway, Slovenia – and,
soon, in India, Bangladesh and Sri Lanka.

For more information, see
www.oaktreepress.com.